The
# Global Great
# Recession

# The
# Global Great
# Recession

## E Ray Canterbery

Florida State University, USA

 **World Scientific**

NEW JERSEY · LONDON · SINGAPORE · BEIJING · SHANGHAI · HONG KONG · TAIPEI · CHENNAI

*Published by*

World Scientific Publishing Co. Pte. Ltd.

5 Toh Tuck Link, Singapore 596224

*USA office:* 27 Warren Street, Suite 401-402, Hackensack, NJ 07601

*UK office:* 57 Shelton Street, Covent Garden, London WC2H 9HE

**British Library Cataloguing-in-Publication Data**
A catalogue record for this book is available from the British Library.

**THE GLOBAL GREAT RECESSION**

ISBN-13 978-981-4322-76-8
ISBN-10 981-4322-76-8

Typeset by Stallion Press
Email: enquiries@stallionpress.com

Printed in Singapore by World Scientific Printers.

*To*

*My beautiful daughters, Katie and Jennie,
and their husbands, Jay and Scott*

# CONTENTS

# PREFACE

*There's no doubt that there is genuine anger, frustration and anxiety in the public at large about the worst financial crisis we've experienced since the Great Depression. Part of what we have to keep in mind here is this recession is worse than the Ronald Reagan recession of the Eighties, the 1990–1991 recession, and the 2001 recession combined. The depths of it have been profound.*

President Barack Obama, in an interview with Jann S. Wenner, *Rolling Stone*, October 14, 2010, p. 39.

The National Bureau of Economic Research (NBER) has long served a useful purpose as the arbiter of recessions — when they begin and when they end. As prestigious as it is, the Bureau erred when it "officially" declared the end of the recent recession as June 2009. Even by this overly conservative ending date, its 18-month duration greatly exceeds the average post-WWII average of ten months. This, despite the fact that the sharp 1981–1982 decline of Reagan's first term happened. In this book I remain steadfast in having named the "Great Recession." Thus, I will not much detour from the conclusion of an earlier book, when I wrote,

As the Dow became more and more volatile, the National Bureau of Economic Research officially declared a recession beginning in December 2007. Most likely, the long recession would be named the second Great Recession of the post-WWII era or the Great Recession of 2007–2010, the longest and most worrisome since the Great Depression of the 1930s. Today the 2010 ending date is a provisional one.[1]

Since, I have amended the name of the episode to the "Global Great Recession." The Great Recession circled the globe. Besides "Global," you naturally raise the question of why the Bureau and I are at odds. The short answer is found in the magnitude of the unemployment rate that continued to bedevil policymakers. It remained disturbingly high, reaching 10.2 percent in October 2009, followed by ten percent rates. Dreadful numbers spilled over into 2010 and got stuck at 9.6 percent in August, September, and October. Worse, the possibility of a significant decline remained remote. Economists were referring to "the jobless recovery" when indeed economic growth was at a snail pace. The economy had stagnated, awaiting more stimulus from monetary policy, as fiscal policy was taken off the table.

There is much more to the story. Before continuing with an overview, I want to acknowledge some important sources for many of the details. I must again be self-referential in the first acknowledgments, those for parts of Chapters 1 to 6. I relied on some earlier publications for much of the material. They include *The Making of Economics*, 4th Edition and *A Brief History of Economics*, 2nd Edition (2011), both published by World Scientific. Also, there is influence from *Economics on a New Frontier* (1968), published by Wadsworth as well as *Wall Street Capitalism: The Theory of the Bondholding Class* (2000) and *Alan Greenspan: The Oracle Behind the Curtain* (2006), both again published by World Scientific. Beyond these books, I cite a number of articles that were published in scientific journals.

For the balance of the book, where the pace picks up, I leaned gently on several sources. These include Carmen M. Reinhart and Kenneth S. Rogoff's *This Time is Different* (2009), David Wessel's *In Fed We Trust* (2009), Andrew Sorkin's monumental *Too Big to Fail* (2009),

---

[1] E. Ray Canterbery, *The Making of Economics*, Vol. III, 4th Ed. (New Jersey/London/Singapore/Hong Kong: World Scientific, 2010) pp. 216–217.

Dean Baker's *False Profits* (2010), Simon Johnson and James Kwak's *13 Bankers* (2010), Nouriel Roubini and Stephen Mihm's *Crisis Economics* (2010), Michael Lewis's *The Big Short* (2010), Raghuram G. Rajan's *Fault Lines* (2010), John Authers' *The Fearful Rise of Markets* (2010), Roger Lowenstein's *The End of Wall Street* (2010), Charles Gasparino's *The Sellout* (2010), Sebastian Mallaby's *More Money Than Gold* (2010), and Maria Bartiromo's *The Weekend That Changed Wall Street* (2010). These comprised my background reading; where I used material directly, citations follow. Besides a sweeping look at public sources, *The Wall Street Journal, The New York Times* and other newspapers also proved valuable. Some of my own work, including the aforementioned books and articles, again comes into play.

We return to the main story. The Great Recession was preceded by the Great Depression, Reaganomics, the rise of the Casino Economy, and a housing market conumdrum. Until Alan Greenspan altered the landscape, housing needed a healthy stock market to prosper. The conumdrum occurs when house prices are driven by historically low long-term interest rates while other forms of investment flounder. By sometime in 2005 the housing industry and construction became by far the driver of Gross Domestic Product (GDP), the broadest measure of economic activity. At a time when short-term interest rates were at historical lows, long-term rates were dominating the economy via the housing-construction nexus. A bubble was inflated, only to be pricked by Greenspan's reversal. In the meantime the wealth distribution became more lopsided.

The George W. Bush administration saw two official downturns, though the Great Recession spilled over "officially" for six months into the Obama administration. According to the NBER, a recession is a significant decline in economic activity spread across the economy, lasting more than a few months, normally visible in production, employment, real income, and other indicators. By this measure, the Great Recession was already longer than the average post-WWII recession by December 2008. There also was the Great Money and Banking Panic of 2007–2009, with 2008 as the year of its greatest intensity. Within this span *The Wall Street Journal* and Maria Bartiromo have the financial insider's turning point as September 15, 2008, when

Lehman Brothers filed for Chapter 11 bankruptcy. But there is much more. Inside the recession came the debacle of the auto industry, which was essentially taken over by the government. Then President Obama, for one among others, did not see the recession ending in 2009. If the NBER had used the unemployment rate as the key indicator, the Great Recession would still be devoid of a happy ending.

What has happened was predictable. To understand why, we only need to visit our early chapters and the original John Maynard Keynes and his stress on uncertainty as well as the Post Keynesians such as Hyman Minsky and Paul Davidson. We will return to recent events and prospects for the future in the final chapter. But first we pay a visit to the Great Depression. While the reasons why may seem obvious, they nonetheless will be explained. Throughout the Global Great Recession, the Great Depression was on the lips of many policymakers, in the USA and abroad.

While many professors of economics and of finance will find much to chew on, this book, written in accessible bites, can be read by laypersons. The only ingredient required is curiosity. As with my books cited above, I write for a broad audience which has, over the years, included undergraduates and graduate students in economics and in finance. As with most of the books I cite, these and others can be supplementary reading for college and university courses.

I must keep the Preface as a preface and end it. After all, this is not the main course. The balance of the book is for your pleasure and instruction.

# 1

# AT INCEPTION

President Barack Obama has had and continues to have much on his plate. Obama signed a massive health-care-reform bill on one fine spring day. On the same day he also had an economic briefing on unemployment, discussions about financial reform, a meeting at the Department of the Interior, a quick lunch, a meeting with senior advisers and then with Senate leaders on ratification of a new nuclear-nonproliferation treaty with Russia, and an Oval Office summit with Israeli Prime Minister Benjamin Netanyahu on devising a model for Middle East peace. Meanwhile TV pundits offered nonstop analysis of the holes in the new financial reform package, while Sarah Palin renewed accusations of Obama's "government takeover" of health care. Worse, more of the American people disapproved than approved of his job performance.

Unemployment has proven to be his Achilles heel. Voters — be they Republicans, Democrats or independents — want to hear more about how the government is going to reduce unemployment without burdening them with higher taxes and fewer benefits. There have been episodes of ups and downs in federal budgets, at home and abroad. Still, from about 1970 until the beginning of the Great Recession, the U.S. federal budget was unbalanced (on average) only by about two percent. Similarly sustainable budget deficits character-ized many nations in Europe and Asia. This all changed during the Global Great Recession. In 2010 the U.S. budget deficit was about ten percent of Gross National Product (GDP). Huge budget deficits emerged in the USA and elsewhere because of rising unemployment and falling national income; tax revenue fell and government spend-ing rose in attempts to stabilize economies in the face of the worst economic climate since the 1930s. Easy money policies accompanied the fiscal ease in most instances. As we will come to know, national budget deficits have been a by-product of financial crisis and they continue after the crisis has cooled. We must consider whether the remedies were sufficiently radical, especially in the United States. Policies proposed to deal with national debt over the long run must be made in the face of rising unemployment.

Our journey begins much before the National Bureau of Economic Research (NBER) officially set the beginning of a recession at December 2007. As we proceed, this specific date, while still important to the few, will fade in importance to many. Since the Great Depression is on the minds of many, we begin there. The Great Depression bears several landmarks — falling prices of ordinary goods and services (deflation), a failing banking system, a liquidity trap, extremely high unemployment, and industrial production lost forever. If any of these terms seem unfamiliar, they will be clear in due course. There are several reasons for beginning here, not the least of which are some common elements that resonate with the Global Great Recession.

The economist's name most often associated with remedies for the Great Depression is the great British economist, John Maynard Keynes. Sometimes he is simply referred to as "Keynes," so great is his fame. During and after the publication of his magnum opus, *The General Theory of Employment, Interest and Money* (1936), Keynes would overthrow the ruling orthodoxy in economics. At first, only scraps of the General Theory were available to a few leading economists. However, some economists were already thinking along the same lines, but they failed to put it all together in one magnificent theoretical framework. Already famous, as early as 1931 Keynes was telling his British radio audience that heightened government spending was necessary to counter the Depression. He only needed policymakers to put his ideas into action.

The policymaker most often identified with the Great Depression is President Franklin D. Roosevelt. The initial policy package was the early New Deal. It was confidence that Roosevelt first addressed. Thereafter, his administration would provide relief funds for the destitute and ignite the federal welfare program. Much of what was achieved during the early and later years of the New Deal helped to relieve much of the suffering from the Great Depression. Very beneficial was unemployment compensation. The banking system had to be rescued with the Federal Deposit Insurance Corporation (FDIC), which had its hands full again during the Great Recession.

There have been other theories, especially ones aimed at inflation or a sustained rise in prices of consumer goods and services. Still, during downturns policymakers have always turned to Keynes. When the downturns are underestimated, as during the Great Recession, government spending and taxation changes are too little too late to quickly restore full employment. Before detailing these outcomes we will consider the writings of the Post Keynesians along with the Keynesians, the rightful heirs to Maynard Keynes. Of them all, the Post Keynesians have been the literal interpreters of "what Keynes really meant." There are disagreements, even among the Post Keynesians. As we will see, Post Keynesianism has flourished not only in the USA but also in Cambridge (England) and in Italy. What I call "primal Keynesianism" received some of its impetus from the other Cambridge (Harvard University).

Though diverse in thought, the Post Keynesians have done a number of things that distinguish them from the Keynesians and the hyphenated Keynesians — the neo-Keynesians. For one thing, they have extended Keynes's doctrine by demonstrating how the income distribution helps determine national income and its growth over time. Their pricing system differs from the orthodoxy (which changes over time). Moreover, some have theorized about the importance of asset pricing, including the pricing of stocks and bonds. Beyond this, they see the wealth distribution as being important in explaining bubbles. It is therefore appropriate to use my integrated version of Post Keynesian economics as a framework for evaluating the Great Recession. In this respect, I amend the surveyed theory with my own vita theory of the personal income distribution. As we will see, it is theory with a common sense explanation.

We complete much of the pre-history of the Great Recession with the rise of Casino Capitalism. Though there is much more to the story, we see the beginnings of the Casino Economy during the brief era of Reaganomics. I say "brief," but note that there remains a splinter group of economists known as "supply-siders," the true believers in everything Reagan. This much we cannot deny; there was another great transformation of capitalism during the Reagan administration and abroad under the leadership of Prime Minister Margaret Thatcher as well as others. They spread the doctrine of fundamentalism in the marketplace. This view has been the major threat to Keynes and Keynesianism. We note nonetheless that when things went wrong during the sharp ensuing downturn, Ronald Reagan and Paul Volcher invoked Keynesian stimulation. After 1980 the banking and finance industries rose to dominance as they devoured a greater share of GDP. Their political and financial power dwarfed the effect of money and banking on the USA and global economy.

We next focus on the housing bubble. At the inception of bubbles, we usually find Alan Greenspan of the Federal Reserve, the U.S. central bank. He helped engineer a crisis and we consider how he mismanaged it. He had a lot of help from subprime mortgages, those beneath the solid, respectable mortgages. The collateralized debt obligation (CDO), a derivative from mostly mortgages, plays an important role in inflating the housing bubble. CDOs became part of a global phenomenon. They and exotic derivatives aided and abetted the collapse of the housing market, which remains on the critical list.

The housing bubble and collapse had implications for Main Street USA where its homeowners reside. By February 2008 Ben Bernanke at the Federal Reserve admitted that a credit crisis triggered by rising defaults in subprime mortgages had reached Main Street. After two hedge funds managed by Bear Stearns had failed, Bear Stearns proper later was to lose half its market value in minutes. To avoid a collapse that would have shaken the financial community, Bear was bailed out by the Federal Reserve and JPMorgan. Conditions in early spring foreshadowed what was to follow: the housing crisis was to affect the overall economy. There were adversities for the banking system that extended into all financial markets and afflicted economies abroad.

Matters were complicated by the growing dominance of banking and the financial sector. The debt held by the financial sector had grown to 259 percent of GDP by the end of 2007. Every dollar of GDP required $2.59 in debt. The United States was in a heavily leveraged situation. Salaries and wages in finance greatly outpaced those in manufacturing. Among other events, the American stock market fell off a cliff in mid-2008. It too had grown to dominate the lives of many. There ensued the Great Money and Banking Panic. Besides the FDIC, the Federal Reserve was often at the center of the action. While the FDIC may have prevented a massive run on commercial banks, the Fed so far had prevented the money and banking crisis from collapsing the economy. It served to ease the credit crunch and the stock market decline. In this process the Fed took on additional powers, powers not granted by any institution but itself. These powers extended into the halls of foreign financial institutions.

Money panics have a lot to do with the history of the Federal Reserve. In the Panic of 1907 the nation turned to 70-year-old J. Pierpont Morgan to save the republic. It was the mortality of Morgan that gave impetus to the formation of a central bank — hence, the Federal Reserve System. As we come to note, there is much more to the story. There was a modern-day panic. During 2008–2009 and beyond Ben Bernanke and the Federal Reserve engaged in some remarkably unconventional policies. The Federal Reserve was to work with the International Monetary Fund (IMF) to assist selected central banks abroad. Swap lines of credit between the Fed and other central banks totaled half a trillion dollars by late 2008.

What brought about such radical policies as near-zero central bank lending rates and unprecedented intervention in bond markets? In 2008–2009 the Fed faced the same conditions that had prevailed during the Great Depression — deflation and a liquidity trap. Great Britain and many European countries were enduring the same conditions. To avoid a second Great Depression, an innovative monetary policy was required. Such actions constituted a massive and unprecedented intervention. Not only did the Federal Reserve operate as a fourth branch of government, it became the lender of last resort to Europe and Japan.

The turmoil in housing and banking had to affect the real economy and the stock market. In late August 2008 stocks fell as the U.S.

Government said personal incomes stumbled in July by the largest amount in nearly three years, while consumer spending slowed. Overseas markets dropped sharply the day after the Labor Day weekend. This was followed in early September by a plunging Dow Jones. There were sharp sell-offs in Asia and Middle East, followed by still more hemorrhaging in Asian and Japanese markets. There was a deep decline in output and employment that could not be prevented by monetary policy alone. Keynesian fiscal stimulus was applied by the Obama administration. The failing automotive industry was largely placed under government control with safety latches for the automobile executives and shareholders. Rising unemployment and declining incomes were the main causes of failing mortgages and loss of homes.

What happened was predictable and avoidable. Still, Alan Greenspan, by his own admission, did not see speculative bubbles emerging much less bursting. Ben Bernanke did not recognize the housing bubble until after the collapse. Both had helped create the bubble environment. Among several who saw the future was Nouriel Roubini. In September 2006 he warned a skeptical International Monetary Fund (IMF) that the USA was likely to face a once-in-a-lifetime housing bust and ultimately, a deep recession. There was a speculative bubble in housing that required central bank action. In Roubini's view, the USA has been growing through a period of repeated big bubbles. Moreover, he saw housing bubbles in many other countries. To understand why Roubini got it right, we need only to read our early chapters, John Maynard Keynes on uncertainty, and the Post Keynesians such as Hyman Minsky on speculation.

Despite surplus labor and idle factories, a vicious circle of falling demand, employment, production, and prices gripped the economy in a deflationary spiral. Bush's $152 billion Economic Stimulus Act of 2008 was overshadowed fiscally by Obama's American Recovery and Reinvestment Act of 2009. Bush's stimulus funds provided tax rebates to low- and middle-income taxpayers, tax incentives for business investment, and an increase in the limits imposed on mortgages purchased by Fannie Mae and Freddie Mac. Obama's $787 billion was directed at the three conventional fiscal policies of spending increases, tax cuts and transfer payments. Some $700 billion was actual fiscal stimulus. Between the two stimulus bills came the remarkable Troubled Asset Relief Program (TARP) signed into law by President George W. Bush on October 3, 2008. As a component of the government's measure to address the subprime mortgage crisis, TARP funds were used to purchase assets and equity from financial institutions to save them. Ultimately some $700 billion of "troubled assets," such as residential and commercial mortgages and securities, obligations, and other instruments based on those mortgages were purchased or insured. As we shall see, fiscal policies also included innovations, as they continue to play a role in the stimulus fight. Federal deficits are a passive way of naturally expanding the economy as Congress has diminishing appetite for discretionary deficit spending and monetary policy is as easy as it can ever get. Mounting public debt is a natural counterpart to slumping output and employment in the USA and abroad.

Just as inequalities in income and wealth incited asset price bubbles, the bursting of bubbles and the accompanying output-employment collapse worsened inequalities. In the spirit of Post Keynesianism, we address the unequal income and wealth distributions in the USA, continuing to draw comparisons with other countries. But the United States is the richest country in the world in the aggregate and when it catches cold, much of the rest of the world suffers pneumonia. In the case of the Great Recession, the U.S. had the pneumonia. Wages comprise the greatest part of incomes in the U.S. and they have been growing unequally. This growth has gravitated to the top. Whatever happens to the income distribution, worse happens to the wealth distribution. This is true at home and abroad.

Technological advancement and lagging education go a long way toward explaining wage disparities. I developed a vita theory of the personal income distribution to explain this phenomenon. The individual's quantity of human capital or inherited skills from birth are added to by education and experience, as well as by age. In turn, the individual's quantity of human capital decides which labor market the person enters. A person "qualifies" for a particular labor market by the state of his or her vita at that point in time. Since labor demand is related to product prices and a changing technology, only the rare individual can predict with any accuracy the derived demand for workers with vitae of his or her type. The approximate wage rate is decided in the marketplace most accessible by the relevant vita. The marketplace wage and income inequalities can be addressed only by public policy in a capitalistic society. (This is only an overview of a theory explained in some detail in Chapter 13.)

The United States and other capitalistic countries have deployed a welfare net to catch those disadvantaged who fall outside of capitalistic good fortune. Compared with other advanced industrialized nations, the American welfare net is full of holes. In great part this is a consequence of the public policy focus on housing and owning a home. As we can now surmise, the cause and effect runs both ways. Bursting housing bubbles lead to inequalities and inequalities lead (especially through wealth) to housing and other bubbles. This is not to say that American governments have failed to respond to business downturns. It's just that policies made during the middle of a downturn, especially one so great, are often hurried, opportunistic, and poorly thought out. This was the case in the current crisis. This is to be expected due to the nature of the dire circumstances surrounding the great financial panic and the rapidity of its unfolding.

Near the end of this book, we consider recent policies and suggest some from my earlier writings. Inescapable is the fact that only federal governments can spend more than its revenues and run budget deficits. Most states and cities must balance their budgets annually or face default. There is a recourse for states and some very large cities that do not face insolvency; they can issue bonds but at increasingly high rates of interest as they become junk. Because of the willingness of financial institutions and households around the world to hold U.S. government bonds, the Treasury can issue U.S. Treasuries equal in value to budget deficits. In turn, the Federal Reserve can keep interest rates stable or at zero, if need be, by buying a large share of the Treasury issues.

During the Great Recession states and cities had no choice except to cut back on the provision of public services such as welfare to balance their budgets. This cut state and municipal employment at a time when the national unemployment rate remained high. These cutbacks in turn contributed to national unemployment. With Medicaid growing out of the necessity of adversity as well as demographics, the states and cities remain in budgetary crisis. However, across all states and cities the total of the budget deficits are small compared with the ability of the federal government to fund deficits through bonds and the bondholding class. The deficits all the way around will be automatically reduced if proper public policy reignites the economic growth process. This is the case unless capitalism on its own can do the job. We have witnessed what capitalism did during three great downturns.

There are ways and means to avoid or stem catastrophes. For example, if the federal government is unwilling to transfer roughly $200 billion to states and cities annually for two years, the Treasury could provide interest-free loans. In fact, they could be the basis for a new fiscal policy. As we come to note, interest-free national bank notes have been used in the past in the U.S. and currently elsewhere. In any case, to be true to Keynes, long-term interest rates should be kept as low as possible to reduce the cost of private business investment in plant and equipment. An important side-effect is the provision of low-cost public infrastructure investment. Eventually the claws of deflation and liquidity traps can be released.

These days the world is adrift in policy proposals. The international financial system has been reformed twice since Keynes wrote about international clearing unions and the prospect of one international currency. The IMF is the logical place to look for reformation. I plug my own plan for a wide SDR band and delayed peg. SDRs are international reserve credits created for IMF-member nations. I leave open the option of an international currency, but recommend that it be SDR based. Look in Chapter 14 for the details.

As I write on December 3, 2010, the U.S. House of Representatives has passed a bill to extend the Bush tax cuts of 2001 for those earning up to $250,000 while allowing the tax rates of higher income households to rise to pre-2001 levels. The Republicans are saying the bill will not pass the Senate. The Democrats are looking for a compromise whereby millionaires and billionaires would be left with higher tax rates while all those below them would enjoy the lower rates. For reasons related to how bubbles are made, in Chapter 14 I opt for the original plan of the Democrats. The compromise is a deal with the devil, but a lot worse could happen. Somehow, and I suggest a middle way, the U.S. and selected other countries will have to deal with the huge lingering budget deficits. The long view should prevail on deficits. The main point that is a winner? The rich can now afford to pay higher taxes while the middle class and poor are being wiped out by the paucity of jobs and incomes.

This brings us to the question of where we are, where we are headed, and the final chapter. At mid-2010 and beyond many of the economic indicators in the USA were very mixed. There was one near-constant — extremely high unemployment. The unemployment rate got stuck at 9.6. percent, then it rose to 9.8 percent in November. In that month the number who had been unemployed for more than six months was approaching seven million, and 20 million more were believed to be underemployed, many having stopped looking for work. On average, there were 4.6 unemployed Americans competing for each job opening. Consumer sentiment was up one month and down the next. The stock market was sharply up or down, depending on what was happening with retail sales and employment at home, budget crises in Europe, and monetary policies in places like China and Japan.

Despite the recent record of strong economic growth in China and India, a restoration of healthy economic growth in the United States is necessary to revive a large share of the global economy. It may seem like a heavy burden, but such is not inconsistent with a full employment economy. Much of the welfare debate and the concern over federal budget deficits evaporate with rapid economic growth. This will not be easy and will require still more innovative policies. The banking system remains in crisis with bank failures in 2010 exceeding those of a banner year in 2009. Foreclosures in housing is still on the rise; home prices continue to fall. At least retail sales were up in early December, spurred on by an otherwise bleak Christmas. The world awaits the next moves by Ben Bernanke and the Federal Reserve Open Market Committee (FOMC) as well as President Barack Obama and the Congress, not to mention decisions by the Supreme Court.

# 2

# THE GREAT DEPRESSION

The Great Depression of the 1930s is the downturn against which all subsequent downturns are measured. This nightmare was frequently mentioned in the process of the Great Recession; policies were aimed at preventing the recession from becoming another Great Depression. There are at least four reasons for discussing the Great Depression. (1) Its return is a source of great fear. The Great Recession and the Great Depression were often mentioned in the same breath. (2) During downturns we return to policies pioneered during the Great Depression as possible remedies. This is no less so in the Great Recession, for there has been a heavy reliance on federal deficit spending. (3) Some of the institutions created during the 1930s remain intact today. These institutions provided a floor under the economy during the Great Recession. (4) The ideas of the great British economist, John Maynard Keynes, parallel in their development the history of the Great Depression. He was frequently cited as the inspiration for both the fiscal stimulus and the incredible monetary ease of the Great Recession.

Though he already was a famous economist by the time of the Jazz Age, John Maynard Keynes (1883–1946), some would say, suffered one glaring defect. He had read Alfred Marshall's *Principles*, attended Marshall's lectures, and hence was a conventional, though brilliant neo-classical. Keynes's neoclassicalism, the revival of classical economics, was doomed by his genius, which eventually made him a scientific maverick and an earth-shaker. Because of him, two generations of economists saw a different world. We have to go back to Karl Marx, who died the year Keynes was born, to find an economist of comparable influence.

Keynesianism, if not the original Keynes, dominated national macroeconomic policy in the United States from the end of World War II until about 1968. Keynes' ideas dominated British economic policy from the mid-1930s until Margaret Thatcher became prime minister in 1979. The Keynesian policy revolution was forged in the fires of the Great Depression that began during the 1920s in England and dominated the 1930s in the United States.

## THE PRELUDE TO DISASTER

The Great Depression cannot be separated from the upheavals of the Great War and the excesses of the Jazz Age. The postwar prosperity was always mixed and uneven. Farmers, in particular, did not share in it for long. Partly because of rising exports during the Great War, agricultural production had soared, and farmers had taken on debt to put more land under cultivation. But after the war, this wartime capacity began to come up against European competition, and prices began to fall, leading in turn to declining farm incomes.

The depression of 1921 accelerated the price slide, and farmers had to produce even more to meet mortgage payments, turning to tractors and more efficient combines and away from workers. But the agricultural cornucopia combined with sated domestic demand pushed prices still lower. With many farms no longer profitable, the bankruptcy rate soared from 1.7 percent of all farms in 1920 to almost 18 percent in 1924 to 1926.

Structural change also beset coal mining, another highly competitive industry. Coal prices were low and falling, and competition from electricity and oil was beginning to tell. The textile industry, too, failed to share in the prosperity. Like agriculture and coal-mining, the textile industry was an old, established industry faced with "too much" competition. A picture of the Flapper, patterned after Zelda Fitzgerald, reveals how little cloth was required for dresses. As skirts came up short, so did textile profits.

And, as early as 1916, the relative position of the railways had begun to slip. Again, capital investment and increased productivity reduced employment. Competition with the railways came from the automotive revolution and the increase in road building, highways subsidized by the government in the same way that rail-beds had been subsidized before. An economy once dependent on railways for its growth now had shifted into high gear with the automobile.

# THE SPECULATIVE BUBBLE

What is remembered with greatest nostalgia is the phenomenal speculative bubble. While some workers were already experiencing hard times, other folks never had it so good. According to one estimate, the five percent of the population with the highest incomes in 1929 was receiving about a third of all personal income. The personal income accountable to the well-to-do such as interest, dividends, and rent was about twice as great as in the years immediately following World War II. While a mere 24,000 families enjoyed yearly incomes in excess of $100,000, fully 71 percent of families had incomes below $2,500. In the race against deprivation, the poor were getting less poor but the rich were beating them four to one. Wealth inequalities in 1929 were even greater. Whereas four-fifths of the nation's families had no savings, those 24,000 families at the tip of the top held a third of all savings. Fully two-thirds of all savings were controlled by the 2.3 percent of families with incomes above $10,000 yearly. Stock ownership was even more concentrated.[1]

Questions of fairness aside, this financial imbalance presented problems of its own. Except for what is purchased as necessities, the large discretionary income of the rich is not dependably spent. It must go for mansions, yachts, Rolls-Royces, and Caribbean travel or else be saved and thus be subject to the even less predictable behavior of producers. It is one thing for producers to issue new equities and bonds to expand their facilities, it is quite another for rich people to buy and sell existing securities among themselves, changing only the

---

[1] These data are gleaned from Maurice Leven, Harold G. Moulton, and Clark Warburton, *America's Capacity to Consume* (Washington: Brookings Institution, 1934), pp. 54–56, 93–94, 103–104, 123; Selma Goldsmith, George Jaszi, Hyman Kaitz, and Maurice Liebenber, "Size Distribution of Income Since the Mid-Thirties," *The Review of Economics and Statistics*, **36**(1), 16, 18 (February 1954); Robert J. Lampman, *The Share of Top Wealth-Holders in National Wealth, 1922–1956* (New York: National Bureau of Economic Research, 1962); James D. Smith and Steven D. Franklin, "The Concentration of Personal Wealth, 1922–1969," *American Economic Review*, **64**, 162–167 (May 1974) and; John Kenneth Galbraith, *The Great Crash 1929* (Boston: Houghton Mifflin, 1954), pp. 177, 180, 182, 191.

prices and ownership of the pieces of engraved paper. The amount of unanchored cash chasing other pieces of paper probably had never been so high.

When such great volumes of savings are held in so few hands, they must be parked somewhere or moved from lot to lot. Despite the obvious trouble that can be caused by cash on the loose, the average citizen threw caution to the restless winds: He wanted nothing so much as getting rich quickly with a minimum of exertion. These excesses began to bubble to the top well before 1929.

By the mid-1920s, a classic speculative bubble inflated over balmy Florida. Miami, Miami Beach, Coral Gables — in fact the whole southeast coast as far north as Palm Beach — basked in the warmth of the great real estate boom. "Ocean view" lots often required telescopes, and Charles Ponzi's subdivision "near Jacksonville" was actually 65 miles west, closer to the Okefenokee than to the Atlantic. Still, nearly everybody acted as if prices of Florida real estate would go forever skyward, and it took not one but two hurricanes out of the autumn skies of 1926 to blow away the bubble. The bigger one showed "what a Soothing Tropic wind could do when it got a running start from the West Indies."[2] It killed 400 people and launched yachts into the streets of Miami.

The collapse of the Florida land boom did not end speculation, it merely ended Florida's prosperity. The rise in stock prices had been rather steady beginning in the second half of 1924. Then the hurricanes blew away the Florida land bubble that October, stock prices dipped a bit, but a recovery soon began. The true stock market boom got underway in 1927, by the end of which the *Times* industrials, predecessor to the Dow, had gained 69 points to end at 245.

What happened next is neatly summed up in a classic book by John Kenneth Galbraith:

> Early in 1928, the nature of the boom changed. The mass escape into make-believe, so much a part of the true speculative orgy, started in earnest

---

2 Frederick Lewis Allen, *Only Yesterday* (New York: Harper, 1932), p. 280.

... the time had come, as in all periods of speculation, when men sought not to be persuaded of the reality of things but to find excuses for escaping into the new world of fantasy.[3]

During 1928, the *Times* industrials gained a remarkable 35 percent, climbing from 245 to 331. Radio had gone from 85 to 420 and Wright Aeronautic from 69 to 289. Radio had never paid a dividend! Trading on the margin — on borrowed money — soared like Wright Aero. The speculator could buy $1,000 of stock with but $100 down.

Investment trust companies had made their first appearance in America earlier in the decade, their numbers growing by leaps and bounds through 1929. Their sole purpose was to buy the securities of other companies and make sponsors richer. J.P. Morgan and Company, for example, co-sponsored United Corporation in January 1929. J.P. Morgan offered a package of one share of common stock and one of preferred to friends, some Morgan partners, for $75. When trading in United began, the stock quickly reached $99 and was resold at a tidy profit.

Even ignoring fraud and larceny, the great surge in holding companies and investment trusts leveraged businesses in the same way that stock buyers were leveraged. Dividends from the firms actually producing goods paid the interest on the bonds of the holding companies. A slump in earnings from production meant a cut in dividends and possible default on the bonds. Such inverted corporate pyramids invite toppling from the bottom up.

Meantime, the American economy had peaked during the summer, and "the most expensive orgy in history," as F. Scott Fitzgerald's epitaph[4] for the Jazz Age reads, soon had to end.

---

[3] Galbraith, *op. cit.*, pp. 11–12. I have drawn shamelessly on bits and pieces of this book in this and the next section. There is no other source on 1929 that blends so magically, information and entertainment. I direct the reader to *The Great Crash 1929* for the more extensive and detailed history of its subject.

[4] F. Scott Fitzgerald, "Echoes of the Jazz Age," *Crack-Up*, p. 21.

## THE GREAT CRASH

The panic of 1929 began on Black Thursday, October 24th. Shortly after a normal opening of the Exchange, prices began to fall on a rapidly rising volume. The stampede of selling by 11 o'clock was so wild, it would have scared even the Merrill-Lynch bull. The collapse of prices being so complete by eleven-thirty, fear became genuine panic. A crowd gathered outside the Exchange on Broad Street, New York City.

The first wave of panic subsided at noon, when word spread of a meeting at 23 Wall Street, the offices of J.P. Morgan and Company. The gathering of bankers pledged to pool their resources and turn the market around. But they could only lean — with their great bulk — into the wind. By Monday afternoon the effort had clearly failed. The *Times* industrials were down 49 points for the day, with General Electric alone down 48. Since the ticker tape could not keep abreast of trading, no one knew how bad it was by the end of the day. The bankers reassembled at Morgan's at 4.30 pm. Now they would try to save themselves, minimizing their losses by selling short. The next day, Tuesday, October 29, was the most devastating, with no buyers at all on many issues. As the *Times* industrials closed down 43 points on enormous volume, alarm gripped Wall Street.

The stock market would continue its relentlessly downward slide. The *Times* industrials, which had reached 331 at the start of 1929, closed at 58 on July 8, 1932. Its stocks had lost 82.5 percent of their value. General Motors had plummeted from 73 to 8. But the low was barely noticed in the press or in the market: Attention by now had shifted to an economy in free fall.

When the crash is viewed in the economist's rear-view mirror, it is clear that early warning signs were abundant: The stock market collapse was a part of the already developing slump. But few were willing to believe this to be the end of the good times, and so the signs were ignored and the trauma made worse.

## THE AFTERMATH

Since the market had become imbedded in American culture and the symbol of prosperity, consumer and producer confidence was crushed by its collapse. Moreover, the decline in stock prices made the (mostly rich) stockholders "poorer," and this slowed consumption spending on luxuries. Finally, the crash broke the circular flow of international financial capital.

United States financial capital flowing to defeated Germany had been funding the circular flow of reparations payments (demanded by the Allies at the Paris peace conference) from Germany to the former Allies, that in due course flowed back to the United States as war debt repayments. As Keynes had anticipated, an economically troubled Germany ceased reparations payments. Not only was the international exchange system weakened, but international trade slumped, further dampening global demand and thus output and employment.

The banking system was problematical even before the crash. The banks held call loans on stock purchases of about $4 billion. As stock prices fell, some banks could not cover their loans by sales of securities and suffered significant losses. In the agricultural states of Missouri, Indiana, Iowa, Arkansas, and North Carolina, bank failures greatly increased in November and December 1930. The Bank of the United States of New York failed. In the absence of deposit insurance, these bank failures led people to increase their holdings of cash and to reduce their bank deposits. Runs led to still more failures.

American banking is based on fractional cash reserves in which, for example, only $10 of cash in hand may support $100 in checking account liabilities, $90 dollars of which can be bank *loans*. The system is so interdependent that a failure of one bank can bring down several more; that is, deposit liabilities too are heavily leveraged. Leveraging works both ways: when things are going up and when they spiral downward. A window with a view from the top of the credit pyramid reveals why the failure of banks holding $600 million, or only three percent of the U.S. money supply, could cause the panic in the winter of 1930.

What had begun as a banking rumble reached a crescendo in the spring of 1933. Bank loans that had been good during the 1920s went sour as the prices of the goods they marketed and the value of real estate collateral plunged. President Franklin Roosevelt came into office on March 4, 1933, and closed all private banks that week by declaring a "bank holiday," an action that prevented the complete collapse of the American banking system.

## GNP AND THE DOWNWARD TRADE SPIRAL

Most economists consider the length of the Great Depression to have been over ten years in the United States — from 1929 until U.S. mobilization for World War II in the waning months of 1940 — granting that within that span there were ups and downs. The fall in gross national product (GNP) from a cyclical peak of $104.4 billion in mid-1929 to a low of $55.6 billion in the cyclical trough in the spring of 1933 comprised the worst part of the Great Depression. By 1933, almost 25 percent of the civilian labor force in the United States was unemployed.

The Federal Reserve had not helped: Its policy at the time was only to increase credit according to the "needs of trade," meaning if business was not interested in borrowing, the Fed did not increase the money supply. It is difficult to imagine a more inept policy, for it caused bank credit and the money supply to fall during bad times. Amidst a collapsing banking industry and a manufacturing industry too frightened to borrow anyway, the money supply slumped by a third over the cycle ending in the spring 1933.

Only the U.S. Congress could rise to this level of incompetence. Under pressure from the farm lobby, Congress passed (and President Herbert Hoover signed) the notorious Smoot-Hawley Tariff in mid-1930, leading to retaliatory tariffs around the world and a trade war in which world trade spiraled ever faster downward. Figure 2.1 pictures this downward spiral more dramatically than could a thousand words.

Not surprisingly, then, some historians and economists use the term "Great Depression" to describe only 1929 to 1933, because the real GNP (in 1929 prices) began recovering thereafter. The establishment of the deposit insurance system in 1933 helped to restore confidence and credit, and the money supply rose sharply in 1934 to 1936. The economy expanded slowly under the stimulus of government job-creation projects and from the gathering business and

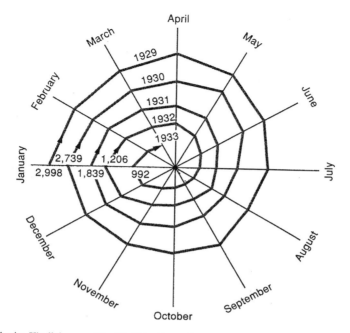

*Source*: Charles Kindleberger, *The World in Depression* (Berkeley: University of California Press, 1973), p. 172. Reprinted by permission.
*Note*: Monthly values in terms of old U.S. gold dollars, millions.

**Figure 2.1:** Contracting Spiral of World Trade, January 1929 to March 1933: Total Imports of 75 Countries.

consumer confidence to $109.1 billion in spring 1937, slightly higher than in 1929. Then, the 1937 to 1938 recession brought real GNP down to $103.2 billion in 1938.

Whether one calls it a separate recession or the last great crisis of the Depression, the downturn lasted from the spring of 1937 to the summer of 1938. During that year, industrial output dropped by about a third and unemployment rose by about a fifth, according to the official data, leaving about 6.5 million people unemployed in 1937 and about ten million in 1938. After six of years of crisis, the unemployment rate was higher in 1938 than it had been in 1931 (see Table 2.1).

The relapse of 1937 to 1938 was partly a result of a sharp reduction of the federal budgetary deficit (see Table 2.2) plus a sharp

**Table 2.1:**   Great Depression Unemployment Rates (Percent of Civilian Labor Force)

|  | Official (%) |
|---|---|
| Peacetime prosperity | |
| 1919 | 3.2 |
| The Great Depression | |
| 1930 | 8.7 |
| 1931 | 15.9 |
| 1932 | 23.6 |
| 1933 | 25.2 |
| 1934 | 22.0 |
| 1935 | 20.3 |
| 1936 | 17.0 |
| 1937 | 14.3 |
| 1938 | 19.1 |
| World War II begins | |
| 1939 | 17.2 |
| 1940 | 14.6 |
| 1941 | 9.9 |
| 1942 | 4.7 |

*Sources*: U.S. Department of Commerce, Bureau of the Census, *Historical Statistics of the United States: 1960 Series* (Washington, D.C.: U.S. Government Printing Office, 1975), p. D46.

**Table 2.2:**   U.S. Federal Government Expenditures and Deficits as Percentages of Current Gross Domestic Product, 1931–1939

|  | Expenditures (%) | Deficit (%) |
|---|---|---|
| 1931 | 4.7 | 0.6 |
| 1932 | 8.0 | 4.7 |
| 1933 | 8.3 | 4.7 |
| 1934 | 10.2 | 5.6 |
| 1935 | 9.0 | 3.9 |
| 1936 | 10.2 | 5.4 |
| 1937 | 8.6 | 3.1 |
| 1938 | 8.0 | 1.4 |
| 1939 | 9.8 | 4.3 |

*Source*: Based on data from U.S. Department of Commerce, *Historical Statistics of the United States, Colonial Times to 1970* (Washington, D.C.: Government Printing Office, 1975); and U.S. Department of Commerce, NIPA, 1929–1976 Statistical Tables, September 1981.

contraction in the money supply. That is, at a time the government was reducing its spending, businesses were not investing despite a call loan rate in New York City that fell below one percent in 1938. And yet — contrary to the neoclassical view — business did not invest, apparently having regained its pessimism about returns on investments in machines, people, and plants. For example, machines more than ten years old, which made up about 44 percent of the total in use in industry in 1925, had risen to about 70 percent by 1940. Thus the recession of 1937 to 1938 came in the wake of confidence in the economy insufficient to bolster business investment.

The devastation did not escape contemporary literature. John Steinbeck's novel, *The Grapes of Wrath*, published in 1939 as the United States struggled to escape the Great Depression, is an intensely dramatic story of the suffering and privation experienced by poor farmers during the 1930s:

> The decay spreads over the State, and the sweet smell is a great sorrow on the land. Men who can graft the trees and make the seed fertile and big can find no way to let the hungry people eat their produce. Men who have created new fruits in the world cannot create a system whereby their fruits may be eaten. And the future hangs over the State like a great sorrow.[5]

Steinbeck's pessimism was widely shared.

## KEYNES'S ACADEMIC PRECURSORS

In addition to John Maynard Keynes himself, others were nibbling away at the edges of conventional economics, among them, Keynes's student, friend, and colleague at Cambridge, Dennis Robertson (1890–1963). When, in 1930, Keynes published his self-described *magnum opus, A Treatise on Money*, it met immediate criticism, notably from Robertson, Joan Robinson (1903–1983) and Sir Richard K. Kahn (1905–1989) at Cambridge,[6] and their dissents aided Keynes, who soon began rethinking his ideas.

---

[5] John Steinbeck, *The Grapes of Wrath* (New York: Viking Penguin, 1939), p. 448.
[6] Others include James Meade (1909–1995), Austin Robinson (1877–1993), and Piero Sraffa (1893–1983). Austin was Joan Robinson's husband.

In a 1933 article, Joan Robinson succinctly explained how measured savings and measured investment can be equal without equalizing the savings desired by households and the investment spending planned by producers. It is the failure of the two sets of intentions — those of the households and those of the businesses — to mesh that creates downturns. By intending to save more and buying fewer Fords, households will leave unsold cars at the dealers. Such cars would be inventoried, and an increase in inventories is one form of business investment (albeit unintended). A pile-up of inventories leads to production and employment cutbacks at the factory Measured savings being equal to measured investment is scant comfort to the dealer when unsold cars, a part of the measured investment, is contrary to his intentions. And unemployment is cold comfort for the automobile worker.

Kahn began with the notion that public employment can have a multiplier effect in the economy. Building on an idea that Keynes had put forth two years earlier, Kahn showed in 1931 that government expenditure on public works will be distributed to workers in the form of wages, a large part of which will be spent on consumer goods and services. Store merchants will then spend a large fraction of their receipts from the consumers on wages, inventory, and so on and on and on. If the government hires 200,000 workers to rake leaves and, as a result, employment in consumer goods industries (secondary employment) is increased by 400,000, then total employment is increased by 600,000. There is thus an employment multiplier of three. It seemed a matter of simple arithmetic.

Meanwhile, the official view could be found in the cheerful oratory of President Herbert Hoover during the first three years of the Great Depression. In January 1930, Hoover said, "business and industry have turned the corner," a phrase repeated sufficiently during those years that "turning the corner" became a proverbial cul-de-sac. Hoover viewed government relief programs to aid the jobless, homeless, and starving as socialist and communist. Nonetheless, even he belatedly set up a public-works program, though wholly inadequate.

In truth, American capitalism was dying, despite bedside affirmations from conventional economists and the President of the patient's early recovery. The occasion is reminiscent of the reassurances given to Alexander Pope while he was on his deathbed. The doctor assured him his breathing was easier, his pulse steadier, and so on. "Here am I," commented Pope to a friend, "dying of a hundred good symptoms."

## KEYNES'S POLICY SUGGESTIONS

Keynes's new ideas steadily evolved from 1931 to 1934, as capitalism was devolving. In the earliest months of the 1930s, Keynes expressed his belief that the fundamental cause of the slump was a lack of new plants and equipment, a result of the "poor outlook" for capital investment. To improve the outlook, profits needed to rise; that would stimulate investment. But greater profits must not be achieved by cutting costs; that would be deflationary. Keynes decided that profits could be raised either by inducing the public to spend a larger share of their income or by inducing business to convert a larger portion of its revenue into investment, but not by both.

At this point, Keynes was still relying in part on neoclassical thinking. An increase in consumption required sacrificing savings otherwise available for business investment. He did not yet envision the pleasurable possibility of both total consumption spending and total investment spending growing simultaneously.

Even so, Keynes told his British radio audience in 1931 that heightened spending was necessary to counteract the Depression, an intuition that proved to be more useful than the advice of the neoclassicals, the ruling orthodoxy. Keynes attacked thrift, a Victorian virtue, because he saw the fallacy of expecting large savings to be offset by investment when there were virtually no investment opportunities in sight. By 1932, for example, American industry was selling less than half of its 1929 output.

Keynes urged families to spend more (as did President George H.W. Bush during a recession in December 1991, by his purchase of socks in J.C. Penney's) and the government to increase its public works expenditures (much as President Bush did in his visit to a Texas highway project the same month). He rejected Arthur Pigou's suggested wage reductions; that would, Keynes felt, only make matters worse.

In 1931, Keynes also served on the Macmillan Committee to investigate and make recommendations about economic conditions in Britain, Anticipating his later theory of the multiplier, Keynes and other dissenting (from the neoclassicals) members of the committee argued that with private unemployment already high, public spending by government would not divert resources away from private investment but would rather have a compounding effect.

Although Keynes admitted that public-works programs might dampen business confidence for a short time, he thought that, on balance, increased government spending would be helpful, even desirable. Keynes was beginning to suggest that, if free markets did not produce working people and humming factories, then it would be necessary for the government to intervene to restore higher levels of economic activity.[7]

Until Keynes, critics of the neoclassicals were easily dismissed; they simply did not understand. But Keynes obviously did, and he had to be taken seriously when he condemned laissez-faire governmental policies. This he did in an essay in 1925 called "The End of Laissez Faire," in which he denied the Smithian principle of natural liberty and the close relationship of private and social interest with enlightened self-interest. Keynes doubted that there would always be enough expenditure to stabilize the economy — that is, he questioned Say's law. But at this point he lacked a counter theory to Marshallian economics: He had only a fuzzy vision.

In retrospect, Keynes's policy suggestions were increasingly on the mark. What was needed now was someone to translate policy suggestions into action. The consequence was to be called the New Deal in the United States.

---

[7] My private correspondence with the late Joan Robinson over several years greatly improved my understanding of the evolution of Keynes's pre-*General Theory* thinking as well as directing me away from some errors in interpretation of the subtler aspects of Keynesian thought. My late colleague and friend, Abba P. Lerner, provided similar guidance even though he and Joan were not always in agreement. In the end, I became the referee where their ideas or opinions collided. Not everyone will agree with my arbitration.

# 3

# PRIMAL KEYNESIANISM AND THE NEW DEAL

## THE EARLY NEW DEAL YEARS

Keynes had sensed a lack of confidence by consumers that blighted the business community. Confidence is precisely what Franklin D. Roosevelt (1882–1945) undertook to restore first when he took office as president in March 1933 and began what became known as the New Deal. Although decried then (and often since) as outright socialism, the program was aimed at saving American capitalism. Those economic policies, though not socialist, were certainly radical by peacetime standards, that is, they attempted to uproot the laissez-faire system and make government an active partner in the conscious steering to the economy. In retrospect, it is best described as "primal Keynesianism."

Beginning in March 1933, Franklin Roosevelt began implementing primal Keynesianism before Keynes had fully developed his revolutionary theory. Roosevelt noted in his first address the "corrosiveness" of lack of consumer confidence: "So first of all let me assert my firm belief that the only thing we have to fear is fear itself — nameless, unreasoning, unjustified terror which paralyzes needed efforts to convert retreat into advance." By May 1933, the Federal Emergency Relief Administration (FERA) was given $500 million to provide relief funds for the destitute, marking the beginning of the federal welfare program.

Relief kept people from starving, but Roosevelt's basic New Deal strategy was to create jobs even while removing people from the charity rolls and restoring their self-respect. It gave Americans dozens of new federal government agencies. Some, like the Civilian

Conservation Corps (CCC), which provided jobs for young males ages 18 to 25 years in conservation work, were successful. Others, like the Agricultural Adjustment Administration (AAA), which raised farm prices by paying farmers not to produce, were not. Pigs were slaughtered and corn plowed under (by government decree), even though people were near starvation and black sharecroppers and tenant farmers were thrown off the uncultivated land.

The government also funded new infrastructure. The Tennessee Valley Authority (TVA) was a socialized hydroelectric power program producing not only electric power but dams, fertilizer, reforestation, and recreational lands. TVA also built the Oak Ridge facility, later to provide research and development for the atomic bomb. Private enterprise, faltering during the Depression, was no longer sacred or exclusive.

To shore up a failing banking system, the Federal Deposit Insurance Corporation (FDIC) was created, insuring bank deposits. The Home Owners Loan Corporation also was established to refinance mortgages and to prevent more foreclosures.

The capstone of the New Deal was the National Recovery Administration (NRA), designed to oversee and enforce the National Industrial Recovery Act (NIRA). Deflation had been bankrupting farms and businesses, while plummeting wages were stalling consumer spending. Manufacturers were encouraged to fix prices with impunity from antitrust laws. Wages were fixed at a minimum and hours at a maximum, and collective bargaining rights were extended to workers. Thus the NIRA proceeded to violate the most revered premises of free markets. The NRA did expand labor-union membership (the United Mine Workers grew to half a million), but business abused the price-fixing laws by fixing prices at high rather than low levels.

The Depression ground on through the mid-1930s, even as the Supreme Court unanimously declared the NRA unconstitutional. Undeterred, Roosevelt set up the Works Progress Administration (WPA) in 1935 (in 1939 its middle name was changed to Projects). The WPA hired workers to build ten percent of new U.S. roads, alongside new hospitals, city halls, courthouses, and schools. It built, for example, the bridges and roads connecting the Florida Keys with Miami. It built Boulder Dam (now Hoover Dam), the Lincoln Tunnel connecting New York and New Jersey, the Triborough Bridge system linking Manhattan and Long Island, the East River Drive in Manhattan, and a warehouse for official gold holdings called Fort Knox. In addition to its construction activities, the WPA employed thousands of down-and-out artists, writers, and musicians in its artistic projects.

The deficit spending was hardly radical in magnitude: Federal government expenditures had risen to 10.2 percent of gross domestic product by 1934, hardly an imposing number by the standards of the more prosperous 1990s when government expenditures averaged about a fifth of gross domestic product. However, as about a fifth of the New Deal federal outlays was budgeted for employment creation and those outlays (and an expanding money supply) had contributed to the recovery in real GNP to 1929 levels sometime in 1937 makes the official unemployment data suspect. Economist Michael Darby has corrected the official unemployment data to include this public employment (see column 2, Table 3.1).

**Table 3.1:** Great Depression Comparative Unemployment Rates, 1933–1938 (Percent of Civilian Labor Force)

|      | Official (%) | Darby (%) |
| --- | --- | --- |
| 1933 | 25.2 | 20.9 |
| 1934 | 22.0 | 16.2 |
| 1935 | 20.3 | 14.4 |
| 1936 | 17.0 | 10.0 |
| 1937 | 14.3 | 9.2 |
| 1938 | 19.1 | 12.5 |

*Sources*: U.S. Department of Commerce, Bureau of the Census, *Historical Statistics of the United States: 1960 Series* (Washington, D.C.: U.S. Government Printing Office, 1975), p. D46; and Michael Darby, "Three and a Half Million U.S. Employees Have Been Mislaid; Or an Explanation of Unemployment, 1934–1941," *Journal of Political Economy,* 84 (February 1976),

Darby's numbers on public employment erase an annual average of six percentage points from the "official" unemployment rate in the years 1934 through 1939. Still, Roosevelt's make-work alphabet of programs did not elevate the economy to full employment, even in the "best" year of 1937. The economy had to wait for World War II and war-related employment to achieve full employment.

## THE FAMOUS KEYNESIAN MULTIPLIER

Meanwhile, Keynes had found the missing link required to complete his new theory. In the neoclassical parable, saving and investment in the loanable funds market set the interest rate. At the same time, the equilibrium interest rate ensures an equality between saving and investment. If saving temporarily exceeds investment, the interest rate will fall (and the amount of investment will increase) until they are equal again and full employment is ensured. As the gloomy months of depression unremittingly rolled on, however, Keynes watched businesses refuse to invest even though interest rates were very low, and he concluded that the level of income and employment must depend on more than simply the equality of saving and investment as set by the interest rate. Once this fundamental flaw was understood, a revolution occurred in economic theory.

Keynes adapted to his own purposes his colleague Richard Kahn's idea of the employment multiplier. It was far from new: many economists had speculated on the multiplicative effects of government spending coming from successive rounds of consumer spending. But none had been able to make it part of an acceptable new theory.

Keynes appropriated Kahn's mathematics as the key link. He used the term investment multiplier: If government or industry invests an initial $1 billion and national income thereby rises by $2 billion, the investment multiplier is two. (Without the data or the statistical tools, Keynes had correctly guessed that the multiplier in England indeed was 2.)

At the risk of some oversimplification, the multiplier relation can be shown in a schematized example. The example has every consumer planning to spend three-quarters of every new dollar of

Table 3.2:  The Multiplier Process

| | Change, Income | | Change, Consumption | | Change, Saving | Initial Change, Investment |
|---|---|---|---|---|---|---|
| Initial increase, investment | | | | | | $5.00 |
| First round | $5.00 | = | $3.75 | + | $1.25 | |
| Second round | 3.75 | | 2.81 | | 0.94 | |
| Third round | 2.81 | | 2.11 | | 0.70 | |
| Fourth round | 2.11 | | 1.58 | | 0.53 | |
| Fifth round | 1.58 | | 1.19 | | 0.39 | |
| All other rounds | 4.75 | | 3.56 | | 1.19 | |
| Totals | $20.00 | | $15.00 | | $5.00 | $5.00 |

after-tax income (Keynes's marginal propensity to consume) and intending to save one-quarter of every new dollar (the marginal propensity to save). To start the process, we presume that business investment rises by $5 billion as a result of improved profit expectations.

Table 3.2 shows what happens. In this process, the $5 billion is multiplied by four to become, in the end, $20 billion of new national income. The multiplier of four derives from only one-fourth of all income increments going unspent.[1] After all rounds are played, the change in saving caused by the change in investment will be equal to the original investment increment. Higher investment spending, either private or public, multiplies itself in terms of national income changes, and out of higher wage disbursements workers are able to save more. Therefore, the initial investment ends up raising enough savings to finance itself.

In neoclassical economics, not only does saving depend mostly on the rate of interest, but any saving increment comes at the expense of

---

[1] A simple mathematical relationship between the marginal propensity to consume (or the marginal propensity to save) and investment expenditures gives the value of the multiplier. It is Investment Multiplier $= 1/(1 - \text{MPC}) = 1/\text{MPS}$. From the numbers in my example, the Investment Multiplier $= 1/(1/4) = 4$.

consumption. The Keynesian multiplier ends this zero-sum game. Consumption depends not on saving but on income. There is a stable psychological propensity in the modern community such that consumers reliably spend more when their income rises and less when it falls. Unlike the Victorians, consumers of this new breed see virtue in buying lavishly and avoiding the pain of abstinence. Scott and Zelda Fitzgerald had glamorized this shift in attitudes during the Jazz Age.

If income is important to consumption, it must also be important to saving, because saving is simply "not consuming." To warrant any particular level of employment, there must be an amount of business investment spending equal to the difference by which total output (at the particular employment target) exceeds consumption. That is, investment must jibe with the employment (and output) desired by society.

Surviving fragments of early drafts of Keynes's *The General Theory of Employment, Interest, and Money* (1936), show that as early as 1932 he was using the multiplier concept in his theoretical system. Yet during these writing and advising years, Keynes was considered by most other economists to be only a thorn in an otherwise flawless rose garden of neoclassical economics.

## ILLUSIONS AND THE NATIONAL INCOME

In the neoclassical parable, freely moving wages and interest rates led to full employment. Keynes circled the neoclassicals like an attorney in cross-examination. Argued Keynes, the free movement of wages and interest rates presumed inevitable in the neoclassical world either (1) will not occur or, *if* it does occur, (2) will not bring about full employment.

Keynes understood massive wage cuts to be an impractical policy notion. Furthermore, even *if* it could be accomplished, a decline in money wages alone would not elevate employment. Even though it would enable producers to reduce costs and thus prices, the money wage decline would also reduce the income that is the wellspring of consumer demand. The boost to total demand in the economy would then have to come from some other source.

What the neoclassicals saw as virtuous thrift rewarded, Keynes saw as employment denied. Higher *intended* saving means lower *desired* consumption, a decline in demand for goods and services resulting in lower production levels, less income from which to save, and therefore less saving than originally intended. This lower than expected saving will match investment at a lower national income level. This equality can be achieved at levels of total demand (and spending) insufficient to employ everyone in the labor force. There was a paradox in thrift.

Total demand is the sum of what is spent by consumers, business investors, and the government. When total planned expenditure exceeds total output, then output rises to meet the demand. Conversely, if total planned expenditure is less than total potential output, then output tends to fall. The tendency, then, is toward a national income equilibrium.

Here is a rare point of agreement between Keynes and the neoclassicals. But they said that this equilibrium is *always* at an output sufficient to maintain full employment, an outcome Keynes denied, contending that the simultaneous occurrence of such natural equilibria in all markets — labor, money, and commodities — at *exactly* full employment was improbable. Furthermore, he said, the failure of the equilibrium process could have dire social consequences.

When total expenditure matched potential output or total supply, say at US$490 billion, the neoclassicals cried "Equilibrium!" and went home early. It had to be equilibrium because any other level of output demand would either be "too low" or "too high." But, Keynes argued, a national income equilibrium does not necessarily coincide with full employment.

Private business investment, dependent as it is on uncertain expectations, cannot be counted on to guarantee jobs for all. At this point government spending comes in. Only the government, contended Keynes, can be expected to take a hand in stabilization policy and increase its net spending (i.e., minus taxes) by the necessary amount.

Suppose current government spending and private spending generates an equilibrium income level no higher than $490 billion and employ no more than 75 million workers, leaving five million out of total labor force of 80 million unemployed.[2] A level of $510 billion would be sufficient to employ the entire labor force of 80 million workers. Suppose the investment multiplier equals four. Keynes would have argued that somehow we need to generate $20 billion in additional output and income to raise output to that $510 billion necessary to employ everyone. With an investment (and other spending) multiplier of four, we need generate an extra increment of only $5 billion (20/4) in spending.

The gap can be filled by a sustained net government spending boost (i.e., minus taxes) of $5 billion. (A spending increase not accompanied by an equal tax increase causes a government deficit.) At the new $510 billion national income equilibrium level, the entire labor force of 80 million would be employed.

However, said Keynes, even this contrived "equilibrium" was unstable — at the mercy of such things as fluxes in profit expectations. The real economy oscillated unsteadily between equilibria, like the billowing and wafting of the Wright brothers' first airplane. Sometimes it would even crash!

## MONEY AND UNCERTAINTY

Once the individual has decided how much of his income he will consume and how much he will save, there is a further decision that awaits him. In what form will he hold this command over future consumption? Rational people do not hold savings in the form of cash or checking accounts, so said Marshall and most other neoclassicals. But holding cash balances for their own sake, countered Keynes, is perfectly rational when the future is cloudy, dark, and foreboding. Uncertain economic conditions can make cash a more attractive asset than bonds, even if stuffed in a mattress and earning no interest. Cash

---

[2] Keynes actually followed neoclassical tradition so that total output increased (with employment), but at a decreasing rate because of diminishing returns. This complication is not necessary to establish the national income equilibrium, and, for simplicity, constant returns are displayed.

as an asset can be like Linus's security blanket in "Peanuts." As Keynes put it, to hold cash "lulls our disquietude."

The rate of interest required for our parting with cash in exchange for earning assets measures the "degree of our disquietude." Certainty is the illusion. Rather than as a neoclassical reward for Victorian abstinence, Keynes saw the interest rate as a reward for illiquidity, the payment needed to overcome the individual's liquidity preference. Thus the amount of money people want to hold decreases only with a rise in the interest rate (the liquidity preference schedule is downward sloping).

This essential difference between Keynes and the neoclassicals is linked intrinsically to the market for bonds. The price of bonds varies with supply and demand, both of which can be unpredictable. However, the dollar amount of interest paid for holding a bond is fixed. For example, take a bond, any bond (except James Bond), that sells for $1,000 and for which the holder receives $100 in interest income per year. The annual interest rate on such a bond is $100/$1,000, or ten percent. If the supply of bonds at that rate and maturity greatly (and often unexpectedly) diminishes, the price of the bond in question — already in the market — will rise. For example, if the bond price doubles to $2,000, the interest rate falls to five percent ($100/$2,000).

Thus a bondholder who buys the bond because the interest return is greater than the zero percent that cash yields can prosper if the interest rate is stable or if the price of the bond rises, providing a handsome capital gain. But if the bond price falls, and if the bond was bought at a relatively high price (low interest rate), a subsequent small drop in its price will cause a loss in the value of the bondholder's capital sufficient to wipe out the small amount of interest income earned from illiquidity. Suddenly, cash is a more attractive asset than a bond.

In Keynes's mind, this point is where the trouble really begins. (The neoclassicals sensed no such trouble.) If bond prices are so high that individuals do not expect them to soar more (i.e., interest rates have bottomed out), the preference for liquidity or hoarding cash and keeping it idle then may be almost unlimited. If virtually everyone holds onto cash instead of bonds, interest rates in the bond market will not decline further. The economy is in what Keynes's friend and colleague Dennis Robertson was to christen a liquidity trap.

If holders of cash and bonds sense doom amidst their gloom, imagine how a firm's CEO might feel about putting funds into a new plant based on sales forecasts over the next 30 uncertain years! Even an exceedingly low interest rate may not incite business firms to borrow money and invest in new plants and equipment. Indeed, if business prospects are sufficiently dismal, a negative nominal interest rate, an impossibility, may be required to stimulate investment.

## Inside and Outside Money Supplies

Where does this money, hoarded or spent, originate? Keynes saw it as coming into existence with debts, which are contracts for deferred payment. Money comes into being because there is a lag between the production of commodities and the receipt of cash. Henry Ford turned out hundreds of Model A's weekly, but they had to go to the dealers and the sales staff had to convince customers to buy them — all of which took time. The time gap is filled by the banking system or by new bond issues, which finances goods in process. Such money is created *inside* the private enterprise system.

In the modern economy, most money is held in the form of checking deposits, a liquid asset for the individual and a liability for First National Bank. Since modern banking is a fractional reserve system, a certain portion of a bank's deposits can be loaned out to business firms. Loans by one bank become new checking deposits for a second bank, which in turn can loan out a large share of these deposits, and so on throughout the banks in the system. In this way, the money supply is enlarged with a mathematical regularity similar to Keynes's multiplier. The money supply grows as long as more loans are being made to businesses for expansion, the financing of inventories, or the financing of production processes.

Other money originates outside the banking system. If it so chooses, the government may also create debt through its deficit spending. The U.S. Government did so, for example, with remarkable regularity during the 1980s and the early 1990s. Governmental expenditures greater than tax revenue can be financed by selling bonds to the central bank, which uses them as backing for loans to commercial banks and for the issuing of currency, thereby increasing the money supply.

The total supply of money therefore depends chiefly on the actions of private commercial banks and those of the monetary authority as both respond to the demands of individuals, businesses, and government. In this way, money is created out of thin air from both inside and outside the private banking system.

## Interest Rates and Uncertainty Upends the Quantity Theory of Money

The supply of money and the demand for money set the level of interest rates. Unlike their role in the crude version of the classical quantity theory of money, money supply changes can influence income and price level only *indirectly*, through the money rate of interest. Then, if expected business sales revenues are sufficiently high and interest rates sufficiently low, firms will borrow from private banks and engage in active investment activity.

If the filament supplier to General Electric sees its sales prospects brightening, it may borrow to buy more modern production equipment to meet its client's needs. Again, however, the interest rate may not fall low enough because of the liquidity desires of the public (a liquidity trap), or else the uncertainty regarding investment prospects may be too great to entice business to invest at *any* rate of interest.

Recall Alfred Marshall's favoritism toward both the quantity theory of money and Say's law and you can see the severe damage done to Marshall's theory by Keynes's view of money. First, the turnover rate of money (V) is no longer stable, much less constant. If the demand for money or liquidity preference is sensitive to interest rate changes (bond price movements) or to mood shifts regarding economic prospects, V might as well stand for volatility. The rate of turnover of money will vary with the swings in the public's desire for cash (liquidity). Indeed, in the liquidity trap the public's desire for liquidity will be infinite. Money balances no longer will stay precisely equal to those funds required for day-to-day household needs and business trade. The desire by individuals and businesses to hold money balances when they expect bond prices to stall in mid-air is one of the broken links in Say's chain of events.

## MONEY AND THE GREAT DEPRESSION

Keynes did not say that money is irrelevant. Rather, he wanted to know how money is an active ingredient in producing income, output, and employment. Nonetheless, his message eluded some of Keynes's interpreters. They were driven by the overwhelming need to move their economy out of the Great Depression, whose conditions included a liquidity trap with gloomy business expectations.

In such a double trap — where interest rates cannot be pushed any lower and business investors are wary — monetary policy is of no avail. The central bank cannot increase the money supply if private bankers are unwilling to make loans. Private bankers will not make loans if they have no takers. Then, the velocity of money (V) sinks beneath a tide of bankruptcies. The central bank ends up pushing on a wet noodle. The interest rate will not fall to zero because individuals do not expect to see bond prices go any higher (or interest rates any lower). Some economists today, such as Paul Krugman of MIT, contend that Japan earlier and, as we will come to note, the USA of 2007–2010 have been in a liquidity trap.

During such a monstrous slump, the only recourse is for the government to spend more than its tax receipts, creating a deficit, and sell its debt (bonds) to the central bank. Not only would the government have to create *outside* money, but it also would have to ensure its use — its velocity — by spending it. The consequent government outlay raises aggregate demand, which leads to a renewed flow of output and increased employment and income, which further has a multiplier effect. The emphasis placed on deficit financing by an important group of Keynes's interpreters, the *fiscal Keynesians*, is better understood in the dimness of what seemed to be the twilight of capitalism.

# KEYNES, HARVARD AND THE LATER NEW DEAL YEARS

The connections between the later architects of the New Deal and John Maynard Keynes were indirect. Although President Roosevelt welcomed Keynes himself to the White House in 1934, the President was quite unimpressed with this "fancified mathematician." As John Kenneth Galbraith has said, the Keynesian Revolution went to Washington by way of Harvard,[3] where Keynes's ideas had blown in like a gale force wind. Washington officials regularly attended Harvard seminars on Keynesian economics.

In some ways, the Keynesians were preaching to the choir. In Washington, Marriner S. Eccles, head of the Federal Reserve Board, had anticipated the ideas of Keynes. Eccles was a business tycoon turned adviser to Roosevelt.[4] The remarkable Lauchlin Currie, once Eccles's assistant director of research and statistics and later the first professional economist at the White House, also was "Keynesian" before the *General Theory*. They and Galbraith were able to place reliable Keynesian economists in various government posts.[5]

The later New Deal also brought the "welfare state," already in place in Europe, to the United States, to the bastion of capitalism where Henry Ford in 1931 could blame the laziness of workers for

---

[3] See John Kenneth Galbraith, "How Keynes Came to America," in *Economics, Peace and Laughter* (Boston: Houghton Mifflin, 1971).

[4] Robert Reich, Secretary of Labor during the Clinton administration, elevates Eccles to virtually the *only* adviser to President Roosevelt with Keynesian ideas three years before Keynes. This may be because Reich relies solely on Eccles's own account, published long after the New Deal ended. For Reich's view, see Robert B. Reich, *After-Shock* (New York: Alfred A. Knopf, 2010), especially Chapters 1 and 2. For the original Eccles, see Marriner Eccle, *Beckoning Frontiers* (New York: Alfred A. Knopf, 1951), especially pages 54, 71–81. Lauchlin Currie was a more modest man, but may have had more influence than Eccles in the latter New Deal days. (I served on the same faculty as the long-lived Lauchlin at Simon Fraser University during a 1969 semester.) The short book by Reich is worth the read because of his stress on the income and wealth distributions.

[5] See John Kenneth Galbraith, *A Life in Our Times: Memoirs* (Boston: Houghton Mifflin, 1981), pp. 68–70.

the calamity shortly before closing a plant and firing 75,000 workers. Ford saw a silver lining in the ragged coats of these men on the road again: "Why, it's the best education in the world for those boys, that traveling around! They get more experience in a few months than they could in years at school."

For all its radical solutions, the New Deal was profoundly conservative. It worked within capitalism — then in critical condition — to preserve that system. What it was failing to do, had to be done — however imperfectly — by the federal government. And it was. Jobs were created and the hungry fed. In the process, the federal government was transformed from a negligible influence on the typical household into a widely felt presence, becoming massive in scale by the end of World War II. So necessary was much of this to the survival of the American political system, it probably would have happened even if John Maynard Keynes had never been born. In the end, Keynesian economics was to justify policies already in vogue.

## LOOKING FORWARD

What was revolutionary is clear. Whereas the English neoclassicals saw full employment as automatic, Keynes said it was not and advocated government action to get it.[6] During slumps, private spending would have to be supplemented by public expenditure, a recommendation flying in the face of the virtue of Victorian frugality — or so it seemed. Keynes's ideas swept the field of academic economics and set the standard for the next 40 years.

There is no agreement today among economists about what is most important in Keynes's theory. Keynes himself, immodest as usual, wrote the famous playwright George Bernard Shaw (a friend and a Fabian Socialist) in 1935, "You have to know that I believe myself to be writing a book on economic theory which will largely

---

[6] For more on the neoclassicals, see E. Ray Canterbery, *A Brief History of Economics*, 2nd Ed. (New Jersey/London/Singapore/Hong Kong: World Scientific, 2011), Chapter 5.

revolutionize — not, I suppose at once, but in the course of the next ten years — the way the world thinks about economic problems...."[7] Robert Heilbroner emphasizes the policy consequences of the revolution: "There was no automatic safety mechanism after all!....A depression...might not cure itself at all; the economy could lie prostrate indefinitely, like a ship becalmed."[8]

Keynes's adherents were themselves divided from the outset, strongly disagreeing on what Keynes *really* meant. The initially dominant Keynesian view was favored by the conditions of the time; the revolutionary antidepression policy carried the day. That Keynes had an enormous impact on antidepression policy in England is not in doubt, and his ideas had a great effect on post-World War II stabilization policies throughout Europe, in Canada, and in the United States. National governments now had an obligation to their constituencies to guarantee sufficient levels of total demand in order to fully employ the nations' labor forces. In Great Britain, this new ethic meant the end of frugality and laissez-faire in government economic policy until the rise of Margaret Thatcher.

The consequence of Maynard Keynes combined with other forces has been a very low level of British unemployment during the post-World War II years up to Thatcherism. In the United States, this new ethic led to the Employment Act of 1946, which committed the federal government to follow policies that would provide employment opportunities for those able, willing, and seeking work. Keynesian economic policies were vigorously pursued by the Truman administration, and a modified Keynesian program was perhaps most successfully followed by the Kennedy and Johnson administrations prior to the escalation of the Vietnam War in 1968.[9]

---

[7] Quoted by Roy Harrod, *The Life of John Maynard Keynes* (New York: Augustus Kelley, 1969), p. 462.

[8] Robert L. Heilbroner, *The Worldly Philosophers*, 6th Ed. (New York: Simon & Schuster, 1986), p. 271.

[9] The details of policy as applied theory during these years are provided in E. Ray Canterbery, *Economics on a New Frontier* (Belmont, California: Wadsworth Publishing Co., 1968).

Keynes did not write the *General Theory* in order to solve puzzles about hypothetical conditions but out of an urgent concern that governments would fail to end the massive unemployment and deprivation of the 1920s and 1930s in Britain and of the 1930s in the United States. After the Vietnam War, U.S. economists shifted their focus to the "equilibrium" tendencies used by Keynes as academic argument, thus obscuring his stress on the uncertainty of the future on economic fluctuations. If we rush unthinkingly into the arms of equilibria every chance we get, we are simply substituting a mechanical analogy for history. At equilibrium nothing can be done — because we are already there.

Over the years there have been many counterrevolutionary theories, but in downturns the policymakers have inevitably turned to Keynesian economics. And in each downturn the fear is expressed that we may have a repeat of the Great Depression. This fear loomed large during the great downturn that began in 2007 in the United States. The economy was more complicated now and Keynes's theory had been greatly amended. Nonetheless, the initial policies directed against the Great Recession were related to those deployed against the Great Depression. If anything, the more current policies were more innovative. In order to fully understand all the new forces, it is useful to broaden our framework. This we do next.

# 4

# A POST KEYNESIAN FRAMEWORK

It often takes adversity to bring diverse strands of economic thought together or, even, to bring diverse people together. In the opening scene of George Bernard Shaw's *Pygmalion* (later a musical, *My Fair Lady*), sundry people are brought together by the common necessity of protecting themselves from a sudden downpour. There, we encounter the impoverished middle-class Clara Eynsford-Hill, with her genteel pretensions and disdain; a wealthy Anglo-Indian gentleman (Colonel Pickering), who seems tolerant enough; an egotistical professor of phonetics (Henry Higgins), who seems exceptionally intolerant; and a pushy, notably rude flower girl (Eliza Doolittle) from the lower class, embodying the essence of vulgarity. These characters never would have been found together except for something like a sudden rain shower.

A number of economists sympathetic to Keynes but not to Keynesianism have long disparaged the vulgarization of the great man's theories and the zealous monetarism that thereby arose. This dissenter movement spent several decades in the economic catacombs. The "sudden rain shower" that brought together diversity extending across oceans and continents was the simultaneous high inflation and high unemployment of the 1970s. This stagflation caused a widespread crisis of faith among "orthodox" neo-Keynesians, those Keynesians classed as "vulgar" by the Post Keynesians.

41

Post Keynesians have flourished not only in America but also in Cambridge (England) and in Italy.[1] On both sides of the ocean they have returned to the classicals' concern with the income distribution. The Americans, however, have focused more on the monetary economy and the Europeans more on a classical real economy.

By their works ye shall know them. The Post Keynesians have done at least the following things that distinguish them from the hyphenated Keynesians.

- They have extended Keynes's doctrine by demonstrating how income distribution helps determine national income and its growth over time.
- They have combined the notion of imperfect competition with classical pricing theory to explain simultaneous stagnation and inflation (stagflation).
- They have used these two concepts — income distribution theory and price markup theory — to forge a new incomes policy.
- They have used the idea of the price markup to replace neoclassical price theory.
- They have conducted a revival of Keynes's ideas on uncertainty, specifically in regard to liquidity preference and business investment, and they have also resurrected Keynes's notion that money is primarily created by the banking system (inside money). As a result, they have defined what monetary policy can and cannot do.

---

[1] Two periodicals devoted Post Keynesian economics, the *Cambridge Journal of Economics* in England and the *Journal of Post Keynesian Economics* in the United States, bear witness to these developments. The founding co-editors of the latter were Paul Davidson (then at Rutgers University, later at the University of Tennessee) and the late Sidney Weintraub of the University of Pennsylvania. John Kenneth Galbraith, one of the founding patrons of the JPKE, was chairman of the honorary board of directors. Joan Robinson and Lord Nicholas Kaldor were among the founding patrons of the *Cambridge Journal*.

# THE INCOME DISTRIBUTION:
# SRAFFA AND KALECKI

With regard to income classes, John Maynard Keynes seemed to be of two minds: His General Theory showed how great income and wealth inequalities led to dysfunctional capitalism whereas his personal comfort was found within his own upper class and the ruling elite. This, even though George Bernard Shaw — converted to Fabian socialism by reading Marx — was only down the street, so to speak, from Keynes and the Bloomsbury group. Clara Eynsford-Hill, one of Shaw's characters and superficially without a trace of vulgarity, nonetheless represents aspects of the middle class (bourgeoisie) which Shaw and Eliza Doolittle reject — that is, Clara is disdainful of people whom she considers beneath her. Keynes too disdained the bourgeois world surrounding Queen Victoria, but they were beneath *him*.

In his concluding notes in the *General Theory*, Keynes had the British opposing the further removal of great disparities of wealth and income for the mistaken belief that a great proportion of the growth of capital is "dependent on the savings of the rich out of their superfluity."[2] As his theory shows, "the growth of capital depends not at all on a low propensity to consume but is, on the contrary, held back by it." Indeed, he proceeds to the conclusion that in contemporary conditions the growth of wealth, so far from being dependent on the abstinence of the rich, as is commonly supposed, is more likely to be impeded by it. One of the chief social justifications of great inequality of wealth is, therefore, removed.[3]

Unemployment is caused by great wealth and income inequalities; this, an economist could easily surmise, is the central idea of the General Theory! After all, investment determines saving, not the other way round. Just when the progressive economist is about to proclaim, "by George, I think he's got it," however, Keynes undoes him; he reopens the closet door to conservatism. "I believe that there

---

[2] John Maynard Keynes, *The General Theory of Employment, Interest, and Money* (New York: Harcourt, Brace & World, 1965), p. 372 [1936].
[3] *Ibid.*, p. 373.

is social and psychological justification for significant inequalities of incomes and wealth, but not for such large disparities as exist today."[4] To the conservative, "large disparities" exist only in the dreamworld of the liberal.

It is not then simply a matter of "Why can't the Keynesians be more like Keynes?" There remains the question: Why wasn't Keynes more like a Post Keynesian? Once again, the shorter our answer, the better. Keynes had the Great Depression on his mind; there was precious little time for pursuing every avenue opened by his General Theory. Keynes's ultimately conservative mission was to save capitalism by relying on the intellectual elite in Britain to implement his social program. Besides, class consciousness was one of Keynes's traits. In an attack on *Das Kapital*, Keynes wrote, "How can I adopt a creed [Marxism] which, preferring the mud to the fish, exalts the boorish proletariat above the bourgeoisie and the intelligentsia, who with all their faults, are the quality of life and surely carry the seeds of all human achievement?"[5] There is no contradiction: Keynes relied on the elite — especially the intellectual elite in Britain — to implement his social program. Eliza Doolittle and the income distribution were left to the Post Keynesians to ponder.

## Sraffa's Attempted Purge of Marginalism

The Cambridge, England Post Keynesians for sure have attempted to overthrow the marginalists explanation for income distributions. For this, they begin with a critique of marginalism that reaches back to the ideas of David Ricardo.

The classical system of fixed input proportions was swept away by the marginalists. In classical production in which equal amounts of, say labor are always combined with a unit of capital, the marginal product of capital is not simply invisible — it is not there! The real wage rate cannot be decided by the marginal physical product of

---

[4] Keynes, *op. cit.*, p. 374.
[5] Quoted in Charles Hession, *John Maynard Keynes* (New York: Macmillan, 1984), p. 224.

labor or the extra units of output from each additional worker. The theory of value or price of the marginalists vanishes with the margin.

Piero Sraffa (1898–1983), Keynes's pupil, was a brilliant and lovable Italian economist who much preferred leisure to publishing. He managed to edit the many volumes of David Ricardo's works during a few minutes or a few hours of daily effort only because he lived so long. Moreover, he finally published in 1950 a slim volume he had written in the 1920s, an enigmatic book with a curious title, *Production of Commodities by Means of Commodities: Prelude to a Critique of Economic Theory*, putting Ricardo in modern dress while providing a devastating critique of marginalism.

Capital goods, contends Sraffa, are diverse, and any measure of the "quantities" of capital in terms of a common denominator (such as another good or money) will vary as the prices of the machines themselves vary. And these prices will fluctuate with wage and profit rates. Therefore, the value of capital (its price times its quantity) is not decided by capital's marginal product, nor is the income distribution decided by the markets for land, labor, and capital.

This book was physically produced, for example, using three machines: A computer, a printing press, and a binder. The money values of capital, however, depend on the price times quantity of all these capital goods (and others) combined. The computer, the press, and the binder all sell at varying prices. Profits can no longer be a return on capital for these prices, or the "rentals" for the services from these capital goods, which themselves depend on the distribution of income between workers and capitalists.

This reincarnation of Ricardo is not as remarkable as the interpretation. No economic explanation of the income distribution emerges, and *that* is its central message. Wages and profits are social and political matters. Like John Stuart Mill, Sraffa thus separates issues of production and economic efficiency from income distribution concerns. Sharing of income among classes is determined not by the impersonal forces of the economy but by class struggle, administered wages, and relative bargaining power.

Sraffa's reincarnation of Ricardo is an abstraction of the system of production and of the way that the real value of goods is decided. Real in this sense means the value of one good expressed in terms of other goods. The real value of any one good is decided by the shares of other commodities required to produce it. At the economy's core are *basic commodities*, goods that cannot be produced independently of each other. Basic commodities appear in two roles — as inputs and as outputs. In agriculture, for example, crops are produced with seed stored from a prior growing season. When such goods are inputs or intermediate commodities, it is helpful to think of them as capital goods. Therefore, capital consists of reproducible capital goods, which are combined with labor to reproduce themselves and other commodities.[6]

At every level of production of a particular commodity, the same ingredients are always combined according to the same recipe. As the techniques of production vary by industry, different products will be produced by different combinations of labor and intermediate commodities. However, in any particular industry, labor and intermediate commodities will be mixed in the same proportions regardless of how much of the final product is being produced. The recipe or technology is not changed, and although demand affects the level of production, it plays no further role in deciding prices. In the system, either wages or profits are a given. Sraffa nullifies neoclassical demand theory even as he leaves open the theory of personal income distribution.

From this framework, Sraffa defines a *standard commodity* as a special kind of basic commodity that serves as an "invariable" measure of value or relative prices, invariable to changes in the income distribution between wages and profits. Such a measure is achieved if a wage-rate change alters the measuring rod itself in the same way that it alters the pattern of prices it is measuring. Adam Smith and David Ricardo had difficulty with labor as a standard of value because labor's current wage did not always reflect labor's past or cumulative contribution to output. Therefore, Sraffa has something else in mind: he sees relative prices (or values) and wages or profits (depending upon which one is "given") decided by the technology used in the

---

[6] Sraffa relies upon a method invented by Wassily Leontief, input-output economics, for which Leontief received the Nobel Prize in Economics. For this reason, it would be correct to refer to this production schema as the Sraffa-Leontief system.

production of basic commodities. In this way, Sraffa answers a question posed by Ricardo: How can the profit rate (as a share of "capital") be determined when the income distribution between workers and producers changes? Also, with such an invariable standard, relative price movements can be correctly assigned either to income distribution changes or to changes in the characteristics of the products themselves. Again, however, we must caution, Sraffa's prices are production prices or physical costs, not market (exchange) prices.

Sraffa points to corn production, an example used (correctly, Sraffa believes) by Ricardo, as a basic commodity in an agricultural economy. Corn was depicted as the only output of agriculture and its only commodity input. As input, corn as food was advanced to the workers and corn as seed was planted. Sraffa's economy is self-replenishing in the sense that gross output must be at least sufficient to pay for all inputs, including labor, so that production can reproduce itself. For example, imagine that corn wages are 35 bushels and the amount of seed corn required is 80 bushels to generate an output of 130 bushels at prevailing technology. In Sraffa's world, only commodity inputs count, so net product is 130 bushels minus the 80 of seed corn, or 50 bushels. Some of this net output would go to wages, supplying the workers with 35 bushels of food and leaving 15 as producer profits. Corn would then be a perfect (invariable) measure of value, because what happens to wages or profits must affect corn both as an output (food and seeds) and as an input (food and seeds), leaving the relative price of corn unaltered. As full employment and fixed technology prevail, gross output is constant. Therefore, an increase in wages (corn payments) would have to come out of profits. "Capital" cannot be substituted for labor.

Suppose wages rise to 40 bushels. With a fixed production technique, the ratio of seed-corn input to gross output would remain the same (80/130), as would the ratio of the number of workers to the amount of seed corn. Moreover, to replace the 80 bushels of seed corn and 40 bushels of corn as food would require outputs of 80 and 40, respectively. A *standard commodity*, then, is a basic commodity whose outputs appear in the same proportions as the reproducible inputs with which it is produced. A unit of such a commodity can be used as a common denominator with which to express the prices of all other commodities.

In the undecomposable core of the economy consisting of production of basic commodities, there is an entire group of commodities that enter into production in the same proportion as they exit from production. In other words, we can identify a *composite* commodity, which is our historically elusive standard commodity of invariable value, one that has the same property as the corn in Ricardo's example. Sraffa shows that the ratio of net output to "capital" inputs in this composite standard subsystem of the economy and the share of net output going to wages in that subsystem determine the rate of profit in the economy as a whole.

This outcome can be illustrated with our version of Ricardo's corn model [I have greatly simplified Sraffa by expressing his model (which includes all prices) in corn-model terms. You would need to understand how to solve a large system of simultaneous linear equations to duplicate Sraffa exactly. However, his results are identical to those derived with my simple illustration.] Recall that the original corn wages of 35 bushels and seed corn input of 80 bushels produces 130 bushels of corn. Profits equal the residual of gross output after the wage payments and the seed corn costs are subtracted, that is, $130 - 35 - 80 = 15$. Sraffa considers only the seed corn as capital (unlike Ricardo, who included the wage advance as capital). The physical profit rate on capital is $15/80$, or 19 percent. After a wage increase of 5 bushels, the profit level drops to 10 ($130 - 40 - 80$). The profit rate drops to $10/80$, or to 13 percent. A higher wage share necessarily results in a lower profit rate because labor is paid from the standard commodity. (If, instead, the profit rate is predetermined or given, the profit rate could be raised and then the wage share would fall.)

The connections among net output, the profit rate, and the wage share can be shown with Sraffa's solution to his system, which is

$$\text{Profit Rate} = (\text{Net Output}/\text{Means of Production}) \times (1 - \text{Wages}/\text{Net Output}).$$

In the first case, where wages are 35, we have

$$\text{Profit Rate} = 0.63(1 - 0.70) = 19 \text{ percent.}$$

After the wage increase,

$$\text{Profit Rate} = 0.63(1 - 0.80) = 13 \text{ percent.}$$

The result for corn as the standard commodity can be extended to a multitude of basic commodities. As wages are not connected with any change in production technology in Sraffa's view, an increase in wages does not change the relative prices of the commodities within the composite yardstick. The composite standard commodity also would be produced with a ratio of inputs identical to the ratio of outputs. Therefore, any jump in wage costs (paid in composite commodity) does not alter this relationship; the consequent change in the prices of inputs is reflected equiproportionately in the prices of outputs so that the input-output ratios remain intact.

Sraffa derives another important result that holds equally for the standard commodity and for other basic commodities. A move in the wage (and profit) rate leaves the ratio of net output to means of production unaltered. In the corn example, the initial ratio of net output to commodity input cost is 50/80, or 0.63. After wages have increased by 14 percent, the ratio of net output to the means of production (the commodity input) is still 0.63. There is no mystery in these numbers: this consequence follows directly from the fixed factor proportions, in which productivity is determined solely by the technical conditions of production rather than from the distribution of product or income between wages or profits.

The invariability of the yardstick, of course, does not mean that prices do not change because the world is not all corn or composite standard commodity. So let us move on to another of Sraffa's intriguing conclusions. As labor and the other means of production are used in unequal proportions in the various basic industries (the ratio of labor to "other inputs" in steel will not necessarily be the same as in corn production), a general wage increase (and profit-rate drop) will cause relative prices to change — say, the standard commodity value of steel compared to corn — because labor will be a larger share of production costs in some industries than in others. Still, the new income distribution will not alter the ratio of net output to the means of production because input requirements remain unaffected. (A change in technology of production also will alter relative prices of basics. The proportions of labor and commodities used in production are altered, and their prices and quantities will vary from those of the old recipe. Therefore, production costs must change.)

Consider the nonbasic commodities, those (including services) that are not used in further production and enter only into final demand. They are strictly consumer goods or services, such as hair-styling or medical treatments. Changes in the prices of nonbasic commodities alone do not alter the relative prices of basics. The reason should be obvious by now.

By definition, a nonbasic commodity is never used in the produc-tion of basics, so a change in the price of a nonbasic does not alter the price of a basic. For example, an increase in the price of hotel rooms does not increase the cost of producing automobiles, because hotel rooms (a nonbasic) are not inputs in the automobile production plant. The impact is limited to changes in the exchange ratios between the nonbasic commodity involved (hotel rooms) and all other commodities.

We need to be judicious in our selection of inferences from Sraffa's abstract world, no matter how appealingly tidy his analysis. As formulated, his results depend crucially upon the presence in a mod-ern economy of a unique collection of industries producing basic commodities, the commodities used to produce each other. The ker-nel of truth in Ricardo's purely agricultural economy must extend to a large area of a modern economy in which nonbasic consumer-goods (and service) industries constitute a fairly small share of total national output. As we shall see, Sraffa's treatment of labor as neither a basic nor a nonbasic service raises questions about the nature of demand. Nonetheless, Sraffa's notion of a standard commodity group in the economy drives a wedge in the neoclassical system sufficiently wide to allow room for new theories of demand and the income distribution.

Sraffa's approach returns economic theory to the classical descrip-tion of production, especially the view of David Ricardo. The classical system of fixed input proportions was swept away by the marginalists, for reasons that will now be apparent. In an industry in which equal amounts of, say, labor are always combined with a unit of capital, the marginal product of capital is not merely difficult to find — it is not there to be found! Profits can no longer be said to be a return on capital because the profit rate varies with the wage rate. Moreover, the neo-Ricardian theory tells us that relative (real) price movements are driven by changes in the income distribution and technology rather than by demand movements. Finally, the income distribution can be altered without changes in net production levels relative to the available means of production. There is little room for the usual supply-and-demand considerations so central to neoclassical price theory because the wages-to-profits relation becomes a social-political question.

Now that we have seen what *doesn't* decide the income distribution, let us turn to a story of what *does* determine it.

## Kalecki's Income Classes: The Workers and the Capitalists

Another contributor to Cambridge Post Keynesianism was the Marxist economist Michal Kalecki (1899–1970). While at Cambridge in 1935 in self-imposed exile from Poland, Kalecki was befriended by John Kenneth Galbraith. "A small, often irritable, independent, intense man," Galbraith relates, "Kalecki was the most innovative figure in economics I have known, not excluding Keynes."[7] Like Sraffa, Kalecki seldom put pen to paper. But when he did, the clarity and depth of his thoughts were powerful.

In 1933, Kalecki had developed a Keynes-style theory of the level of employment, prior to and independent of Keynes's General Theory. Kalecki's income distribution views, however, were more in tune with the Ricardian and Marxian chorus about income classes. In fact, Kalecki's theory can be summed up in the adage, "The workers spend what they get; the capitalists get what they spend." It would have made a marvelous line for one of George Bernard Shaw's plays.

---

[7] John Kenneth Galbraith, *A Life in Our Times: Memoirs* (Boston: Houghton Mifflin, 1981), p. 75.

The national income or product can be measured from either the income side or the expenditures side, so:

*Income*

> Profits (capitalists' income) + wages (workers' income)
> = National Income.

*Expenditures*

> Investment + capitalists' consumption + workers' consumption
> = National Product.

In this schema, all workers' wages are spent entirely on necessary goods, so wages must equal the workers' expenditures on consumption goods — the food, shelter, clothing, and transportation required for life and for work. (In reality, of course, today's workers spend income on some goods and services that are not strictly necessities, but Kalecki is using Marx's and John S. Mill's notion of cultural subsistence.) Sraffa's system reveals the inputs necessary to produce particular outputs; Kalecki's defines the amounts of necessary consumption goods.[8] A worker receives, say, $40,000 per year in income and spends $14,000 on food and drink, $10,000 on housing and utilities, $6,500 on durable goods such as an automobile and a washing machine, $4,000 on medical care, $4,000 on clothing, and $1,500 on miscellaneous goods and services. ($40,000 income = $14,000 + $10,000 + $6,500 + $4,000 + $4,000 + $1,500 expenditures.) No savings are accumulated by the worker and therefore, no net wealth. Consumer installment purchases are assumed zero.

If we further simplify by saying that all profits are diligently plowed back into the business to purchase new investment goods, savings as well as investments are equal to profits. The capitalist is the

---

[8] The author has created this bridge in E. Ray Canterbery, "Galbraith, Sraffa, Kalecki and Supra-Surplus Capitalism," *Journal of Post Keynesian Economics*, 7, 77–90 (Fall 1984). This article contains more detail on how the ideas of Galbraith, Sraffa, and Kalecki can be synthesized. See also Canterbery, "A Theory of Supra-Surplus Capitalism," Presidential Address, *Eastern Economic Journal* (Winter 1988).

lone saver in this simple economy. The capitalist's profits will equal the sum of the value of their purchases of investment and consumption goods. A diligent capitalist might receive $800,000 in annual profits, which he divides between $700,000 for new machinery to replace some outmoded equipment in his plant and $100,000 for living expenses ($800,000 profits = $700,000 investment + $100,000 consumption). Since investment equals savings, savings = profits – capitalist's consumption.

The first surprise? Capitalists can add to their current share of the national income (profits) by having increased their investment spending in a prior period. Investment, Keynes' style, is multiplied in terms of total output. Out of a larger output come greater profits.

More shockingly, even if the capitalists consume their profits in the style of the savings and loan executives of the 1980s — buying yachts, building vacation homes, supporting lovers — they experience no decrease in profits income. Capitalists' income is not vulnerable to *how* it is spent because increases in the purchase of goods lead to higher levels of production. Capitalist profits are like the water of the artesian well: No matter how much water is taken out, the well never empties.

The accumulation of capital is both the rainbow and the pot of gold! If a greater share of national output is devoted to investment goods, the level of employment in the investment sector will be greater and since investment equals profit a greater share of the national income will go to the capitalists. Conversely, if a greater share of output is devoted to consumer necessities, the workers snatch a larger piece of the national income pie.

Although the capitalists are masters of their own universe in this sense, Kalecki saw outside elements, such as uncertainties regarding profitable investments, causing unavoidable fluctuations in profits.

A Kaleckian view of production can be made to conform with Sraffa's subsistence model (in Chapter 1 of *Production of Commodities*). This synthesis is not surprising if we pause to appreciate the unbroken lineage from Ricardo to Marx to Kalecki and from Ricardo to Marx to Sraffa.

Let us retain the above distinction between the worker and the capitalist income classes. Suppose further that the economy is divided

Kalecki-like into two distinct industries, one producing necessary consumption goods, the other producing necessary investment goods, mostly machines and buildings. In Sraffa's admittedly simple world of fixed technology, the amount of business investment and the prevailing production technology then decide the level of employment as well as the division of labor between the production of necessities and the manufacture of investment goods. This technology and the prevailing level of capacity to produce (the size of plants equipped with vintage technology) also decide the total amount of each class of good produced.

The introduction of subsistence wages into Sraffa's model transforms it into a Kaleckian world of income distribution. Workers' incomes generate a flow of spending that decides the quantity of necessities manufactured. The quantity of investment goods produced is determined by the entrepreneurs' expected future profits. These investment goods are combined, of course, with labor effort. Suppose one worker is employed for every two machines in steel production — that is, machines and workers are utilized in a 2:1 ratio. If steel production is doubled, even though more workers and more machines are used, the increase in the units of each must be such that at the higher level of output each worker still is using two machines and the 2:1 overall ratio remains intact. That is, capital and labor are combined in fixed proportions in the short run.

Investment goods are produced in part by investment goods. It is helpful here to imagine Sraffa's commodities being produced with commodities. Machines and labor have to be combined in order to reproduce machines. Therefore, the sales receipts of the investment-goods industry from the necessities-goods industry must cover the investment-goods industry's labor costs plus the cost of the machine-babies, that is, the investment-goods industry's own machines. Those required investment outlays are equal to the profits of the investment-goods industry.

Obviously, the combined profits from both industries must equal the value of produced investment goods. With equal predictability, real wages (money wages adjusted for the price of necessities) equal the amount of necessities produced. Likewise, the profits from both industries combine to purchase the output of the investment-goods industry. This means that the larger the investment-goods industry of the economy, the greater will be the profits for capitalists! As leaders, the capitalists are their own followers.

The distribution of income between workers and capitalists becomes the hallmark of this approach. The division of income between wages and profits is the mirror image of the distribution of national output between consumer necessities and technologically necessary investment goods. The allocation of labor between the production of necessities and investment goods has already been decided by the technology for producing the two general classes of goods.

Now we have a result identical to that in the national income account schema. If a greater share of national output is devoted to investment goods, the level of employment in the investment sector will be greater relative to the consumer necessities sector, and (given that investment = profits) a greater share of the national income will go to the capitalists. Conversely, if a greater share of output is devoted to consumer necessities, the workers will have a larger piece of the national income pie. However, there remain some major difficulties with this Sraffian-Kaleckian system.

After introducing his classical subsistence model, Sraffa moves on to a production surplus economy, one that produces commodities in excess of labor's physiological necessities plus actual depreciation of all the means of production. In Sraffa's model of the surplus economy, basic commodities or goods that appear as inputs *and* outputs are necessities *only* in a *technological* sense.

In the surplus economy, nonbasic commodities or goods and services entering only into final demand include both consumer necessities and luxuries — even for workers. Only in Sraffa's subsistence model are basic commodities necessities in consumption as well as in production. In his surplus economy, Sraffa makes no attempt to separate the allocation of extra-subsistence wages between necessary and "luxury" consumer goods. Kalecki's simplified model does not allow workers to consume luxuries. Moreover, Sraffa's treatment of labor as neither a basic nor nonbasic service in the surplus economy raises additional serious questions about the nature of demand.

Ironically, then, a critical insight into the advanced economy lies hidden in the model so quickly dismissed by Sraffa, his subsistence model in which both necessary consumption and necessary capital goods coexist. Such a model reveals that labor is best treated as a basic "commodity" or, better, basic service, because labor is still necessary to produce subsistence commodities. Labor is an input and an output in the (at least) self-reproducing economy. Nevertheless, in the long run just as the standard commodity must change with new technology, the quantity of consumer "necessities" must change as what is necessary is redefined.

## THE VITA VIEW OF THE PERSONAL INCOME DISTRIBUTION

In the traditional world of economics wages and profits are factor payments to labor and capital. In the economy we have been describing, this isn't so. Income payments are made to persons and therefore we are concerned with the personal income distribution.

Beyond his subsistence model wherein labor requires a subsistence wage in order to meet basic physiological needs, Sraffa provides no guide to the distribution of surpluses. What happens then to Sraffa's and Kalecki's theories when — as is the case in a modern economy — we find some "workers" with sufficient incomes to indulge in nonspending, that is saving? If such persons purchase income-producing financial assets, they can then share (albeit indirectly) in total profits. The incomes of such persons then include labor earnings plus some capitalistic profits. In this case, of course, the "working class" receives a larger share of the national income than that derived from their labor efforts alone.

Because such earners also receive some nonwage income — interest on savings accounts, rents, or profits — more than two income classes exist, and the simple distinction between "workers" and "capitalists" dissolves. Such income intervals would identify the personal income distribution. However, this refinement of the income distribution does not alter Kalecki's general conclusions as long as there is one group that receives only profits income.[9] Such a group of income receivers does exist (coexist?) in modern capitalistic societies.

In short, the reliance on a stereotyped income division between workers and capitalists is an inadequate explanation for the income distribution of an affluent society. Moreover, it tells us little about the characteristics of the labor receiving differential income payments beyond the color of their collars. We need to know more about why different households occupy varied places in the income distribution Our concerns go beyond the extremes of Tiger Woods' $110 million for playing golf, Jay Leno's $32 million as a talk-show host, or Taylor Swift's $17.2 million for singing. A pharmacist in El Paso, Texas earned $143,000 while a library director in Springfield, Illinois earned $36,000. The CEO of Xerox in Rochester, N.Y. earned $900,000 while the owner of a recycling company in Cadet, Missouri earned only $36,800. A real-estate appraiser in Vail, Colorado earned $215,000 while a copy editor in Corvallis, Oregon earned only $25,000. A family physician averages about $160,000 a year; a specialist averages $267,000.[10] Generally, the more specialized the occupation, the higher the income. Incomes vary with a myriad of occupations, gender, and location. Unionized workers generally earn more than like-occupied nonunion workers. The personal income distribution is highly unequal. More unequal still is the wealth distribution. The members of these diverse income classes end up spending their incomes in equally distinct stores, restaurants, and nightclubs. My vita theory provides a more eclectic explanation. Sraffa and Kalecki leave open the possibility of new theory of the personal income distribution.

A vita is a brief summary of the main attributes and events of one's life, a kind of autobiographic sketch. The vita theory is a way of saying

---

[9] See Luigi L. Pasinetti, *Growth and Income Distribution* (Cambridge, England: Cambridge University Press, 1974).

[10] For these incomes and for many other occupations for spring 2010, see *Parade*, April 11 (2010), cover and pp. 4–14.

that an individual's life history is important in deciding his or her income, and that income is important in deciding the person's life.[11]

The main thrust of a vita theory can be simply stated. Imagine that one labor market exists for each general class of labor, such as plumbers, medical doctors, electricians, or elementary school teachers. The individual's quality as a productive member of the economic system determines which labor market that person enters. A person "qualifies" for a particular labor market by the state of his or her vita at that time. The vita begins with birth, when race, sex, religion, national origin, inherent or initial mental and physical capacities, inheritances, and family background (endowments) are duly noted.

The autobiography is added to over the life span by education, other training, and experience. An individual does have some control over the length and depth of his autobiography. However, production "recipes" change in the long run. Because labor demand is related to technology as well as to product and services demand, only the rarest of individuals can predict with any accuracy the amount of future demand for workers with his or her own emerging or mature autobiography. Beyond this, specific labor supply conditions are a collective outcome that is beyond personal control.

Thus, given his vita and the characteristics of the applicable labor market, the individual's basic wage rate depends upon the average wage for such services. Upon closer examination, however, the individual's personal income exhibits differentials from potential labor market earnings. The differentials — occupational, geographic, interindustry, union-nonunion, discriminatory, and so on — often can be traced back to the first vita stage, the birth vita. Second and third stages are the precareer vita, and the career or mature vita. Speaking in terms of life stages highlights those events and times in which the individual often loses control over important choices. At birth, the genetic code has already determined one's initial or innate

---

[11] A detailed development of the vita theory of the personal income distribution (including the mathematics) appears in E. Ray Canterbery, "A Vita Theory of Personal Income Distribution," *Southern Economic Journal*, **46**, 12–48 (July 1979).

IQ, sex, race, and initial state of health. The precareer vita is the time for education, when earning qualities can be enhanced. For example, 35 percent of all white householders earned $30,000 or more in 1981 while 15 percent of black householders earned as much. Of these above-average whites, 63 percent were college graduates compared with 14 percent who had completed elementary school education. Of the above-average blacks, 47 percent were college graduates whereas seven percent had completed elementary school. Education adds substantially to the income of blacks, though not nearly as much as to that of whites. Education beyond that which is mandatory and free normally depends heavily upon parental contributions. Individuals thus have only moderate control over their precareer vitae because voluntary schooling and training is often directly related to inherited material endowments. By maturity, the options of the individuals are greatly narrowed. From the view of earnings prospects, the autobiography is for the most part written, although one new consideration enters at this life stage — years of experience.

The labor force, the supply side of the labor market, consists of those people who are of working age, who wish to work, and who have either precareer or mature vitae, which identify the person's occupational characteristics. In the short run, individuals can enter only that labor market they "fit"; in the long run, they potentially can change their characteristics and qualify for a different labor market, perhaps one with a higher wage rate. In general, however, the number of vitae directly applicable to the labor market decreases with increases in skills, special aptitudes, and required credentials. For example, the number of people who qualify as unskilled labor greatly exceeds the number who qualify as medical doctors. Similarly, the possibilities for substitution of different types of labor are greater among occupations with unskilled labor markets. The least labor substitution occurs within the most specialized occupations. At the higher skilled extreme, in fact, the professional occupation *is* the labor market.

There is no assurance that all vitae will be employed at any particular time, for employment levels depend upon demand. However, it is presumed that, wherever involuntary unemployment exists, it involves those of lowest ranked employment vitae, including young people with precareer vitae who lack job training or are being newly considered for on-the-job training.

During production and employment expansion, upward occupational mobility can occur. However, labor institutions — craft unions and industrial unions — are a major part of the real-world conditions for mobility. Industrial unions, for example, organize entire industries. They consist of persons with diverse autobiographies and occupations, including both the unskilled and the semiskilled. The main economic effect of the industrial union is the negotiation of a wage floor for its members. However, the industrial union attempts to gain some of the advantages of the craft union through apprenticeship regulations, seniority practices, and (in some cases) discrimination. These practices alter the mobility conditions for union workers as they attempt to change occupations within the unionized plant.

The vita theory points toward a structural view of labor demand. In the short run, employment and wages are not always determined by the same forces. In describing such a process, we lose the determinism of the neoclassical labor market but gain some realism.

In the short run, product prices, the state of technology, and industrial competition are givens. Employment is a fixed proportion of production so the quantity of labor demanded is tied directly to the production level. With fixed capital-to-labor combinations, employment levels are unrelated to the wage rate and therefore vary with output levels.

Technological progress can alter demand for a particular labor type in two ways. First, it can change labor-quantity requirements. Though capital and labor complement each other in the short run or even the intermediate run (two workers may be needed for each new machine), they can become substitutes for each other in the longer run. The long-run trend of wages in the concentrated sector is known to be upward, and it is not surprising that the main purpose of new equipment in industrialized economies is to reduce labor employment. Technological change also exerts a more indirect effect on labor demand. A new, more complex technology can cause a shift to labor of a different type altogether. Workers who once combined the ingredients for frozen cakes may be unqualified to monitor the automated machines that now perform this task, and unemployment of these workers results.

The labor markets dominated by industrial unions are akin to "administered" wages and prices. If the labor union is strong, industry's ability to pay the demanded wage is enhanced by its ability to impose price markups upon the consumer. The industrial union's tool is the wage rate rather than the labor supply. This means that in the short run employment is not related to the wage rate, and the wage rate is related to employment only if full employment extends across all labor. (At full employment, wages can be bid up by Keynesian excess demand.) Therefore, a high wage can be associated with a high unemployment rate because employment is decided by the level of production.

Union labor sets the pace for the wage structure across the industrial economy. Moreover, the price markup is not limited to concentrated industries. Competitive industries producing industrial or consumer necessities can pass along rising costs because the industry or consumer supplied does not have an alternative to the product.

The long-run labor supply is related to what individuals expect the wage rate to be, because the supply over time represents the maturing of vitae that have been directed along a career path designed years earlier. In the long run, increases in the expected market wage rate, for whatever reasons, are likely to attract new entrants, and the labor supply for that class of worker is increased. Even in this longer run, it is probable that the labor supply will be controlled in craft union areas. It is not mere historical accident that skilled workers were the first to organize in craft unions and successfully raise wage rates.

The actual and expected wages rates may tend to converge for industrial labor, but this by no means assures a full employment equilibrium for such labor. The substitution of newer industrial processes that require less labor may have advanced to the point that long periods of idleness are traded off for higher wages. Full employment under such conditions might require extraordinarily high production levels and glut of goods. An unused supply of unskilled labor is a characteristic of recent experience in the United States, England, and Western Europe.

The vita theory explains several kinds of wage differentials. If we impose the assumption of "rational man" or "superrational man" with respect to income, these differentials represent an opportunity for a worker to move from a low-wage market to a high-wage market. Unfortunately, the mobility of labor is a complex, difficult, and cumbersome process. Studies attribute only 53–69 percent of migration to purely economic motives, leaving considerable room for the motivations of regional preference, health, education, housing, marriage, lifestyle, and an so on.

Nonetheless, according to the vita theory, a higher wage rate for individuals depends upon their mobility. Significant upward mobility requires the acquisition of a "higher quality" set of skills, whether in response to changing technological requirements or because of the individual's desire to increase income and status. Despite the training and education that require a substantial amount of time and personal investment, this search for higher earnings may end with still another barricade. The individual may not receive the wage rate of the labor market and occupation of his choice because of genetic characteristics — race, sex, nationality. Even age is a source of discrimination that can bar a worker from receiving the desired wage. Studies suggest that more than half of the earnings differential relates to racial discrimination. In short, earnings and income differentials are wider than wage differences. Under such circumstances, the best advice is that children be very selective with regard to their parentage.[12]

The vita theory sheds some light on labor market conditions during the Great Recession in the United States. By October 2010 the jobs crisis brought an unwelcome discovery for many of the unemployed. Job openings in their old fields existed. Yet they no longer qualified for them. Some companies asked staffers to take on a broader array of duties — duties that once were spread among multiple jobs. By now, someone who hoped to get those jobs must meet

---

[12] See John Brittain, *The Inheritance of Inequality* (Washington, D.C.: The Brookings Institution, 1977).

the new requirements. The importance of the precareer vita is high-lighted by the distribution of unemployment in September 2010. For those with less than high school education, the unemployment rate was 15.4 percent; with high school completed, 10.0 percent; some college, 9.1 percent; bachelor's degree or higher, 4.4 percent.

In the light of the vita theory, an economy of workers demanding only minimal necessities cannot be described as robust. If we are looking for an "invariant" measure of value from the demand side, the quantity of necessities per worker seems a better candidate than Sraffa's composite standard commodity. Nevertheless, in the long run, just as the standard commodity must change with new technology, the quantity of "necessities" will change as workers redefine what is necessary. Whether necessities are a constant or a variable market basket of goods and services, their quantities and prices will determine their dollar value and the required dollar value of the wage bill. For example, in the autumn of 1980, the Bureau of Labor Statistic (BLS) estimated the annual cost of a "lower" consumption budget for a four-person family in the urban United States at $14,044. This household's budget included expenditures on food, shelter, furnishings, transportation, clothing, personal care, and medical care. If $14,044 represented the cultural subsistence requirements for an average family in the urban United States, the wage bill paid to the household had to be at least $14,044.

Surpluses, a characteristic of the capitalistic economy, are production increments in excess of what is required merely to sustain life. Although it cannot be denied that there are American households that exist at the biological subsistence level, ours is indisputably a supra-surplus economy, or Galbraith's affluent society.

The estimate for the "higher" consumption budget for a four-person family in the urban United States in 1980 was $34,409, nearly 2.5 times the lower budget. The "intermediate" budget was estimated at $23,134. Does this mean that the higher one's income goes, the greater the number of necessities the individual must meet? The answer, though not definitive, is illuminating. In an economy such as ours, we need to distinguish between absolute physical necessities and "wants." The satisfaction of a greater number of wants is usually associated with higher standards of living. Leaving aside the question of whether people continue to be better off at higher and higher income levels, we can say with certainty that the ratio of the dollar value of absolute biological necessities to the wage bill paid to the U.S. higher-income family is much less than one.[13]

The vita theory also sheds light on the wealth distribution. Again, the birth vita sets the upper and lower levels of wealth. It is difficult, though not by any means impossible, to overcome disadvantages from sex, race and household endowments. Women in 2010 had wages equal to about 87 percent of men's wages. Black people, especially women, had much lower wage levels than white people. Rich households tend to perpetuate themselves; again, there are notable exceptions. The stark reality is found in the figures for the wealth distribution in the United States and worldwide.

## THE PRICE MARKUP AND PRICES

### The Imperfection of Competition and Kalecki's "Degree of Monopoly"

The struggle between the working and the capitalist classes shapes not only the income distribution but also classical-style pricing. In turn, the combination of these forces provides one explanation for stagflation — that dreaded combo of stagnation and inflation.

Kalecki was very much into the world of imperfect competition in which production was the business of only a few firms in each industry or oligopoly. A firm can raise its own price right along with its production costs if other firms in the industry do likewise. When General Motors, once the most efficient of only three American producers of automobiles, signs a union contract with the United Auto Workers of America for higher wages, the corporation also raises prices more or less in proportion to the wage hike. Chrysler and Ford then follow suit.

---

[13] An interesting distinction between necessities and comforts is made by Tibor Scitovsky in *The Joyless Economy* (New York: Oxford University Press, 1976), pp. 106–131.

The "degree of monopoly" was the outcome not only of industrial concentration but also of tacit agreements, selling agents, and advertising. In one of his last published papers, Kalecki explained how high markups (of price over costs) would encourage strong trade unions to bargain for higher wages, since oligopolistic firms had the ability to pay them. There is a wee bit of Galbraith (see later) in that paper.

## The Price Markup and the Price Level

The introduction of imperfect competition in macroeconomic theory is due not only to Kalecki, John Kenneth Galbraith, and Joan Robinson, but also to Sidney Weintraub (1914–1983) at the University of Pennsylvania. Kalecki's and Weintraub's vision of pricing in the manufacturing sector can be dramatized in Kalecki's cryptic style — markup.[14]

An example will clarify the role of the markup. If the wage cost per personal computer is $700 and the markup is ten percent, the profits flow per unit of production if $70. If one million PCs are sold yearly, industry profits are $70 million. If wage costs rise to $800 per unit, the unchanged markup rate of ten percent over current costs will now generate an earnings flow of $80 million, given the same number of units sold.

If money wages are administered by union-management agreements, the balance of income is provided by the markup over wages, most of which will be retained profits (profits plus depreciation) and dividend payouts. Capacity utilization may move up and down with

---

[14] Whereas Kalecki's markup applies only to manufacturing, Weintraub's is more general and applies to all industries, including those that are nearly competitive. A markup pricing rule is now widely used in orthodox econometric modeling. See Otto Eckstein ed., *The Econometrics of Price Determination* (Washington, D.C.: Board of Governors of Federal Reserve System, 1974); Arthur Okun, *Prices and Quantities: A Macroeconomics Analysis* (Washington, D.C.: Brookings Institution, 1981); and William D. Nordhaus, "The Falling Rate of Profits," *Brookings Papers of Economic Activity*, 74(1), 169–208 (1974).

demand, but the firm usually will stick with the markup that achieves its target level of retained profits. This target depends on its dividend payout ratio to stockholders, its amount of debt relative to its equity, and (according to some Post Keynesians such as the late Alfred Eichner) its perceived investment needs. According to Weintraub, even highly competitive firms price according to a markup rule. The price markup target's highest limit is determined by the current number of firms in the industry and by the firm's perceived price elasticity of demand or consumers' sensitivity to price changes. Generally, the fewer the firms in the industry and the lower the sensitivity of consumers to price increases (the lower the price elasticity of demand), the higher the upper limit to the price markup.[15] Although the margin of prices over current costs already reflects the market power of the firm in a concentrated industry, even a fixed markup allows for a higher price when the unit cost of production goes up.

Income in excess of cultural subsistence leaves a demand wedge and breathing space for producers. The price markup is the breath of fresh air that fills the void. Although the stylized income division between workers and capitalists creates the Marxian drama of a "class struggle," Kalecki understood that such a razor-sharp division cannot fully explain the income distribution and its effects in an "affluent society" (Galbraith's term). The new upper middle-class

---

[15] See Canterbery in "A Theory of Supra-Surplus Capitalism," *op. cit.* and "An Evolutionary Model of Technical Change with Markup Pricing," in William Milberg, *The Megacorp and Macrodynamics* (Armonk, New York and London, England: M.E. Sharp, 1992), pp. 85–100.

The motivation for investment "needs" has been variously attributed to market share, growth, and power goals. These explanations have been put forward, respectively, by Alfred S. Eichner, *The Megacorp and Oligopoly: Micro Foundations of Macro Dynamics* (Cambridge: Cambridge University Press, 1975); Robin Marris, *The Economic Theory of "Managerial" Capitalism* (New York: Basic Books, 1964); and John Kenneth Galbraith. To the extent that borrowed funds are used to finance increments to the capital stock, new financial assets are created in the process of business investment. Hyman Minsky takes this position in his *John Maynard Keynes* (New York: Columbia University Press, 1975).

consumer, once satisfied with a black Model T, must now be motivated to buy a streamlined, racy, colorful machine designed for maximum road comfort and perhaps fulfilling exotic fantasies. These new attributes of the automobile lend themselves to persuasion through advertising.

Ironically, the markup is used most directly by commercial and investment bankers. Bankers have a prime rate for the "least risky" short-term loans to business. It is a rate "marked-up" from the federal funds rate, the interest rate changed by the federal reserve for loans to private banks. Many mortgage loan rates are based on the ten-year treasury bond (with a markup). As we shall see, these cascading interest rates played a role in the Great Recession.

## Stagflation

How do we get from firm and industry pricing behavior to the general price level? We begin with the old equation of exchange. If

$$(\text{Price level}) \times (\text{real output}) = (\text{money national income})$$

or

$$(\text{Price level}) = (\text{money national income})/(\text{real output})$$

then stable prices require that money income grow no faster than real output. If the money income per employee rises no faster than output per employee (productivity), the inflation rate is pleasantly zero.

Money wages then become central to the price level. The money wages are inflexible downward, because to reduce money wages violates an implicit contract with the worker or perhaps a written labor contract, which often has been negotiated by an industrial union. If the Teamsters' Union signs a contract for a 30 percent wage increase divided equally over a three-year term, no one would expect the second year increment to be sliced to, say, five percent. In the short run, therefore, product prices must adjust to money wages and the cost of production rather than vice versa. There is a revised sequence in which the price level and inflation are resolved after the money wage rates are determined. Money wages, outside Sraffa's system, are determined by social-political conditions.[16]

This Post Keynesian view exposes the possibility of simultaneous inflation and unemployment (stagflation). The short-run response to any consumer resistance will be not wage or price slowdowns but slower production. Substantial production cutbacks will lead — with a lag — to worker layoffs. This view, too, can explain why recession teamed up with inflation, peaking in 1973 to 1974 and again in 1979 to 1980, following soaring world oil prices. A similar camel-like pattern is found in the UK, Germany and France. Oil, a necessary input in the production process, raises through its price the unit cost of production. Even with a constant percentage markup, the price of output will rise.

## INCOMES POLICY

The Post Keynesian explanation of the income distribution and the price level leads to a third kind of economic policy to supplement Keynesian fiscal and monetary policy. All incomes policies were widely discussed by economists during the 1970s era of stagflation. If the tenacious advocacy of deficit spending characterizes the fiscal Keynesians, the relentless pursuit of an incomes policy distinguishes the Post Keynesians.

Some fiscal Keynesians, such as James Tobin, nonetheless joined hands with the Post Keynesians to endorse an incomes policy. An incomes policy blatantly requires that wages or profits be "controlled" in some sense. The profit margin will be whatever it will be because of the relative consistency of the price markup. However, as time goes by, wages go up and the price level with them.

---

[16] Money wages are endogenous in the manner described in Canterbery's vita theory of the labor market: See E. Ray Canterbery, "A Vita Theory of Personal Income Distribution," *op. cit.*

## What to Control? Wages or Profits?

Firms prefer, if anything be controlled, it be wages: Unions favor the control of profits. Equity and political problems quickly emerge with the control of wages alone. A variable markup can be a source of profits-push inflation so that the part of profits not retained by corporations for financing investment also would require regulation. Dividends and corporate salaries might be taxed at a rate that keeps them in line with the growth of wage income. Irrespective of whose ox is gored, all incomes policies have the same theme: Money income changes are to be geared to the pace of productivity.

Real-world incomes policies have ranged all the way from voluntary wage and price guidelines to the mandatory wage and price controls long advocated by John Kenneth Galbraith. Such measures were utilized in different forms and with varying vigor by the Kennedy, Johnson, Nixon, Ford, and Carter administrations.


## The TIP Proposals

An alternative to wage and price guidelines or controls is tax incentives, smart-targeted to modify the behavior of labor unions and concentrated industry. Incentives and deterrents of the price mechanism are used ju-jitsu style against itself. One tax-based incomes policy (TIP) was developed by Weintraub and by Henry Wallich (1914–1989), once a governor of the Federal Reserve Board.

TIP works this way. Whenever a corporation grants a pay increase in excess of an established norm — say, six percent — the firm granting the pay raise would be penalized by an increase in its income tax. If a firm increased the average pay of its workers by, say, ten percent rather than by six percent, the firm might be required to pay ten percent more in taxes on its profits. The wage-salary norms would be the average increase of wages and salaries of the firm, so that above-average wage stipends could be awarded to meritorious workers. The goal would be to confine average money wage increases to the gains in average labor productivity in the economy.

What is the premise underlying TIP? Individual businesses will be encouraged to resist unreasonable wage demands only when they are convinced that resistance also will come from other firms and industries. TIP tilts the individual firm in the direction of yielding only noninflationary average wage increases. The laborers would benefit from real wage gains as inflation subsides.

A TIP is a very flexible policy: It can provide a penalty for a wage increase above the norm, a reward for a wage below the norm, or both. The neo-Keynesian Arthur Okun (1928–1980), once economic adviser to President Johnson and later associated with the Brookings Institution, preferred carrots to sticks. If a firm holds its average yearly rate of wage increase below six percent and its average rate of price increase below four percent, Okun's plan would give the employees of the firm a tax rebate (carrot) and the firm would receive a rebate on its income tax liabilities.

A TIP of the carrot persuasion was proposed by President Jimmy Carter in October 1978. However, the incentive was indirect, a kind of diced carrot. It would have provided tax relief for those workers who stayed below their wage norm if the annual inflation rate ended up above seven percent. Congress rejected the initiative.

Conditions have changed since the original TIP proposal. For one thing, the effective average corporate income tax rate, the original tax penalty based for TIP, has been approaching zero. For another, net interest income as a share of national income increased 14-fold between the end of World War II and 1990. Therefore, it appears essential to obtain a new federal revenue source to exert downward pressure on interest rates as well as a TIP that acknowledges monetary interest as a new, increasingly important source of rising production costs. In order to deal with these problems, in 1983 I proposed: (1) an equitable value-added tax (VAT) as a new revenue source and as the ideal tax base for the immediate implementation of TIP; and (2) a simplified personal income tax program that would satisfy those critics of VAT who viewed it as inequitable. Several of the features of the simplified personal income tax have been implemented by

Congress: VAT remains in limbo.[17] Later, we shall return to this VATIP proposal.

## MONEY AND THE FINANCING OF INVESTMENT

There is a finance connection between profits and funds for the firm's investment. The markup and investment plans are inextricably linked — in one direction or the other, and perhaps in both Because of the degree-of-monopoly, prices do not reflect *current* demand conditions; they are more closely tied to *expected* future demand. At times capacity will exceed current needs, but this situation is no problem for an oligopoly.

Kalecki, in particular, sees the oligopoly ensuring its needs for investment funds through its pricing powers. The sensitivity or price elasticity of the demand by workers for necessities is essentially zero. Therefore, producers can raise prices with impunity and raise revenues from consumer necessities in excess of the costs of production as a source of funds for the purchase of investment goods.

Machines and labor have to be combined in order to reproduce machines. Therefore, the sales receipts of the investment or capital-goods industry from the necessities-goods industry will cover the investment-goods industry's labor costs plus the cost of the machine-babies: That is, the capital-goods industry's own machines. Those required investment outlays equal profits of the investment-goods industry.

The combined profits from both industries must equal the value of produced capital goods just as real wages (money wages adjusted for the price of necessities) must equal the amount of necessities produced. Likewise, the profits from both industries combine to

---

[17] See E. Ray Canterbery, "Tax Reform and Incomes Policy: A VATIP Proposal," *Journal of Post Keynesian Economics*, **5**, 430–439 (Spring 1983). A later, more detailed version of the proposal appears in E. Ray Canterbery, Eric W. Cook, and Bernard A. Schmitt, "The Flat Tax, Negative Tax, and VAT: Gaining Progressivity and Revenue," *Cato Journal*, 521–536 (Fall 1985).

purchase the output of the investment-goods industry, creating even more profits for the capitalists.

This stylized Kaleckian fable once again has savings = profits = investment. It is instructive, even accurate, as far as it goes. Prior to the 1980s, most fixed capital investment in the United States was financed from retained profits. The giant firm had the power to select a percentage markup over production costs (mostly wages) sufficient to complete its investment plans, much of the time without going hat in hand to a banker or the capital market for funds. That power had diminished somewhat as more foreign markets have been opened to U.S. goods and services. In turn, American corporations have gone to the bond market for funds.

## "Inside Money"

In Kalecki's and other, more sophisticated explanations of where funds come from for investment, retained earnings or expected profits can be used to obtain bank loans or issue corporate bonds. That part of debt which is bank credit constitutes Post Keynesian "inside money." Moreover, depending on preferences for debt compared with equity financing, the corporation can issue new equities in the stock markets for financing investment needs. Oddly, during the Great Bull Market of the 1980s and the 1990s, U.S. corporations, in the aggregate, retired more equities than they issued so that negative amounts were "raised" in the equities market.

Post Keynesians Paul Davidson and Basil Moore, like Keynes, Joan Robinson and Kalecki before them, suggest that the supply of money comes into existence, as Keynes and Kalecki describe it, with private debts ("inside money"). Therefore, the money supply is related to debts created by contracts to purchase or produce goods. Because production takes time, the agreements or contracts for the goods are denoted in money units to be paid on delivery. However, the production costs have to be paid during the time of production, so that producer debt may be incurred prior to any sales revenue whatsoever. This process enables producers to operate reasonably well under conditions of uncertainty.

In turn, borrowing from banks and issuance of new corporate bonds add to the money supply unless the increase in loan activity is offset by actions from the monetary authorities — in the United States, the Federal Reserve System. New loans in a fractional reserve banking system create new checking deposit amounts. In this way, changes in the nation's money supply are in great part decided by business activity itself. That is, in contrast to the monetarists, we have $M \leftrightarrow$ GNP.[18] The money supply (M) and GNP is a two-way street.

The largest and most strategic savings reside in the corporation, held as financial assets in the form of bonds or other securities. Altered expectations can cause shifts in these financial asset holdings and worsen an economic downturn. This happens because the price of bonds held by firms tends to be very low immediately preceding the downswing (interest rates being very high). A time of high interest rates also coincides with a sluggish stock market, so that although the price markup can be held constant or even perhaps increased, a slump in consumer demand may culminate in a smaller profits flow and therefore less retained earnings (savings). Even the giant corporation is then reluctant to cash in its bonds at a capital loss or borrow at interest rate peaks in order to expand its facilities or replace aging equipment. This liquidity reluctance can be a monetary source of instability in investment.

## The Money Supply and Monetary Policy

Demand deposit creation by the firm and by loans to the firm starts the money-supply train. A contraction in the money supply engineered by the central bank has little direct impact on the private sources of giant firms driven by the real economy. It has an indirect

---

[18] This is Keynes's original view of the money-national income interaction. It is also the interpretation of Keynes used by Sidney Weintraub, *Capitalism's Inflation and Unemployment Crisis* (Reading Massachusetts: Addison-Wesley, 1978), pp. 66–77, and by Paul Davidson in "Why Money Matters: Lessons from a Half-Century of Monetary Theory," *Journal of Post Keynesian Economics*, pp. 57–65 (Fall 1978), and in *Money and the Real World* (New York: Wiley, A Halstead Press Book, 1972).

effect insofar as the corporation is reluctant to liquidate bond holdings that are dipping in price. Nonetheless, as long as its sales revenue is growing, the giant firm willingly issues additional stock or borrows from the largest banks, banks that are too large to fail.

For competitive firms such as small businesses and the fragmented construction industry, quite a different tale unfolds. Even with MasterCharge, the small firm does not have the markup clout of the giant firm. Small businesses (considered the highest-risk firms and dependent on costly trade credit) are the first to experience difficulty obtaining loans during periods of tight money. Moreover, higher interest rates for housing and construction, as every home buyer knows, have similar effects. The value of interest payments usually is greater than the face value of the mortgage itself. Rather than reflecting the productivity of capital, the interest rate is a major cost of buying the product. A tight money policy only exacerbates stagflation as it reduces production and creates rising prices simultaneously![19]

The Post Keynesian's effort to reduce the reliance on such a perverse monetary policy has led them to the aforementioned third way, an incomes policy.

## Minsky and Financial Fragility

Hyman Minsky (1919–1997), a laconic but persistent American Post Keynesian with Italian connections, connected the dots between Kalecki's markup, retained earnings, and inside money to financial volatility. Minsky emphasized how the retained earnings from the markup levered by debt could finance the acquisition of additional capital assets. The capital assets acquired by the nonfinancial firm may be purchased out of the existing plant and equipment (corporate takeovers, mergers, etc.) or through the production of new

---

[19] For those who wish to take the mystery out of money and interest rates, they can do no better than read George P. Brockway, *The End of Economic Man*, Revised (New York and London: W.W. Norton and Company, 1993), especially Chapters 3, 8, 11 and 13.

investment goods. Only in the latter case will new increments and industrial capacity be added to the economy's productive potential.

Minsky's theory of investment focuses on how Keynesian uncertainty, speculation, and an increasingly complex financial system lead to business cycles. Any sustained "good times" stagger off into a speculative, inflationary binge and a fragility of financial institutions. Minsky's ideas are no longer orphans; events have overtaken his explanation.

Since business debt has to be serviced (scheduled payments on principal and interest made), Minsky suggests that such cash flows (and debt servicing commitments) determine the course of investment and thus of output and employment. In this manner, Minsky has extended Post Keynesian monetary theory to include not only credit, but the special problems connected with financial speculation in a capitalistic system.

The boom may end because of price resistance by consumers. After all, it is because the price elasticity of demand for many products is nonzero that the amount of markup is limited. The boom may end because the central bank begins to contract credit. The hope, eventually, is that wages and thus costs and inflation will slow.

Any slowdown in wage rates, however, does not alter contractual debt commitments so that the burden of debt rises during disinflation or deflation. Debt-financed investment decreases, and purchases of investment goods financed by money supply increments decline. Business firms will begin to pay off debt instead of buying new plant and equipment. As in Keynes, employment falls with the decline in use of the existing capital stock. Once again, business conditions are at the mercy of uncertainty and financial market behavior.

The leveling-off of prices brings financial distress for certain participants and industries. Firms, including farms, have counted on a particular inflation rate for their products in order to service their mounting debt. (The same could be said for middle-class homeowners, who since World War II have counted on the appreciation of houses as a source of net worth.) Yet, those most in the know in the financial markets, the insiders, take their profits and run. This is the start of a race toward liquidity as financial assets are cashed in.

As Keynes had it, the holding of money "lulls their disquietude." Outright financial panic can be avoided only if (1) prices fall so low that people move back into real assets; (2) the government sets limits to price declines (e.g., agricultural price supports), closes banks (e.g., the "bank holiday" of 1933), and shuts the exchanges; or (3) a lender of last resort steps in, as the Federal Reserve did in the financial turbulence following the Penn-Central collapse (1969–1970), the Franklin National Bank bankruptcy (1974–1975), the Hunt-Bache silver speculation (1980), and the stock market crash of 1987 and as the Federal Deposit Insurance Corporation (FDIC) did in nationalizing Illinois Continental Bank (1984) or banks since. Such interventions prevent the complete collapse of the value of assets.

Liabilities such as junk bonds and other financial innovations of the boom are validated as the central bank refinances the holdings of financial institutions. This propping-up of capitalism creates the base for still further expansion of credit during the economic recovery, a process that helps to explain the inflation following the financial crises of 1969 to 1970, 1974 to 1975, and 1980. Goods inflation, but not financial speculation, was tamed by the near-depression of 1981 to 1982. In a similar way, inflated housing prices were tamed by a slump beginning in 2007, about which more later.

## THE GLOBAL SPECTRA

Charles P. Kindleberger (1910–2003), longtime professor of economics at MIT, extends Minsky's theory to the global economy. Kindleberger sees pure speculation spilling over national borders. International links are provided by exports, imports, and foreign securities. Indeed, interest rates in the United States during the 1980s and 1990s would have been much higher in the absence of massive purchases of U.S. Treasury securities by foreigners.

At the same time, however, these foreign purchases add to the credit pyramid that will again tumble should such speculators again lose confidence. Kindleberger points a finger at the enormous external debt of the developing countries, accelerated by rising oil prices (up to at least 1979, we must add), "as multinational banks swollen with dollars tumbled over one another in trying to uncover new foreign borrowers and practically forced money on the less-developed countries (LDCs)."[20] At the international level, however, there is *no* lender of last resort, though the International Monetary Fund has in some recent times tried to be, but with mixed results. Later we will have much more to say about the trade balance and about countries other than the United States.

## WHITHER ECONOMIC GROWTH?

Economic growth is the long-term trend rate of growth in real gross domestic product (GDP). The business cycle is reflected in the movements of GDP above (inflation) and below (recession) this historical trend.

In much of Keynes's theory, the economy appears as a sequence of snapshots rather than as a continuous moving picture and thus is more applicable to the business cycle than to the problem of economic growth. The same might be said, although to a lesser degree to Kaleckian theory. Even a snapshot showing us the way we are today reveals little about what our economic conditions might be over the years.

The dynamic version of Keynes, building his theory to bridge a period of time, originated with Sir Roy Harrod, was extended by Lord Nicholas Kaldor, and is on the grand scale of Malthus, Ricardo, and Marx. Harrod shared the stage with Esvey Domar at MIT. Robert Solow was to build a popular neoclassical growth theory.

Kaldor suggests that the ratio of savings (and thus investment) to income in an economy depends upon the distribution of income. We can best see the explanation for this phenomenon in Kalecki's description of the behavior of workers and capitalists. Kaldor also begins with a Sraffa-like fixed relation between labor and capital so that the number of workers per machine in any particular industry remains constant. This assumption, of course, means (again) that the

---

[20] Charles P. Kindleberger, *Manias, Panics and Crashes: A History of Financial Crisis* (New York: Basic Books, 1978), pp. 23–24.

capitalists have positive savings, and — as in Sraffa — the rewards to capital and to labor are not based upon their productivities.

The income distribution is thus variable (unlike Keynesian or neoclassical economic views), and neoclassical-style wage or price adjustments do not guarantee that the economy will grow along a smooth path. In this simpler version of the model, therefore, profits are the only source for financing investment. In turn, the level of profits depends upon the level of investment goods demand by producers. When demand slackens, the level of production in the affected industry falls below the capacity of its plant and equipment to produce it; in other words, the physical facilities of production are underutilized. When this happens, the national income is on the downswing. Whether existing profits will be invested depends upon the attitude of the producers about future sales prospects. Even though there is an upward trend in the economy's capacity to produce goods and services, variations in demand can swing actual national output away from the growth trend line as well as toward it.

If production techniques (technology) and the money wage rate are givens, the faster the growth rate of national income, the higher will be the ratio of profits (nonwage income) to wages. Now we are fully in the world of Kalecki. The relatively high level of profits will result in a higher level of investment and a greater share of national income going to capitalists. Kalecki and Weintraub arrive at the same destination by route of the markup deciding the capitalists' share. Thus, the focus remains on the distribution of income even in the growth process. Money wages are decided outside the production process (they are among the givens) and reflect the bargaining power of unions relative to management's ability to pay.

How can a division of income described so long ago by the classical economists be at all relevant to a modern industrialized economy? Supra-surplus capitalism is dominated by large corporations so that a great share of the economy's savings do come out of the corporate sector. Therefore, the savings-out-of-profits behavior of large corporations is a key determinant of the distribution and level of income because profits are the prime source of investment expenditures. Following Keynes, then, we can see that investment expenditures are the main factor deciding the level of economic activity. Whenever such expenditures are insufficient to keep the national income and product growing at a steady rate, the economy will turn downward in a cyclical pattern beneath the trend line. Nonetheless, the strength and duration of booms shape the trend rate of growth.

Harrod and Domar dramatized a major element that had been glossed over by Keynes. With respect to the investment multiplier, Keynes neglected to mention that continuous investment augments the capacity of firms to produce goods because it adds to the number of machines and plants. In order, therefore, to warrant this extra capacity, it is not enough to experience a one-time increase in investment of a fixed amount. Investment, a reservoir for "supply" in the Harrod-Domar view as well as a source of demand in Keynes's view, must grow at a sufficient rate to generate enough (multiplied) income to buy (given the propensity to consume) enough goods to warrant the available equipment and plant; otherwise, plants and equipment will not be fully utilized. IBM must not only build and equip a new plant, it (or a firm in another industry) must build a second plant lest the demand for office equipment be inadequate to justify the first plant.

As harmless as the Harrod-Domar thesis might sound, it raised a perplexing question about the future of capitalism. The dual role of investment, generating both demand and industrial capacity, implies that an unplanned capitalism is inherently unstable. There is little reason to presume that some natural law will equalize the rate of growth in income (multiplier) with the rate of growth in capacity (a second multiplier) from a given growth of investment. If expanding investment gives rise to a growth rate of demand less than that of capacity, the resultant unwarranted or excess capacity will cause a recession. Even if demand and capacity expand at the same rate, this rate may not be sufficient to employ the entire labor force at *its* growth rate. Keynes's greatest dread, unemployment, might follow. Conversely, if demand grows faster than capacity and the labor force, inflation is the likely result.

We have seen that a dynamic yet stable economy depended upon an unlikely triple coincidence. As a result of the growth rate of investment, demand and the industrial capacity to satisfy it must expand at the same pace. Following upon the heels of the Great Depression, the Harrod-Domar views seemed to throw some light upon the darker side of capitalism, its tendency toward bust and boom. Thus, the Harrod-Domar view is in the tradition of Keynes's disequilibrium economics.

Those who would construct growth theories that depict an economy in which steady and stable growth is possible reject Harrod and Domar's premises. This "dynamic duo" had assumed that, given the state of technology, the ratio of labor to capital is fixed in the production of any particular commodity. If such a relationship is fixed, changes in wage rates or the return to capital would not alter the labor and capital mix.

Two American economists in the mid-1950s were associated with the evocation of a new neoclassical ball game suggesting the opposite. The key new player was Robert Solow, Paul Samuelson's younger colleague at MIT.[21] Solow on first and Samuelson at shortstop abandoned the presumption that production takes place at fixed proportions of capital and labor. In the neoclassical growth form, the interest rate is responsive to changes in the levels of savings. Variations in the interest rate then will lead to adjustments in the capital-to-labor mix. All these adjustments are sufficiently fine that the economy never really diverges from its stable path. Thus, the threat to capitalistic stability is eliminated.

The development of neoclassical growth theory soothed the nerves of Harrod-Domar readers by showing how changes in labor's wage and capital's price would keep the capitalist economy on a path of steady growth. The economy could be compared to a long-distance jogger who never changes pace and yet runs forever. Neoclassical growth theory still dominated macrodynamics in the

---

[21] Robert M. Solow's seminal article is "A Contribution to the Theory of Economic Growth," *Quarterly Journal of Economics*, 70, 65–94 (1956).

later 1970s: the theory, like the economy, had the endurance of the long-distance runner.

It is possible to combine the fixed factor proportions theory with variable factor proportions. Once plant and equipment is in place, the ratio of capital to labor is set. One thing that can change this fixity is technology. If the technique of production changes, so too do the capital to labor ratios. A given state of technology can characterize an industry for a long period of time, perhaps ten years. Then, advanced equipment requiring less labor can come on the scene. The introduction of the new technology requires an increment of investment spending. Once the expenditure is made, a new capital-labor ratio prevails, again, for a possibly long time.

## CONCLUSIONS

If Keynes were alive today he might not be a Keynesian; instead, he most likely would be a Post Keynesian. Much of his social vision, which began to take form in the 1920s and which was vindicated (in his mind) during the Great Depression, was lost in the neoclassical Keynesianism. Although Keynes's early interpreters made good use of his antidepression nostrums, the Keynesians' version of what Keynes meant was not enduring. It did not work well when turned against inflation, and it displayed fatal weaknesses in its premises of perfect competition in product markets and a general equilibrium, as certain as certainty.

The grand neoclassical synthesis was music to economists' ears. The arrangement was always there; it only needed a fine-tuned economy and somebody to write the lyrics. The United States provided the one during the 1950s, and the youthfully indiscreet John Hicks supplied the other. Though the result was a small measure for the neoclassicals, it was turned into a major score for the modern monetarists who next came center stage.

The born-again neoclassicals in the guise of monetarists were not finished with Keynes. Economists would question equilibrium only at the risk of being defrocked. When inflation was too great to be explained by the merely rational economic man, the super-rational economic man was invented. Keynes's theories were taken out of historical time because the past, present, and future are indistinguishable in equilibrium. Keynes had the neoclassicals right where they wanted him!

Although many neo-Keynesians have never been able to understand Post Keynesians because they see no reason for trying, some differences between the two schools are not great. As I noted, some neo-Keynesians, including 1981 Nobel Prize winner James Tobin, endorsed incomes policies. And Nobelist Robert Solow says, "some of Post Keynesian price theory comes forth from the belief that universal competition is a bad assumption. I have all my life known that." But, he also adds: "I have found it an unrewarding approach and have not paid much attention to it."[22] Paul Davidson has suggested that Solow has since relented and now embraces a larger part of Post Keynesian theory. Still, Solow's growth theory would stand apart from Post Keynesian theory.

We will use the above Post Keynesian framework to evaluate recent economic history, especially that of the Global Great Recession. We will find the vita theory of the personal income distribution to be a useful theory for that left vacant by Sraffa and Kalecki. Included in the mix will be Hyman Minsky's theory of speculation in financial assets. Not far from our minds will be the deflation and liquidity trap of the Great Depression as well as the Keynes's style policies invoked during the New Deal.

---

[22] Arjo Klaner, *Conversations with Economists* (Totowa, New Jersey: Rowman & Allanheld, 1984), pp. 137–138.

# 5

# THE RISE OF CASINO CAPITALISM

*No matter what anybody says, there is a maldistribution of wealth in this country that I think is very unhealthy. It's very easy to fall into the mode of saying, well this whole thing is casino and paper money. I don't think everyone in the financial community is a rogue — it's just that that's the way the world is.*

Felix G. Rohatyn,[1] Lazard. Quoted in Andrew Ross Sorkin,
"Deal Maker Looks Back, and Sighs,"
*The New York Times*, October 19, 2010, p. B1.

Capitalism is Faustian in scope: It has many faces. Another great transformation of American capitalism began during the Reagan administration; some of the same forces were imported by England during the Thatcher years. It all began with Reaganomics, which required the convergence of three powerful forces. The first was monetarism; as Milton Friedman had told Ronald Reagan, monetarism could bring down inflation with only a temporary slowdown in production and employment. The second force was the rising influence of the neo-Austrians and their desire to free the entrepreneur from the state. The third force was the dream of the supply-siders to free the rich from "excessive" taxation. From these forces came the rise to power of the New Right in the United States during the late

---

[1] Mr. Rohatyn's revealing memoir, *Dealings: A Political and Financial Life* (Simon & Schuster) was released in November 2010.

1970s and early 1980s, beginning with Austrian economist Ludwig von Mises in Vienna and coming to rest on the front steps of the White House with Ronald Reagan.

As with monetarism, the rise of the New Right was a reaction to the stagflation crises of the 1970s. We have already noted how stagflation was the rain shower that brought together the diverse Post Keynesians. Whereas all Keynesians are united in expecting some role for government in the economy, the New Right places its faith in free-market capitalism. The New Right sees the market as the solution to all economic problems, the *only* solution.

The neo-Austrians' initial link to political power emanates from the establishment in 1974 of the Charles Koch Foundation; it has since become the Cato Institute in Washington, D.C., a public policy institute. Koch, the head of Koch Industries, established his foundation to seed the views of laissez-faire economists such as Ludwig von Vises, Ayn Rand's favorite economist. The shared goal of the neo-Austrians and the Cato Institute is to greatly shrink the government. Although they would have preferred an Ayn Rand to a Ronald Reagan as President, his was the only game in town. In part by design, but mostly by error and accident, monetarism and Reaganomics built a bridge to casino capitalism.

Casino capitalism was the basis for the bubbles and busts that were to culminate in the Great Recession.

## THE FEDERAL RESERVE'S EXPERIMENT WITH FRIEDMAN'S MONETARISM (1979–1982)

Still, monetarism preceded Reagan's presidency. The inflation beginning in the late 1960s (made much worse by the OPEC cartel during the 1970s) and Milton Friedman's ascension led to a monetarist experiment, which began in the final months of Jimmy Carter's presidency. Paul Volcker, then head of the Federal Reserve System, made sure that the growth rate in the money supply dropped roughly in half during the first six months of the experiment. The fed funds rate, close to ten percent in mid-summer 1979, by early 1980 had nearly doubled, soaring to 18 percent. Even the highest rated corporations began to pay 14 percent or more for loans.

Faced with a financial Armageddon, the Carter administration pressured a reluctant Volcker to invoke a little-used countermeasure, the Credit Control Act of 1969, to regulate the credit of financial institutions. The immediate reduction in borrowing had an equally quick and sickening effect on the economy. In the second quarter of 1980, the real gross national product (GNP) plunged at an annual rate of nearly ten percent. Volcker's monetarism and the Carter administration's regulatory error had caused a very sharp business recession, riding on the back of the lengthy, painful recession of 1973 to 1975. Even so, the deep but short recession ended before the monetarist experiment. Volcker began to remove the new controls only two months after he imposed them. The Fed began pumping money into the economy, only temporarily reversing the experiment.

Carter was defeated in the presidential election of 1980, in great part because of what monetarism had wrought and despite warnings from White House advisers of the consequences of Federal Reserve policy. It was an economy in which only the infectious optimism of Ronald Reagan and supply-side economics, the economics of joy, could turn things around, or so it was thought.

As Reagan came to power, the recovery from the Carter administration's 1980 recession was incomplete: The unemployment rate still hovered near eight percent. Volcker, now by Reagan's side, faced the continuation of the stagflation malaise, a condition of simultaneous inflation and unemployment afflicting Great Britain and Western Europe as well. Of the twin abominations, Paul Volcker and Ronald Reagan — by then both under the influence of scientific monetarism — considered inflation by far the greater evil.

Reagan fervently believed what Friedman had told him; monetarism could defeat inflation without a noticeable decline in production or rise in unemployment. Reagan believed that Volcker had failed because he had not persevered in his first duel with the inflation demon. In an influential meeting with Volcker, Reagan urged him not only a return to tighter monetary policy but an even tighter monetary policy. As a biographer has noted, "Reagan...believed the way a child believes — ardently and absolutely. He believed in Reaganomics; therefore Reaganomics had to be."[2]

Volcker once again cranked up monetarism, slowing money supply growth after mid-1980 and continuing to decelerate its growth in 1981. The cooperation between the self-proclaimed "politically independent" monetary authorities and the Reagan administration was inspirational, what with the White House and the Fed in unaccustomed agreement: The money supply would grow by no more than a meager 2.5 percent per year. A few blocks from the Fed, the White House staff was singing hosannas about how nominal GNP would be growing at an annual rate of 12 percent between 1980 and 1984. Any economists failing to believe in the religion of the money supply was turned into salt by the *Wall Street Journal*.

## SUPPLY-SIDE ECONOMICS

Like the pamphleteers of mercantilism, the supply-siders relied on dramatic arguments rather than numbers and facts. Supply-side economics was a media event led by Wall Street journalist Jude Wanniski (1936–2005), writer Bruce Bartlett (1931–), and pop sociologist George Gilder (1939–). All three writers make devoted reference to the neo-Austrians. Still, just as monetarism was a reaction to the perceived failure of Keynesianism to end stagflation, the "supply-side" economics identified with Reaganomics was thought to be a way out of the stagnation.

Monetarism and supply-side incentives, the first scene in the Reaganomics script, would restore the classical utopia. Super-tight money would break inflation while supply-side tax cuts would expand employment and production. Modest personal income tax cuts for workers would cause them to work harder, bolstering productivity.

---

[2] Edmund Morris, *Dutch: A Memoir of Ronald Reagan* (New York: Random House, 1999), p. 447.

Dramatically large tax cuts for the rich, especially on capital gains, would incite them to save more. The surge in savings would lead to higher levels of business investment.

Lurking behind the supply-side ideas was the classical's old friend Say's law, in its crudest expression; "supply creating its own demand," and the first scene stealer. As Bartlett correctly wrote (at the age of 30), "in many respects, supply-side economics is nothing more than … Say's law of markets rediscovered."[3] Say's law connected Reaganomics to economic growth. Saving races the growth engine because of the guaranteed transmission of saving into investment. The engine always races no matter how chilly the investment climate, since every dollar saved never leaves the race track.

Thus, the higher purpose of the rich lay in their saving. Reaganomics sought out the upper-income class (over $50,000 a year in 1980 dollars) for personal savings because that was where the money was. This incentive provided the moral grounds for lowering marginal tax rates for the well-to-do. As a failsafe, special tax benefits to corporations such as larger tax credits, lower tax rates, and faster depreciation would add still more incentives for investment.

Gilder gave a further boost to the supply-siders even while embracing neo-Austrian entrepreneurship in his *Wealth and Poverty*, required reading for Reagan's 1981 White House staff. The saving to investment connection revealed to Gilder, the author most frequently quoted in Reagan's speeches, the truth: "To help the poor and middle classes, one must cut the tax rates of the rich."[4] The welfare state,

---

[3] Bruce Bartlett, *Reaganomics: Supply-Side Economics in Action* (New Rochelle, N.Y.: Arlington House, 1981), p. 1. After serving as an adviser to President Reagan, Bartlett had a career of serving conservative Republicans (congressional committees, writing, adviser to President George H.W. Bush, and so on). However, he became a critic of President George W. Bush's economic policies and in 2009 at the age of 58 wrote a book endorsing Keynesianism and demoting Reaganomics as suitable for the 1970s and the 1980s only. [See *The New American Economy: The Failure of Reaganomics and a New Way Forward* (New York: Palgrave Macmillan, 2009).] The other supply-siders remain supply-siders.
[4] George Gilder, *Wealth and Poverty* (New York: Basic Books, 1981), p. 188.

Gilder further surmised, motivates the poor to choose leisure over work and is a great disincentive. Moreover, entrepreneurs would play their historically heroic role once they were freed from the shackles of taxation.

The centerpiece of supply-side economics, the Economic Recovery Act of 1981, as promised, cut personal tax rates. Whereas Reaganomics stressed those tax incentives presumably affecting the supply of labor and productive capacity, the full program went further. The federal government's role, expanded by the New Deal programs of the 1930s and by World War II, was to be reduced, except for national defense and the penal system, which were to be enlarged. Finally, Reagan would *balance the federal budget by 1984*, the year that George Orwell had "the clocks striking thirteen."

Judging from the tax cut results, the richest Americans were most in need of motivation. Consider the reductions in the *effective* income tax rate, the true rate paid rather than simply the tax rate from the IRS schedules. The effective income tax rate on the super-rich, the top one percent, had been reduced by 7.8 percentage *points* by 1984. The effective tax rate for the very rich, the top five percent, dropped by 4.2 percentage points and, for the simply rich, the top ten percent, 3.1 percentage points. Moreover, the top tax rate on unearned income from interest payments fell steadily from 70 percent in 1980, to 50 percent in 1982, to 38.5 percent in 1987, and to 28 percent in 1988.

Not only did the rich enjoy much higher incomes — be they from salary, stock options, interest payments, or capital gains — each family now could keep a much larger share of any gains. The average tax break for the super-rich, the top one percent, was $52,621 by 1989. The total value of these tax cuts for 1982 through 1990 was nearly $2 *trillion* (in 1985 dollars), a value roughly equal to the entire gross domestic product (GDP) for 1960. By 1992, under President George H.W. Bush, the average tax break for the super-rich had risen to about $78,090 on incomes averaging $676,000.

We now turn our attention to the second scene in the Reaganomics script.

## The Laffer Curve and the Mantra of the Balanced Budget

A link was missing: How, with massive tax cuts, would the federal budget be balanced? As "balancing the budget" further fed the media frenzy, the missing link was filled by Arthur Laffer, a former business professor at the University of Southern California. The Laffer curve, the Rosetta Stone of Reaganomics, was drawn for Wanniski on a napkin in a Washington, D.C., "insiders" hotel bar by Arthur Laffer, and was given celebrity status in Wanniski's book, *The Way the World Works.*

The Laffer curve traces the relationship between tax rates and government revenue. At two extremes (zero percent and 100 percent), there will be no revenues for the government. As tax rates rise above zero, the provision of public goods essential for markets to operate (justice, defense, law and order, and primary education) contributes to productivity, output, and, thus, tax revenue. However, as tax rates are raised further, relative price changes cause a decline in the after-tax rewards of saving, investing, and working for taxable income. People begin to shift out of these activities and into leisure, consumption, and tax shelters. The national output and income base on which tax rates apply is eroded, and the tax revenue from higher tax rates falls. Most economists believed otherwise; tax rates were well below this range of perversity.

As tax rates fall from "excessively" high rates, workers become more productive, the economy grows, and tax revenue grows even faster. The federal budget is automatically balanced.

The opening scenes had been written and the movie set built.

## The Angst of Insider David Stockman

David Stockman, the President's first budget director (1981–mid-1985) and once an unabashed supply-sider, quickly saw defects in the program. In the words of a Christmastime 1981 confession, the "Kemp-Roth (the name of the original supply-side tax bill) was always a Trojan horse to bring down the top rate."[5]

A Trojan horse? Supply-side economics was rolled into the enemy camp of labor with a horseload of entrepreneurs. Rather than a Calvinistic response by workers, all the President's men were counting on a literal interpretation of Say's law and on self-styled neo-Austrian entrepreneurship for the stimulation of output, either Puritanical investors or super-alert entrepreneurs. The supply-side theory, in Stockman's view, was really new clothes for the naked doctrine of the old "trickle-down theory"[6] in which benefits to the rich "trickle down" to the workers. After all, the need to cut welfare for the poor and give tax benefits to the rich implied that the working poor had *too much* money and the rich *too little*.

Thus, even though the various tax cuts would increase disposable income, their conjectured effectiveness did not stem from their effects on Keynesian aggregate demand, which were presumed to be nil. Rather, following the neoclassical lead, the effectiveness of tax reductions would come from their changing of relative prices and inducing decision-makers to substitute productive activity (investment, work and exchange) for leisure and idleness, causing output to rise. The Howard Roark's of the world — no thanks to God Almighty — would be free at last to play their role under free-market capitalism. (Reagan never seemed to fathom the atheism of Ayn Rand.) The shift away from leisure and consumption toward productive activity would enhance economic growth.

---

[5] Quoted by William Greider, "The Education of David Stockman," *Atlantic Monthly* (December 1981), p. 46. Stockman's confessions had been made to journalist-friend Greider.
[6] *Ibid.*, p. 47.

# THE SEQUEL

## The Deep Recession of 1981 to 1982

Sequels often promise more but deliver less than the original movie. In this regard, the outcome of the supply-siders' proclamation was not unique.

Even Ronald Reagan's optimistic glow could not prevent the calamity. The tight monetary policy of the Federal Reserve combined with rising budget deficits sharply raised interest rates, overwhelming the business tax cuts aimed at encouraging capital formation.[7] Earlier, in 1979 and 1980, the line of "voluntarily" unemployed workers was rapidly growing but apparently not fast enough to keep inflation under control. Still, following the monetarists' prescription to the decimal point, Paul Volcker managed to move the unemployment rate much higher. The nominal GNP growth rate during Reagan's first presidential term was not, of course, at the scripted but wildly improbable yearly rate of 12 percent. In mid-summer 1981, it was the *unemployment rate* that was approaching 12 percent and the highest rate since the Great Depression.

Where were those heroic entrepreneurs when they were most needed?

## The National Debt Explodes (1980–1992)

Had the government revenue targets been military ones, though doubtless improved by a handsomely funded Pentagon, the supply-siders

---

[7] In reaction to the massive tax revenue losses, in 1982 Congress repealed a scheduled further increase in accelerated depreciation allowances and eliminated safe-harbor leasing, a 1981 provision that allowed unprofitable companies to sell their tax credits and depreciation write-offs to profitable ones. These 1982 tax changes left the expected return from plant and equipment investment about 17 percentage points (rather than 28) above the pre-Reagan tax treatment return. In the deep economic slump, however, sales were not sufficient to warrant investment in new capacity and the tax cuts could provide no stimulus.

would have missed them by roughly a continent. *Budget deficits* began to shatter historical records. A slumping national income meant sluggish tax revenues, especially at the lower tax rates. Reagan's tax cuts combined with the explosion in military spending and the deep recession took the national debt from $908 billion to $3.2 trillion, or *more than treble that accumulated by all of his 39 predecessors, beginning with George Washington.*

Soaring federal budget deficits and debt accumulation did not end with Reagan's second term, President George H.W. Bush comforted those habituated to continuity as the federal deficits continued their rise, reaching nearly $400 billion by fiscal year 1992. The national debt weighed in around $4.0 trillion in 1992. Unable or unwilling to reduce the deficits, Bush left it to New Democrat Bill Clinton to cut the deficits by some 50 percent during his first term, move to a balanced budget sometime in 1998, and build his proverbial bridge to the twenty-first century with budget surpluses.

What had gone so horribly wrong?

## The Arithmetic of Modern Monetarism in Action

Even if we accept the monetarist's arithmetic, Volcker's monetary policy does not add up. We need look no further than MV = PT, the classical equality for monetarism. In the modern monetarist equation from Friedman, real output or real GNP replaces the T. If we express all values in the equality in percentage changes or growth rates, the growth rate in the money supply plus the growth rate in its velocity equals inflation plus the growth rate in real GNP. That is, the modern monetarist equation becomes

Percent Change, M + Percent Change, V = Percent Change, P + Percent Change, Real GNP.

The sum on the right side of the equal sign is the growth rate in *nominal* GNP.

In this way, the great promise of monetarism reduces to simple, if wholly embarrassing, arithmetic. Reagan-Volcker's planned pace for the money supply was a meager 2.5 percent for 1980 to 1984.[8] Suppose President Reagan's advisers had asked the obvious question: "How great would the percentage change in the income velocity or turnover rate of money have to be to give their targeted money GNP growth rate (on the right side of the equal sign) of 12.0 percent?" The answer, of course, is 12.0 percent minus 2.5 percent or 9.5 percent. The growth rate in the velocity of money, a variable Friedman failed to mention to Reagan, would have to be an astounding 9.5 percent! Yet, the *average growth rate* in velocity was *only* three percent for the entire postwar era, 1946 to 1980. More important, this historical three percent growth rate of velocity added to a 2.5 percent growth rate for money (again, summing the two rates) would allow nominal GNP to grow only 5.5 percent a year, not 12 percent. At a White House inflation wish rate of six percent, the real growth in GNP would be –0.5 percent annually (5.5 – 5.0). *Real GNP declines!* In fact, that's what happened.

In 1981 to 1982, job prospects were appalling, and expected returns from investment dismal and increasingly uncertain, seemingly a Keynesian situation. Households and corporations, however, not only held onto money but placed it in highly liquid financial assets, reducing the income velocity of money. Contrary to the ideas of either Adam Smith or Keynes, personal and corporate savings were pouring into financial assets instead of into real business investment. Without rising spending by consumers and business, output falls.

---

[8] An alternative measure of the money supply, M2, was relatively stable during this time, The Federal Reserve, however, was using only M1 as its guide. Later, the Fed would look at a variety of measures of the money supply. M2 includes not only currency, checkable accounts and traveler's checks (M1) but also small-denomination time deposits, savings deposits and money market deposit accounts, money market mutual fund shares (non-institutional), overnight and term repurchase agreements, overnight Eurodollars, and a consolidation adjustment. Obviously, as Wall Street invents more instruments in which liquid assets can be held, whatever comprises the money supply changes. The other measures, M3 and L, include larger denomination deposits plus financial instruments of long maturities. The search for the "correct" measure of the money supply goes on.

Thus, Volcker's tight monetary policy only diminished inflation at the steep cost of a deep recession, just as it had before.

Rabo Karabekian, Kurt Vonnegut's fictional artist-collector in *Bluebeard* (1987), describes well the outcome. Rabo, back in 1933, is looking in the Grand Central Station in New York City for the address of his mentor. Rabo is musing, "the Great Depression was going on, so that the station and the streets teemed with homeless people, just as they do today. The newspapers were full of stories of worker layoffs, and farm foreclosures and bank failures, just as they are today."[9] Just as they were in 1981 to 1982.

All things considered, the fiscal revolution was stunning, but the President did not get everything he asked for.[10] Although federal income taxes for the "average family" actually rose by one percent, a large number of major corporations such as US. Home, Dow Chemical, General Electric, General Dynamics, and Boeing received a negative income tax (refunds or other tax benefits) during 1981 to 1983 even while earning large profits. Not satisfied, President Reagan pushed for still more domestic program reductions in his second term.

---

[9] Kurt Vonnegut, *Bluebeard: The Autobiography of Rabo Karabekian (1915–1988)* (New York: Delacorte Press, 1987), p. 85.

[10] The U.S. Congress rejected Reagan proposals that would have: greatly reduced social security benefits for workers taking early retirement, disability benefits for veterans, federal aid to low-income families for home-heating expenses, spending on the Food Stamp program; eliminated school-lunch programs for middle- and upper-income children; increased payments by Medicare patients for most hospital stays; greatly reduced spending on primary and secondary education programs for the disadvantaged and handicapped; greatly reduced the student loan program; cut spending for highway and bridge construction; raised interest rates on farm disaster and Small Business Administration loans; sharply reduced general welfare payments; eliminated the Legal Services Corporation and Juvenile Justice programs; drastically cut the budget for maternal and child healthcare, including programs for low income women who are pregnant; and cut deeper than Congress would allow numerous other domestic programs, including energy conservation, the Environmental Protection Agency, federal mortgage insurance commitments, economic development grants, American Indian assistance, job training, Medicaid, and community services grants.

## Keynes Redux: Reagan's Ersatz Keynesianism

History, as in F. Scott Fitzgerald's novels, is replete with irony. By 1980, Keynesian economics was at a nadir among U.S. economists; the Reaganomics near-depression greatly altered this perception. For one thing, unemployment compensation and other programs from the New Deal placed a floor under disposable income and therefore the decline in consumer spending. Just as Ronald Reagan and his family had been helped by the programs of President Franklin Roosevelt during the thirties, the poor and the unemployed were being served again by the same kinds of assistance. The Reagan administration looked to gains in consumers' disposable income to stimulate Keynesian effective demand.

Fiscal Keynesianism became the way out of the malaise. Federal Reserve officials, in near panic as the 1930s flashed before their eyes, in the summer of 1982 began to pursue an incredibly expansive monetary policy. Monetarism was scrapped. The tremendous increase in federal military expenditures (about seven percent annually in real terms), although a part of Reagan's original budget plan, provided a sorely needed Keynesian demand yank for the depressed economy. President Reagan and the supply-siders began to defend vigorously Keynesian budget deficits greatly in excess of amounts acceptable to the many modern Keynesians.

## CASINO CAPITALISM

A legacy of Reaganomics was the greatly enlarged importance of Wall Street in American society. The central message of Ronald Reagan was that not only were American corporations free to do whatever they wished, so could people with wealth. The perpetuation of these policies by the Clinton Administration, often at the expense of those near the bottom, astonished and angered many Old Democrats.

Little distance separates wealth from Wall Street. The securities held by the wealthiest households were on the balance sheets of Wall Street firms. Wall Street became the eye of a hurricane of financial vortices soon to engulf and shape a financially fragile American economy. During 1983 to 1989, the United States imploded into Las Vegas — hence, the term "casino economy."[11] A similar kind of speculative bubble rose over Tokyo.

This unnerving transformation reached an apogee of financial speculation somewhere around the mid-1980s, conflated into a Great Stagnation during the early 1990s, only to reignite into a speculative orgy during the last half of the 1990s. Many seemed to have rediscovered the Veblenesque pleasure in the making of money on money or financial assets rather than depending on profits from goods production. Others, out of greed, rediscovered the Gatsbyesque advantage of stepping beyond the bounds of propriety. The society began to resemble a giant money market fund in which the central function of households and businesses would be speculation.

## Private Sector Debt Explodes

The debt epidemic soon spread to the private sector. Business balance sheets shifted from equity financing (issuing new corporate stock) to debt financing (issuing corporate bonds). In 1983, equity and debt issuance were $4.8 billion and $4.0 billion, respectively, a conservative business persons' dream. In every year of the eighties thereafter, net equity issuance was negative while corporate net bond issues soared (to about $30 billion in 1989). The rich comprised a subculture of bondholders.

Although the post-recession 1980s has been biblically called "the seven fat years," closer inspection makes it look more like simply a rebound from the deep recession of 1981 to 1982. By mid-1984, the U.S. economy had recovered only to its pre-Reagan level, much like the 1935 to 1937 recovery had reached

---

[11] I first introduced the term "casino economy" in *The Making of Economics*, 3rd ed. (Belmont, California: Wadsworth, 1987), pp. 342–343. See also E. Ray Canterbery, "Reaganomics, Saving, and the Casino Effect," in James H. Gapinski, editor, *The Economics of Saving* (Dordrecht/Boston/New York/London: Kluwer Academic Publishers, 1993).

the pre-Depression GNP level. A contrast can be drawn between two periods highlighted by tax reductions — the decade of the 1960s and that of the 1980s. Real GNP growth during the 1960s amounted to 45 percent, greatly higher than the 28 percent of the 1980s. Industrial production expanded by 57 percent during the 1960s, but only by 29 percent during the 1980s. The unemployment rate never rose above 5.7 percent (1961) during the sixties; it never fell below seven percent during 1980 to 1986, peaking at 9.6 to 10.7 percent in 1982 to 1983. Moreover, financial manipulation and speculation soared.

Since the ownership of interest-bearing debt is highly concentrated, rising interest rates shifted the income and wealth distributions toward greater inequality.[12] The rising share of interest income made the income distribution more lopsided and when converted into securities added to the inequality of wealth. When only a few have the bulk of the "bullion," they have to become wonderfully imaginative as to where to put it. As providence provided, increasingly deregulated financial institutions became remarkably innovative in creating new financial instruments (CDs, jumbo CDs, junk bonds, options, and so on) in which wealth could be stored momentarily for quick appreciation. Put differently, if the rich are to speculate, they had to have an ample supply of chips. Initially, chips were supplied in the form of new Treasury bond issues; later, additional chips were provided by a new means of corporate acquisition, takeovers by leveraged debt.

## Michael Milken Creates the Junk Bond Market

With the path to liberated markets being smoothed by Milton Friedman, the freeing of markets for moneymaking became a moral imperative for Reagan. The sole responsibility of business,

---

[12] In 1995, ten percent of families owned 89.8 percent of bonds, and 88.4 percent of corporate stock and mutual funds, with the top one percent alone owning half of all stocks and mutual funds. Finally, the richest ten percent held 71.6 percent of household net worth (value of assets minus value of liabilities).

wrote Friedman, was to increase its profits, a faith echoed in Reagan's speeches. Word about the "magic of the market" spread quickly from the Reagan White House to the countryside. The key phrases on Wall Street were: (a) The Reagan administration was against all government regulations affecting *any* market, including bond markets; (2) If money could be made doing something — anything — it was an immoral act not to "just do it" (with needless apologies to Nike). Michael Milken was a natural by-product of this free-market revival.

Milken, an intense business student at the University of California at Berkeley during the mid-1950s, was reading about low-grade and unrated corporate bonds while other students were mellowing out on marijuana. Later, as a securities salesman at Drexel, Milken preached a new gospel. To Milken, the higher yield on low-grade bonds simply reflected a risk well worth taking at such high expected returns. He was convinced that the *only* problem with low-grade debt was its lack of liquidity or quick convertibility into money.

Eventually, Milken dispelled customers initial aversion to high-risk bonds. Milken's sales ability solved the "lack of liquidity" problem; he attracted financiers who saw no stigma attached to low-grade securities. As their returns met or exceeded their expectations, the early buyers became enthusiastic backers of Milken.

By early 1977, Milken already controlled a quarter of the national market in high-yield securities. He had become a *market-maker.* Milken could assure the holder of bonds that he would buy their bonds whenever the holder wanted to cash out or go liquid. In turn, Milken could resell the securities, keeping any difference between the unpublished "buy" and "sell" prices he amassed. Only Milken and a few colleagues knew of the widening spreads between the buy and sell prices, a source of rising richness for Milken.

The Securities and Exchange Commission (SEC), the main regulatory agency for the securities markets, did not register the offerings and the Milken Market went unregulated, just as Friedman, Reagan, and the supply-siders fancied. Milken always operated with more knowledge than any buyer or seller because he *was* the low-grade bond market.[13] Those buyers and sellers on the other side of the market might as well have been smoking something; they were no match for Milken's secret information. Thus, much of the "magic" of this market came from Milken's concealment of the key to it.

A half century trend favoring risk aversion and apposing excessive debt ended during the 1980s.

## Junk Bonds Lead to LBO Mania

The merger trend in the United States has a long and glorious history, dating all the way back to the era of the robber barons. Concentration is as American as motherhood, apple pie, and John D. Rockefeller. The only things changing were the nameplates on the imploding industries and the methods of acquisition. A new method — leveraged buyouts, or LBOs — was a 1980s' innovation.

The largest American manufacturing corporations, by size of total assets for 1947 to 1983 were oil, automobile, computer, steel, communications, and chemical producers. Those are the industries at or well past their product cycle peaks. Exxon (formerly Standard Oil of New Jersey) was still at the top of this heap in 1983, followed by General Motors, Mobil Oil, Texaco, Standard Oil (Indiana), E.I. Dupont de Nemours, Standard Oil (California), Ford, and General Electric.

Few giant corporations have been broken up by the antitrust authorities — those initially empowered at the turn of the nineteenth century to do something about the giant trusts of the robber barons — and few mergers have been blocked. For example, Standard Oil was "broken up"; now there were three Standard Oils

---

[13] Many more details about Michael Milken and many other Wall Street characters can be gleaned from Pulitzer Prize-winning reporter James B. Stewart's *Den of Thieves* (New York: Simon & Schuster, 1991).

among the top ten corporations instead of only one.[14] Even among the 500 largest industrial (manufacturing and mining) corporations in 1983, the top 25 garnered 41 percent of their total sales and the top 50, more than half.

Despite the slippery slope on which the junk bond market was built, it led to a new era of leveraged buyouts (LBOs) during the 1980s and 1990s, and, ultimately, to downsizing the working class. Though *being* the junk bond market was highly lucrative, Michael Milken saw still bigger money in mergers and acquisitions. A corporation, a public company, would be bought out by a group of financiers with money generated by selling junk bonds to insurance companies, banks, brokers, and S&Ls. In this wonderful arrangement, the financiers did not have to use any of their *own* money. Moreover, all those handling the transactions, including the CEOs selling their own companies and Milken, made tens of millions of dollars.

Some new forces would sustain Milken at a time when his business otherwise would have been slowing. During the Reagan years, a conglomerate rush, the merger of unrelated enterprises, was encouraged by both tax policy and by an antitrust policy most notable for its aggressive laxity. By 1983, the arrangement of mergers had become a growth industry led by a legendary Texas tycoon by the misnomer of Slim Pickens. Fortuitously, by 1985 Michael Milken and his Drexel colleagues had more client money than they could place. To increase the supply of junk bonds, they began to finance corporate raiders such as Pickens, Carl Icahn, Ronald Perelman, and, notably, Kohlberg Kravis Roberts & Co. (KKR).

The KKR executives from 1984 to 1989 borrowed more money through Drexel than any other client of the junk-bond firm: KKR

---

[14] The Rockefeller Standard Oil trust was "dissolved" by the U.S. Supreme Court in 1911. The "old" Standard Oil was divided into separate companies whose operations were allocated to different areas of the United States. Generally, each of these same Standard companies remains the dominant factor in each of the original marketing areas. Among the dominant stockholders of each company are the Rockefeller family, Rockefeller "interests," and the Rockefeller Foundation.

became the dominant takeover artist.[15] Insurance companies, banks, and S&Ls virtually stopped financing the buying of capital goods, drilling for oil, or building houses; they instead lent billions to KKR in their purchases of junk bonds from Milken. KKR completed nearly $50 billion in acquisitions during the 1980s, culminating in the purchase of RJR Nabisco for $25.4 billion in late 1988, then the largest takeover in history and sufficiently notorious to become not only a book but a TV movie. These takeovers of large corporations generated billions of dollars' worth of junk bonds, for even the use of leverage diminishes the value of outstanding bonds of former blue-chip corporations to junk. Milken's salary and bonus continued to climb — exceeding $440 million in 1985 alone.

Conglomeration and its consequences are symbolized by the bidding war for Marathon Oil Company. Mobil, which earlier had acquired the Montgomery Ward department store chain (apparently, it was widely speculated, in order to drill for oil in Montgomery Ward's aisles), tried to buy Marathon. Contrary to the claims for the effects of the supply-side tax incentive program, Mobil expressed an interest in buying existing oil reserves rather than going to all the time and trouble of actually looking for new reserves. In its boldest gamble since the company was put together by Andrew Carnegie and J.P. Morgan in 1901, U.S. Steel bid against Mobil for Marathon. As a result of its successful acquisition, U.S. Steel, now USX Corporation, became the nation's 12th largest industrial company.

By the spring of 1990, RJR Nabisco nearly sank into bankruptcy from the cost of keeping its junk-bond debt afloat. KKR, too, was close to sinking. These savings, including those from seniors' social security checks, went, not into new software development or factories, but into junk bonds with values eroding in the high tide of debt. However, unlike many senior citizens and the S&L's, not only did KKR survive the storms, but by the mid-1990s it was again listing shares of companies it owns on the New York Stock Exchange and expanding its operations.

---

[15] The complete story of KKR is told in George Anders, *Merchants of Debt: KKR and the Mortgaging of American Business* (New York: Basic Books, 1992).

If net new industrial capacity came out of these acquisitions during the 1980s, it does not show up in the data. Net fixed investment as a share of net national product fell from 5.7 percent in 1970 to 1979 to 4.8 percent in 1980 to 1988. More important, the growth rate in capital services in private business dropped from 4.2 percent in 1950 to 1959, to 4.0 percent in 1970 to 1979, to 3.2 percent in 1980 to 1988, and to 1.3 percent in 1985 to 1988. Productivity also slowed.

This massive consolidation and restructuring was financed by a new breed of financiers. It is a breed well-described by Tom Wolfe in his novel, *The Bonfire of the Vanities*, published in November 1987 just as the bubble was beginning to burst. Sherman McCoy, Wall Street's top bond salesman and the "master of the Universe," lives in a sumptuous 14-room duplex apartment on Park Avenue, the street of dreams! He worked on Wall Street, 50 floors up, for the legendary Pierce & Pierce, overlooking the world! He was at the wheel of a $48,000 roadster with one of the most beautiful women in New York — no Comp. Lit. scholar, perhaps, but gorgeous — beside him! A frisky young animal! He was of that breed whose natural destiny it was to have what they wanted![16]

This unreal McCoy was going broke earning a million dollars a year. As one of those "serious bond dealers representing Wall Street," the Master of the Universe wore a blue-gray nailhead worsted suit, custom-tailored in England for $1,800, two-button, single-breasted, with ordinary notched lapels. On Wall Street double-breasted suits and peaked lapels were considered a bit sharp, a bit too Garment District. His thick brown hair was combed straight back. He squared his shoulders and carried his long nose and wonderful chin up high.[17]

During the first half of the 1980s, much of the power of commercial bankers and S&Ls had shifted to Wall Street arbitrageurs such as the Master of the Universe, Ivan Boesky, Robert Rubin,

---

[16] Tom Wolfe, *The Bonfire of the Vanities* (New York: Farrar, Straus & Giroux, 1987), p. 80.
[17] *Ibid.*, p. 50.

investment bankers such as Milken at Drexel as well as the old reliable J.P. Morgan and Company, and stock brokers. In this fast-moving decade, Wall Street nonetheless was scandal-ridden by 1985 and closer to its Trinity Church graveyard by 1987. The Street suffered a fate similar to that of the Master of the Universe; once again, life was imitating art. The great stock market crash of 1987 and the mini-crash two years later, however, did not end the speculative fever nor the new importance of Wall Street in the economy. It simply provided a buying opportunity for those already made richer by tax cuts, interest payments, and capital gains.

## The Bursting of Bubbles

For nearly four decades beginning in the mid-1950s, new credit was added to the debt pyramid at a faster and faster pace. Speculative bubbles in real estate and in financial markets during the 1980s were driven by an acceleration in new credit. But toward the end of the Reagan era, the pace of growth slowed dramatically as Chairman Alan Greenspan of the Federal Reserve shifted toward a zero-inflation goal. This reversal of a 40-year trend meant lower real estate values and a slowdown in earnings growth for both financial and nonfinancial corporations.

Weaknesses in real estate were visible by the mid-1980s, but the great stock market crash of October 1987 was the most dramatic omen that the first phase of speculation was about to end. By this time, the S&L industry already had virtually collapsed. By mid-1990, the U.S. Treasury predicted that more than 1,000 S&Ls — more than 40 percent of all thrifts — would have to be taken over by the government. Private sources put the figure closer to 2,000, virtually the entire industry! The final cost to taxpayers could be over $1 trillion, or $4,000 per person. The total number of properties to be sold by federal regulators would eventually rise to one million (a figure excluding the tens of thousands of homes repossessed by commercial banks).

There were close ties between the junk bond dealers and the bonfire of the S&Ls, between Michael Milken and, as examples,

Tom Spiegel of Columbia Savings & Loan and Charles Keating of Lincoln.[18] By the end of the 1970s, the S&Ls were paying interest rates of 12 or 13 percent to attract deposits and receiving a pittance from their residential mortgages. By 1982 they were effectively wiped out. In order to "save" them, the White House and the Congress agreed to let thrifts lend money for just about anything. Moreover, *anyone* now could open an S&L. Rogues and outright criminals saw the possibilities. When Willie Sutton was asked why he robbed banks, he answered "because that's where the money is." That's why Charles Keating formed the notorious Lincoln Savings and Loan. Columbia, Lincoln, Vernon, and many of the others inflated their assets with junk bonds.

As the leveraged companies such as Integrated and Campeau began to fail in 1989, the junk bond market began a monumental collapse. Led by the plunge in takeover stocks, there was a "mini crash" of the stock market on October 13. Defaults were the order of the day, and the junk bond assets in the S&Ls approached worthlessness. In the end, nearly every savings and loan that was a major purchaser of Milken's junk was declared insolvent and taken over by the government.

Meantime, commercial banks got caught in the squeeze. A nationwide glut of excess commercial and residential properties was pushing rents down, depressing the value of bank assets. Banks foreclosed on $25 billion worth of commercial properties in 1991, or 32 percent more than in 1990. Although fewer than ten banks per year had failed in the United States from 1943 to 1981, the tide had turned.

What happened to key developers suffering foreclosure is revealed by the fate of Charles Croker, the central character in Tom Wolfe's *A Man in Full*. The setting is Atlanta, Georgia, a late-century

---

[18] This connection is established in a wonderfully entertaining way by Michael Lewis, *Liar's Poker* (New York: W.W. Norton, 1989), pp. 205–228. Lewis, now a journalist, was a bond salesman at Salomon Brothers during much of the 1980s. A lively, detailed account of Michael Milken's lucrative life of crime at Drexel Burnham Lambert Inc. is provided by James B. Stewart, *op. cit.*

boomtown full of fresh wealth. Croker, once a college football star, is now a late middle-aged Atlanta conglomerate king whose outsized ego has at last hit up against the reality of overdue bank loans. Charlie has a 29,000-acre quail-shooting plantation, a young and demanding second wife, but also a gigantic, half-empty office complex built with a huge unpaid debt.[19]

Because of banks lending to developers like Charlie Croker, the FDIC, which has insured bank deposits since 1933, went broke for the first time in 1991. Bank failures drained the fund as 882 banks failed between 1987 and 1991. Unlike the failures of many small banks during the Great Depression, these were tumbling giants. Only 11 percent of commercial banks actually posted losses in 1991, but those banks held more than a fifth of the $3.4 trillion in total system-wide assets. Banks were once considered by the Federal Reserve to be "too large to fail"; now they may be too large to save.

When nonfinanical corporations can no longer service their soaring debts, they too fail. These failures had risen to nearly 1,400 a week in 1987, retreated to a level of about 900 a week by 1989, and then soared to over 1,700 in 1991, rising still higher to 1,800 in early 1992. The same principal and outcome apply to households. Total personal bankruptcies skyrocketed more than 150 percent during the 1980s to a record 720,000 in 1990.

The further consolation of industry and of financial institutions was turned over to the federal government and to the Federal Reserve System, including taxpayer bailouts of S&Ls, commercial banks, and giant insurance companies. Much of the financial industry was being liquidated by the time that Michael Milken was being sentenced to ten years in prison on November 21, 1990 (only to be released in 1993 on a greatly reduced sentence). In 1996, Michael and his brother, each still among the Forbes 400 richest Americans, invested $250 million to create Knowledge Universe (KU), an educational-services company. Within two years, KU acquired

---

[19] For the "full" story, see Tom Wolfe, *A Man in Full* (New York: Farrar Straus Giroux, 1998).

30 companies and has more deals pending. Some things never seem to change. Who, people were beginning to ask, would bail out the typical wage earner?

Reaganomics was the impetus for the takeovers by the financial wealth holders, and the end of its fallout is not yet in sight. It is difficult to know where all those federal funds and tax breaks went. In a sense the funds were gone with barely a trace, reminiscent of the experience of Rabo Karabekian, Kurt Vonnegut's aforementioned fictional artist-collector in *Bluebeard*. All of Rabo's own paintings had destroyed themselves because of the unforeseen chemical reactions between the sizing of his canvases and the acrylic wall paint and colored tapes he had applied to them. Yet, people had paid handsome amounts for his paintings.

As Rabo remembers, "...people who had paid fifteen — or twenty- or even thirty thousand dollars for a picture of mine found themselves gazing at a blank canvas, all ready for a new picture, and riglets of colored tapes and what looked like moldy Rice Krispies on the floor." Yet, Rabo had been assured by advertisements that the Sateen Dura-Luxe paint would "...outlive the smile on 'Mona Lisa.' "[20] People had paid handsomely for Rabo's paintings; now they were gone with barely a trace, and so was the money. Yet, Rabo continued to amass a fortune from his collections and resales. Rabo was like a junk bond dealer and the holders of his paintings, owners of deposits in the S&L's.

## THE GROWING INEQUALITY DURING THE 1980s

The Reaganauts' Trojan horse tactic was as successful as it had been for the Greeks in their Trojan War victory of 1200 B.C. Affluent Americans made robust real-income gains, while poorer Americans actually experienced income losses during 1980 to 1984. With about half of American families enduring real-income losses over Reagan's first term, some liberal Democrats were diminished to jokes about the

---

[20] Vonnegut, *op. cit.*, pp. 19–20.

Reaganomics tide "raising all yachts." As family income grew more slowly during the 1980s than in the 1970s or between World War II and 1973, the rich got richer while the poor were getting poorer throughout the Reagan years. The abrupt shift to greater inequality provided $11,317 per family more in 1988 than in 1979 for the top five percent and a loss of $1,200 per family in the bottom three-fifths. The share of income received by the upper one percent soon would be greater than that of the bottom 40 percent!

Any "trickle-down" benefits were illusive. The U.S. official poverty rate had declined to 11.7 percent and 25.1 million persons in 1979, but had rebounded to 13.1 percent and 31.9 million in 1988. In that same year, one of every five children lived in poverty. The poor also were getting poorer, as the gap between actual incomes and the poverty line rose from 8.9 percent in 1973 to 1979 to 15.5 percent in 1979 to 1988.[21]

What happened to wealth inequality was even more dramatic. When we look at those racing to finish the 1980s with the most toys, some were already near the finish line. At the starting line the Federal Reserve Board's survey of consumer finances shows that families in the top two percent — nearly or actually the super-rich — already owned some 39 percent of corporate and government bonds and 71 percent of tax-exempt municipals. The wealthiest ten percent, the simply rich, then owned 70 percent of the bonds and 85 percent of tax-exempts.[22] Most of the values of the holdings of corporate stock and other financial assets also was held in a few hands.

Incredibly, as Reagan's two-term national debt or the value of Treasury bonds outstanding soared to $3.2 trillion, his tax cuts had given rich Americans a $2 trillion windfall for their purchase. Tax breaks for the very wealthy enabled them to buy something

---

[21] See Lawrence Mishel and David M. Frankel, *The State of Working America, 1990–1991* (Armonk: M.E. Sharpe, 1991), p. 168. Additional, related historical data are developed and presented in this important book and its later editions.

[22] The categories of richness are defined in E. Ray Canterbery, *Wall Street Capitalism: The Theory of the Bondholding Class* (Singapore/New Jersey/London/Hong Kong: World Scientific, 2000).

like $700 billion of Reagan's new bond debt. Even the distribution of these holdings was tilted toward the upper one percent or super-rich, and still more to the upper 0.5 percent or supra-rich. Most, if not all, of these extra dollars went into securities portfolios. Not only were the bonds — in massive quantities — initially created during the Reagan years, but so were the means to buy then. The tax breaks continued through the end of the twentieth century.[23]

Among households, the massive interest payments by the U.S. Treasury blessed the few holding bonds, while crowding out federal expenditures. Since only three percent of all families then directly held any bonds (public or corporate), the top one percent of wealth holders, the super rich, got half of all interest payments going to households, while the top five percent divided up the residual fifth. Compound interest alone was creating new millionaires and billionaires. By the late 1990s, still only four percent of all families directly held any bonds. The 1980s decade's entire increment of disposable income is more than accounted for by the rise in the share of interest income.

Meantime, the entrepreneur's share of national income declined drastically, hardly a Golden Age for entrepreneurship. Productive capitalism builds factories, but the casino economy redistributes and concentrates income and financial wealth.

The interest income trend outlived the Reagan-Bush years. In 1998, Americans paid as much in taxes as interest payments to the bond holders as they paid to run the navy, air force, army, marine corps, intelligence agencies, and the defense administrators and staff. That's about 14 cents of every federal government dollar spent! Largely because of the growth of the bond markets, 13 cents of each

---

[23] The massive tax cuts for the rich combined with the torrent of new Treasury bonds was the impetus for what I have called the rise of the bondholding class in *Wall Street Capitalism, ibid.* Much of what follows is a summary of facts and ideas developed in that book; for the details and other ideas, see the original. See also E. Ray Canterbery, "The Theory of the Bondholding Class," *Journal of Economic Issues* (June 2002).

dollar of personal disposable income (personal income after incomer taxes and social security deductions) was coming from interest payments by 1995. In bold contrast, only four cents of each dollar of income came from stock dividends.

## A NET WORTH PERSPECTIVE: WHERE THE MONEY WENT

Economists generally do not like to look at net worth or wealth. If we are to understand the effects of the shift to a casino economy, however, we will find the answers in balance sheets.

Inflation in the prices of ordinary goods and services during the 1980s and 1990s declined, while the prices of financial assets boomed. Moreover, the values of tangible asset values were declining or stagnant, even as debt burdens soared. When we consider the distribution of assets by type — financial or tangible — we can further understand why wealth inequalities widened so rapidly.

The supra-rich (top 0.5 percent of families) held 45.5 percent of corporate stock and 43.5 percent of outstanding bonds in 1983, whereas the lower 90 percent of American families held only 10.7 and 9.7 percent, respectively. For real estate, the source of a typical family's net worth, the shares are nearly flipped, about half of all real estate being held by the lower 90 percent.

The great disparity between financial asset inflation and tangible asset deflation or stagnation had adverse effects on the lower 90 percent during the 1980s. In the 1983 to 1989 period, the average wealth of the top one percent, the super-rich, rose from $7.1 million per household to $9.0 million. This is the *average.* Meanwhile, wealth fell for the bottom fifth (from −$3,200 to −$18,100 per household and for the next fifth (from $12,300 to $10,100).[24] Michael Milken had made $3 billion in his junk-bond deals during a few years ending in 1989, and was one of the

---

[24] See Lawrence Mishel, Jared Bernstein, and John Schmitt, *The State of Working America, 1998–1999* (Ithaca and London: Cornell University Press, 1999), pp. 258–275.

ten richest persons in the United States. It would be easy to conclude that — since the rich were getting richer — business firms must be too. This would be easy, but like so many easy things, would be wrong. Drexel Burnham Lambert Inc., Milken's own firm, filed for bankruptcy protection on February 13, 1990.

As to other firms, if the change in net worth of businesses is combined with that of households, the annual growth of net worth per adult is a flatliner during the 1980s. Moreover, from 1982 to 1992, the net worth of the nonfinancial business sector grew at the feeble pace of 0.62 percent yearly. The growth of net worth in the economy apparently had switched from business firms to selected families. The United States was getting poorer even as its elite was getting richer.

By the time of the presidential elections of 1992, the country seemed to be mired in a dark, foreboding malaise. A troublesome recession, beginning July 1990, ending officially in 1991, and followed by several years of snail-paced growth gave character to the Great Stagnation even as the greatest American bull market in stocks began to roar.

## CLINTONOMICS: CONTINUITY WITH THE FEDERAL RESERVE

Historically, a frequent complaint has emanated from New York and Washington: "Those politicians inside the beltway do not understand Wall Street's needs." Unlike so many disputes, the quarrels between The Street and Washington have ended. The head of the Federal Reserve System, two successive Treasury secretaries, and the bondholding class, itself a joint product of Washington and New York, have moved Wall Street's agenda into the White House. As President-elect, Bill Clinton virtually turned over White House economic policy to Alan Greenspan and to the Treasury heads, all choices of Wall Street. By mid-April 1993, the administration had embraced the preferences of the financial market players for budget deficit reduction and free trade, a dream program for Eisenhower Republicans.

## Greenspan and Clinton: An Unholy Alliance

The initial alignment of Clinton and Greenspan seemed as unlikely as that of Venus and Mars. In the 1950s, Alan Greenspan, well to the political right of the Eisenhower Republicans, was drawn into the tight little New York circle led by Ayn Rand. Greenspan had been one of the first students at the Nathaniel Branden Institute, the "think tank" founded to further the ideas of Ayn Rand. Rand's other followers called Greenspan "the undertaker" because he always dressed in a black suit, much like the one he wore to her funeral. Greenspan later took to wearing only blue, perhaps so he would seem less the villain to blue collar workers.[25]

Greenspan was a member of a radical right group known to themselves as The Collective and, to Rand, as the Class of '43, named for the year of her novel, *The Fountainhead*. The Collective converted Greenspan into a lover of free markets, a man not only suspicious of do-gooders but having a righteous hatred of government. Greeenspan told the *New York Times* in 1974, "What she [Rand] did — through long discussions and lots of arguments into the night — was to make me think why capitalism is not only efficient and practical, but also moral."[26] Whatever irony attends a free-marketeer becoming the world's most powerful bureaucrat is exculpated by the revelation that Greenspan, the Howard Roark of central banking, was the lonely hero freeing Wall Street from the chains of government. Greenspan never strayed from his radical ideology, though as head of the Federal Reserve he stated it with less clarity.

---

[25] A much more detailed account of the Clinton-Greenspan years appears in E. Ray Canterbery, *Alan Greenspan: The Oracle Behind the Curtain* (New Jersey/London/Singapore/Hong Kong: World Scientific, 2006).

[26] Quoted by Steven K. Beckner, *Back From the Brink: The Greenspan Years* (New York: John Wiley and Sons, 1995), p. 12. Beckner first became acquainted with Greenspan through his writings on the virtues of laissez-faire economics and the gold standard in Ayn Rand's journal. Later, Beckner covered Greenspan as a financial journalist in Washington. For the most part, Beckner's book is laudatory, though what Beckner praises Greenspan for, others might condemn him.

In sharp, dramatic contrast to Greenspan's pedigree, Clinton was a Southern populist who had governed the poor, backward state of Arkansas. He was one of the New Democrats; they were more centrist than the old Democrats, but they nonetheless wished to retain the social programs from Franklin Roosevelt's New Deal. They still believed that the federal government had an important role in maintaining full employment. It was, they believed, the responsibility of the federal government to increase opportunities for the poor, because the rich had the resources to care for themselves. Moreover, Clinton had run for president on a platform of public investment in the infrastructure such as roads, airports, bridges, and schools. By his run for a second term, nonetheless, these issues had long since been abandoned unless "building a bridge to the twenty-first century" is considered a new infrastructure.

## Greenspan's Financial Market Strategy

A new psychology came forth: Slow economic growth was good because it led to higher bond prices and hence a bullish stock market. Interest rates were to be kept low not by an easy money policy but by managing to keep the economy soft. Even the hint of a speed up in economic growth created a chill on Wall Street. If necessary, the Fed would raise short-term interest rates so that longer-term or bond interest rates might fall.

Greenspan pictured bond holders and traders as "highly sophisticated," by which, he meant that they expected the federal budget deficit to continue "to explode."[27] With such vast federal expenditures, inflation would inevitably soar. In Greenspan's view, the budget deficits from government spending, not soaring oil prices, had induced the double-digit inflation of the later 1970s. Wary investors in long-term U.S. Treasury bonds then demanded higher returns because of the expectations on deficits. This unfavorable spin on federal deficits was the new twist in the post-Reagan policy strategy.

---

[27] Bob Woodward, *The Agenda: Inside the Clinton White House* (New York: Simon & Schuster, 1994), p. 69.

## Public Infrastructure is Sacrificed to Reduce the Federal Budget Deficit

Clinton's economic team came to conclude that without Greenspan's cooperation, they were doomed. With visions of stock market crashes, depression, and collapsing banks dancing in his head, Clinton assured everyone that a major deficit reduction plan was already in the works. Clinton, the extraordinary mix of true Democrat, populist, Southern pulse-taker, man-of-the-people, and brainy policy student was out: The Washington-Wall Street establishment had swooped down and stolen Clinton's economic policy.

Gradually the 30-year bond rate did come down, and the capital gains of bond holders went up. There followed an undramatic but steady expansion of GDP. In the interest rate-sensitive sectors of the economy, real GDP rose by 11 percent, while the noninterest-sensitive sectors showed virtually no growth. Greenspan and Lloyd Bentsen, the Secretary of Treasury, credited the growth to "the financial markets strategy."

The Greenspan-Clinton alliance nonetheless had the life span of a butterfly. In January 1994, Greenspan told Clinton and his economic advisers that inflation expectations were mounting. Two weeks later the Fed raised short-term rates, with the Fed raising rates a third time on April 18, 1994. The long-term benchmark rate moved higher than any time in Clinton's first term. Greenspan had broken his promise to the president to bring interest rates down if Clinton narrowed the deficit. By the end of this process, Greenspan had raised the fed funds rate seven times.

The same parts of the economy very sensitive to interest rate reductions are equally or even more sensitive to interest rate increases. By early 1995, signs of an economic slowdown appeared. Moreover, a Republican-dominated Congress was pushing for deficit reduction through spending cuts and greatly reduced tax rates for the rich, using Reaganautic rhetoric. Meanwhile, President Clinton was taking a beating in the polls, despite the only significant deficit reductions since the Nixon administration.

During most of the decade, Greenspan relied on the relationship between the actual unemployment rate and the natural rate (or the

Non-Accelerating-Inflation Rate of Unemployment or NAIRU). Generally, Greenspan used pre-emptive strikes, raising interest rates before even the natural rate flashed the accelerating signal. Though the Federal Reserve had estimated the natural rate at 5.3 percent for 1994 to 2000, the actual unemployment rate, at 4.3 percent in May 1998, had reached a 28-year low and inflation was near zero. Despite the deflationary reality, the Fed continued to fret during 1995 to 2000 about impending inflation. Certainly, this natural bias against inflation and full employment pleased the wealth holders.

Despite the *financial markets strategy* being in disarray, job improvements during the campaign, Clinton's adoption of the Republican agenda, and a lackluster campaign from Bob Dole was sufficient to reelect Clinton in 1996. Meanwhile, Greenspan's strategy had created the greatest bull market in stocks in American history. Though it was his creation, he began to worry that the bubble might burst, a concern echoed in an address in December 1995 about the possible "irrational exuberance" of the market. Thereafter, unable to talk the stock market down, the Federal Reserve generally conducted itself in a manner least likely to precipitate the greatest stock market crash in American history.

In early September 1998, when Greenspan merely hinted that he was as likely to *lower* as to raise interest rates, the Dow made its then-largest point rise ever, a 380-point leap in one day.[28] The Dow swung wildly — hundreds of points from week to week, sometimes from day to day, sometimes within the day. The extreme volatility visiting the financial markets during the final years of the twentieth century was unprecedented. In an apparent effort to contain financial market hyper-volatility, President Clinton reappointed Greenspan to head the Federal Reserve for a fourth term a full half year before his third term was to end.

As before, those whose net worth or wealth improved the greatest with booming financial markets were the rich. Projections have the largest increases (in percentage) going to the top one percent.

---

[28] The day was Tuesday, September 8, 1998. The percentage gain of 4.98 percent, however, was only the 58th largest ever in percentage terms.

Wealth for the super-rich in the 1989 to 1995 period grew an estimated 11.3 percent (a $1 million average gain). Meanwhile, the bottom fifth moved closer to breaking-even with a net wealth gain of –$18,100 to –$4,900 while the second fifth at least saw a gain in average household wealth (from $10,100 to $12,300). Still, even with bull market gains, households in the middle fifth of the wealth distribution had a lower level of wealth in 1997 than they had in 1989![29]

## THE CLINTON LEGACY: ENDING THE PROGRESSIVE AGENDA

In his second term, President Clinton abandoned domestic economic policy concerns and was looking to foreign policy achievements as a way to elevate his historical place among American presidents. He had fought Greenspan and Wall Street and had lost: Progressives were deeply disappointed with his capitulation to Wall Street.

The Clinton administration presided over the final phase of a historical shift to monetary policy at the exclusion of fiscal policy. The Reagan Revolution had created so much federal debt (intentional or not) that it left no room to use intentional deficits to stimulate or slow the economy. Besides, political rhetoric had shifted from using the federal budget as a stabilizing force and toward a mantra of balancing the federal budget. Then, budget surpluses were touted and, *finally*, the elimination of the national debt altogether. Since the Federal Reserve buys and sells government securities in the conduct of monetary policy, a national debt of zero would make the conduct of monetary policy virtually impossible. If monetary policy is condemned to the same trash heap as fiscal policy, there will be no need for macroeconomics.

These forces have created and sustained a class rich beyond common imagination. Soon, euphoria combined with price volatility would engulf the sale of bonds, public and private, providing new

---

[29] See Mishel, Bernstein, and Schmitt, *The State of Working America 1998–1999*, *op. cit.*

profit opportunities for daily traders. After huge capital gains had given the bond market long-denied respectability, playing the bond market — joined at the hip by a gyrating but bullish stock market — required the agility of a racquet ball champion. The bondholding class, as I call it, carved out of soaring inequality and now operating in a newly deregulated financial environment, would contribute not only to the reversal of fortunes of the lower 95 percent of families, but to the creation of a financial casino.

The completion of the "Reagan Revolution" continued to be promoted by the GOP majority and the editorial page of *The Wall Street Journal*. In 1997, Clinton signed onto a "trickle-down" package of capital gains and inheritance tax cuts. The richest one percent of households once again benefited by the far the most, with each paying $15,000 less in taxes. The bottom 20 percent of U.S. households saw their taxes rise by an average of $40 a year. The second 20 percent saw no change, and the middle 20 percent gained only $140 a year. New Democrats, it has been said, are the pragmatists who are able to compromise with the GOP. By that standard, if by no other, Bill Clinton was the most compromised Democrat president in history. In winter 1998 while Greenspan's words still were moving financial markets, the president was impeached by the GOP he had emulated. *That* is the way the world *really* works.

## THE DRAMATIC SHIFT FROM BASIC COMMODITIES TO NONBASIC SERVICES

We turn to Sraffa for the language to describe the outcome. As noted, basic commodities are commodities used to produce commodities. They are the stuff of the manufacturing sector. We can think of the economy as divided between the nonfinancial and the financial sectors. As the financial sector amassed more and more assets, it became a bigger part of the national economy. Between 1978 and 2007, the financial sector grew from 3.5 percent to 5.9 percent of the economy (measured by contribution to GDP). In this sector financial wealth is held in the form of stocks, bonds, mortgages, and derivatives. It is where all savings are parked. Its

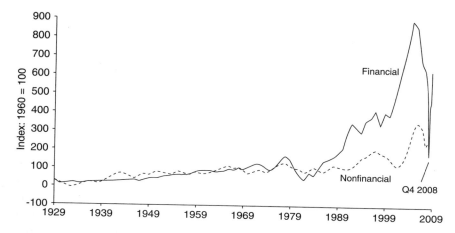

*Source*: Simon Johnson and James Kwak, *13 Bankers* (New York: Pantheon Books, 2010), p. 61.
*Notes*: Bureau of Economic Analysis, *National Income and Product Accounts*, Tables 1.1.4.6.16.
Financial sector excludes the 12 Federal Reserve banks. Annual through 2007, quarterly Q1
2008–Q3 2009.

**Figure 5.1:** Real Corporate Profits, Financial vs. Nonfinancial Sectors.

share of real corporate profits (adjusted for inflation) climbed even
faster, as shown in Figure 5.1.

From the 1930s until around 1980, financial sector profits grew
at roughly the same rate as profits in the nonfinancial sector. But from
1980 until 2005, financial sector profits grew by 800 percent,
adjusted for inflation, while nonfinancial sector profits grew by only
250 percent. Financial sector profits were to plummet at the peak of a
financial crisis in the fourth quarter of 2008, but quickly rebounded;
by the third quarter of 2009, financial sector profits were over six
times their 1980 level, while nonfinancial sector profits were little
more than double those of 1980. The profits growth rate in the
financial (nonbasic) sector was at the expense of profits in the nonfinancial (basic) sector. The aforementioned sharp dips of 1978–1983
as well as the reversals of the 1990s are also illustrated in Figure 5.1.

Salaries and bonuses among bankers also dramatically increased.
In 1978 average per-person compensation in the banking sector was
$13,163 (in 1978 dollars) — about the same as in the private sector

overall. From 1955 through 1982, the average banker's compensation fluctuated between 100 and 110 percent of average private sector pay. Then banking pay took off, until by 2007, the average banker was making over twice as much as the average private sector employee, a trend driven by the stupendous growth at the top end of the income distribution. The industry of the employee had a lot to do with wage differentials. These trends are highlighted in Figure 5.2.

In 1990, Salomon Brothers paid its top traders cash bonuses of more than $10 million, shocking at the time. In 2009 the head of a commodities trading group at Citigroup received a $100 million bonus. The real money was in hedge funds; in 2007, five fund managers earned at least $1 billion each for themselves, led by John Paulson, who made $3.7 billion successfully betting against the housing market and the mortgage-backed securities built on top of it. We will soon return to the housing market. Larger and more profitable, the financial sector grew in every way imaginable during the last three decades. At the same time, it became more powerful.

What was true for banking was true for the entire financial industry. Vast amounts of money combined with the laissez faire of Wall Street spun ever-larger amounts of money into the bank accounts of

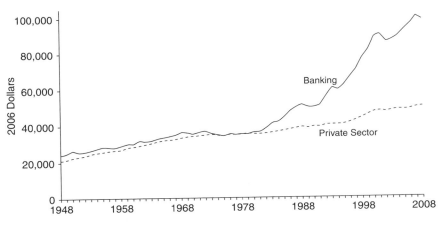

*Source*: Johnson and Kwak, *13 Bankers, op. cit.*, p. 115.

**Figure 5.2:**   Real Average Annual Compensation, Banking vs. Private Sector Overall.

top traders, salesmen, and bankers. Taking high levels of education into account, finance still paid more than other professions. Thomas Philippon and Ariell Reshef found an "excess relative wage" in finance — the amount that cannot be explained by differences in education level and job security — grew from zero around 1980 to over 40 percentage points earlier this decade; 30–50 percent of excess wages in finance cannot be explained by differences in individual ability. They also found that deregulation was one factor behind the recent growth of compensation in finance. Figure 5.3 shows the relationship between the unadjusted relative wage in the financial sector — the ratio between average wages in finance and average wages in the private sector as a whole — and the extent of financial deregulation, as calculated by Philippon and Reshef.[30]

The calculation of the "excess relative wage" by Philippon and Reshef can be thought of as an applied exercise with the vita

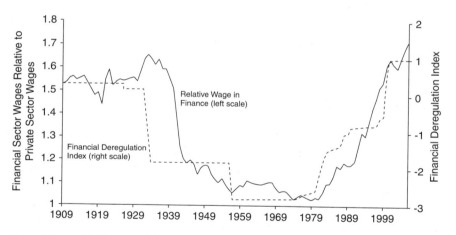

Source: Thomas Philippon and Ariell Reshef, "Wages and Human Capital in the U.S. Financial Industry: 1909–2006," Figure 6.

**Figure 5.3:** Relative Financial Wages and Financial Deregulation.

---

[30] Thomas Philippon and Ariell Reshef, "Wages and Human Capital in the U.S. Financial Industry: 1909–2006" (working paper, December 2008), Sections 3.4 and 3.5.

theory. All the characteristics of labor are the same in the financial and nonfinancial industries. The main different variables are the profits and the ability to pay of the financial industry compared with the nonfinancial industry. There is Sraffa's trade-off between profits and wages, but it occurs *across* industries. There is an inverse relationship (with a lag) between financial profits (and wages) and wages in the nonfinancial industry. These are the relations beginning around the early 1980s. Making money with money is valued much more highly than making money with commodities, including plant and equipment.

In finance rewards for success grew much, much faster as traders' potential bonuses climbed into the millions and then the tens of millions. In 2008, a bad year for most banks, 1,626 J.P. Morgan Chase employees received bonuses of more than $1 million; at the smaller Goldman Sachs, 953 received bonuses of more than $1 million, and 212 received bonuses of more than $3 million. By the 2000s, it was investment banks and hedge funds, where smart college graduates could expect to make millions. Banking and finance became more and more popular among the young and privileged of the ivy league.

## CONCLUSIONS

Like the advertisements for "sateen Dura-Luxe paint," Reaganomics did not yield the benefits it had promised and Clintonomics kept Reagan's fiscal revolution alive. Only the smile of "Mona Lisa" seems authentic.

The failures of Reaganomics revived Keynesianism — originally designed by Keynes to save capitalism from itself — at a time when neoclassical Keynesianism appeared comatose. Still, casino capitalism seemed unstoppable at the start of the twenty-first century. Financial deregulation during the 1980s and 1990s opened the door for heretofore unheralded abuse. The initial euphoria of intense competition among suppliers of credit has floundered on the shoals of massive bankruptcies, mergers, and even greater financial concentration.

After 1980 all this culminated in a shift out of basic industry and into nonbasic industry. The unequal income distribution in the USA was translated into a still more unequal wealth distribution. The wealth was held in the form of financial assets on the balance sheets of financial institutions. Real investment in basic commodities stagnated while financial assets soared. The wealth distribution shifted from once rich producers of oil, automobiles, steel, furniture, appliances, and electronics to the holders of financial assets. One characteristic shared by both basic and nonbasic industries was concentration of the industries among the few.

# 6

# THE HOUSING BUBBLE CONUNDRUM

As we are beginning to realize, the seeds of the Global Great Recession were sown long before the downturn. The massive shift in the income and wealth distributions beginning with Reaganomics set the stage. When so many financial assets are in the hands of so few, Wall Street becomes anxious to find new financial instruments. Out of these financial innovations, bubbles can be made. At their inception, we could usually find Alan Greenspan.

Alan Greenspan never thought that his days of dealing with bubbles had ended with the 1987 stock market crash and the total unraveling of the Nasdaq in 2000–2001. By now he was claiming "risk management" to be the main role for the Federal Reserve. Greenspan and his neoconservative cousins had created enough risks to make risk management a growth industry. Again, Mr. Greenspan and company were busily creating conditions so volatile that only a whirling dervish could dodge them all.

Thanks to the stock market bubble and especially the bursting of the Nasdaq, wealthy people and institutions needed to shift their funds into different assets. Those 35 to 55 percent returns in securities had essentially disappeared except in hedge funds which were again under pressure, some even collapsing. The housing market, especially second homes, vacation homes and investment condos became the new playground for the rich. Ultimately, as ever, families that couldn't afford to play did get in on the action and would be the most vulnerable, just as they are in stock market crashes. They have little to lose, but it is all they have.

# HOW THE FED CAN STIMULATE HOUSING CONSTRUCTION AND DEMAND

The conventional wisdom among real-estate, finance and economics professors is that a bubble cannot form in housing — in part, because housing is not simply straw, brick or timber, but Home Sweet Home. Reminding ourselves that current conventional wisdom is the equivalent of conservative ideology and Greenspan is an ideologue, we naturally expect him to take the same position. We need recall, however in the interest of full Fed disclosure, Greenspan's pattern of taking opposing stances on everything, sometimes on the same day, seldom in the same speech. Though usually never mentioned explicitly, the housing and construction industries are central to Fed policy. As a basic industry housing construction is also central to economic growth.

Now we will review the Fed's open market operations in order to understand the Fed's influence in housing. To stimulate business activity, the Fed provides more reserves to banks for overnight lending (as fed funds). In turn, this act of increasing the reserves in the banking system lowers short-term interest rates. Since private banks mark-up all other loans such as the prime rate from the fed funds rate, the interest rates of longer maturities are lowered. The first effects are to reduce interest rates on credit cards issued by these private banks. Next, housing and construction are especially stimulated by lower interest rates. Employment and incomes in those industries increase, thus stimulating other parts of the economy through the *Keynesian multiplier effect*. To slow down business activity, the Fed provides fewer funds to banks for overnight lending so as to hopefully raise interest rates across the spectrum. In turn, credit card debt is reduced and the construction industry slows down, eventually taking most of the balance of the economy with it. In these two processes, overall credit is expanded and contracted.

## ALAN GREENSPAN ACTS

The foregoing explains why during 2001–2003 Alan Greenspan embraced housing as a new miracle economic driver. The economy had been faltering at the turn of the century and Greenspan needed some source of stimulus for the economy. He saw it in real estate as he lowered the fed funds rate in stair-step fashion through mid-2003. Mortgage rates and credit card rates are tied to the prime loan rate and five or ten-year bonds, all of which are tied to the fed funds rate. Lower interest rates were combined with financial innovation in the way of adjustable-rate mortgages that set off a boom in housing. Before Greenspan, the USA had been bubble free for a half century.

Meanwhile, the stock market had been under tremendous pressure since it peaked in March 2000. In 2002 the Nasdaq declined another 32 percent, while the S&P 500 sank 24 percent. From its peak in 2000, the Nasdaq would tumble a shocking 74 percent, the S&P 500 a substantial 43 percent. Throughout the sharp run-up on the stock markets Greenspan denied that there was a bubble, while at the same time saying that if a bubble were to exist, the central bank and others would not know about it until after it burst. But since a bubble could not exist (in his mind), he could easily ignore the unmistakable sound of air going out of the stock market as it entered bear territory.

With the stock market no longer available for pulling along the economy (nor the associated profits on Wall Street), real estate seemed to be the only motor left to start. New financial products that included derivatives, asset-backed securities, collateralized loan obligations, and collateralized mortgage obligations (CMO's) had made firms and individuals independent of specific institutions for funds. All this contributed to a more flexible and efficient financial system. At the time this meant that regulated banks were being superseded by unregulated markets. It was to make the financial system *ultimately* more vulnerable. These "innovations" led to the financial market turmoil of late 2007 in which many large financial firms approached bankruptcy. They were innovations of the neo-Austrian variety rather than the more substantial Schumpeter species.

Attractive mortgage rates bolstered the sales of existing homes and made possible the use of the home equity loan. Low mortgage rates encouraged homeowners to take on larger mortgages when refinancing their homes. This provided still larger home lines of equity.

At the time this seemed to be a safe thing to do since the housing market had not been a source of speculation during most of the 1990s. Still, the growth rate of mortgage debt outstanding accelerated until by 1998 it was galloping at an annual rate of 9.5 percent. Wall Street stood ready to securitize this rising mortgage debt. Government-sponsored enterprises such as Fannie Mae and Freddie Mac were also rapidly expanding their activities. Sharply falling interest rates added fuel to the smoldering fire.

Greenspan suggested that the usual analogy between the stock market and the real estate market was imperfect. Unlike the stock market, sales in the real estate market incur substantial transactions costs and, when most homes are sold, the seller must physically move out. The turnover in the stock market is something like 100 percent yearly whereas the turnover of home ownership is less than ten percent yearly. Besides, the market for a home is local; a home in Portland, Maine is not a good substitute for a home in Portland, Oregon; the national housing market is a collection of local segmented markets. Nonetheless, his arguments did not prevent the housing bubble.

By October 2002 the real estate market was experiencing multi-year gains. Between the autumns of 1997 and 2002, the average home price in the USA rose 42 percent. In particular cities the increases were much greater — 75 percent in Boston, 88 percent in San Francisco, and 67 percent in New York City. People were moving out of the stock market and were seeking wealth in real estate. Many households had turned themselves into a quasi-ATM machine. As interest rates continued to fall, homeowners refinanced their houses with mortgages in excess of the value of their homes, and then borrowed on the "equity." Whereas homeowner's average equity equaled 70 percent of the house's market value in 1997, in 2003 it was down to 55 percent.

This nascent housing bubble nonetheless sustained the demand for new construction. In short, mortgage markets were a powerful stabilizing force during the first couple years of the economic growth slowdown. In still other words, the home ATM machine was doing well. In turn, the ATM machine had a powerful effect on consumer spending. All this happened during a time when other asset values were being eroded. Housing had saved the day.

Just to be sure, Greenspan cut rates for the 13th time on June 25, 2003. This brought the fed funds rate down to one percent, where it would remain for nearly a year. By July 2003 home prices had gone up 20 percent during a bear market in stocks. Many analysts began to fear that when home prices did start to go down, they would fall remarkably far. In Japan, home prices were down to less than half what they were during the Japanese bubble.

## THE CONSEQUENCES OF ASSET INFLATION

The first signs that the beneficial side of rising home values were vanishing emerged as early as near the end of 2003. Prior to the death of irrational exuberance, the foundation of rapidly growing wealth was in securities. The equity ascent — off to a flying start after 1994, peaking in early 2000 — was a source of great accumulations of wealth at the very top. Wealthy bond holders also did remarkably well. Those ordinary people with financial assets in their pension plans went along for the ride, but also for the fall. Overall, $5 trillion in the market value of corporations was lost from March 2000 to October 2002. This period defined the end of the dot-com bubble. The value of real estate, somewhat more democratically held, began to accelerate well before the bottoming-out of Nasdaq equity prices in 2004.

For an interminable time, Alan Greenspan denied that the U.S. was in the early stages or *any* stages of a housing bubble. He noted the great demand among hardworking immigrants for houses (on Greg Norman's exclusive golf course resorts?). Housing, he said too, is a local market, making it virtually impossible to experience a national housing bubble. Moreover, he added, it's hard to speculate in a house a family lives in because, when they sell, they have to buy another and pay all those closing costs.

Despite Greenspan's romantic window on poor immigrants, a realist should not be surprised to find that rich people own more mansions and estates than the poor or the middle class. Although it may be embarrassing to the neoconservative wealthy family to see typical families benefit from asset inflation, the transfer of wealth out of securities and into large homes, as well as into palatial second homes on beaches and golf courses, did not leave *upper* middle class households behind. Aided by exotic financing innovations so praised by Greenspan, many were buying homes and condos that they couldn't afford.

At a time when an article in the *Wall Street Journal* by James R. Hagerty in 2003 was raising a few red flags, Greenspan continued to say that there was no bubble in housing. However, the oracle's past record in bubble spotting ranks right up there with the captain of the *Titanic* in spotting serious icebergs. Greenspan once said that there is no way to identify a bubble until it bursts; he also told fellow economists on January 3, 2004: "...our strategy of addressing the bubble's [the Nasdaq bubble] consequences rather than the bubble itself has been successful." Although the economists at the AEA gave him a standing ovation and muttered about his greatness, others were reminded of the inadequacy of the life boats on the *Titanic*. If the captain of money policy chose not to address a "bubble" that he could not identify but nonetheless dealt with "its" consequences, doesn't that mean that he knew of a bubble before and after?

## SPOTTING A HOUSING BUBBLE

As with the Nasdaq, and contrary to Greenspan, it *is* possible to know a bubble when it pops up. A bubble in housing prices is different but has some shared characteristics. Buying is based only on anticipation of rising prices rather than on fundamentals. Expectations of returns are based on recent gains rather than on historic norms. Some historical norms can change, but not over a fortnight. Buyers lose all respect for risk and refuse to believe that higher returns are closely linked to higher risks. In housing, as in other assets, at some price the focal perceived risk is "not being on board" rather then "possibly losing money." Minds lose the battle of rationality against irrationality and greed.

Greed and agreed, housing is different in an important respect. We can't inhabit the shares of Microsoft stock, no matter how many shares we have. Normally, buying and selling properties requires paying commissions and other "transactions costs." Normally, it takes months or even a year to sell a house above the current market price. As finance people put it, the market for houses is not as liquid as that for securities; it takes considerable time to "cash out" of a house or other property. This much we grant Alan Greenspan for normal times.

Nonetheless, a house is a home only in normal times. It is precisely when a house isn't a home that a housing bubble exists. During the bubble, price appreciation overwhelms six percent commissions and closing costs; besides there are ways to buy at pre-construction costs that require no costs before the deal is closed and the property cannot be resold (flipped) before closing time. During a bubble, a house can be sold the day it goes on the market. What normally is an illiquid market becomes liquid. Besides, through a process called securitization a bundle of real estate properties can be packaged and resold as a piece of paper; houses are converted not to homes, but to derivatives.

Still, Greenspan has a point about real estate markets being local. Real estate agents live and die on that premise. Of course, this idea is modified by securitization or even by real estate management trusts (REITS). All of which brings us back to the *Wall Street Journal*.

James Hagerty cites a study by house-price gurus Karl E. Case of Wellesley College and Robert J. Shiller of Yale University; they find that national measures of housing trends can be misleading. While house prices rise gradually along with slow growth in most families' personal incomes, states with cities short of land for residential construction such as in California (Bakersfield, Riverside-San Bernardino, Los Angeles-Long Beach, Redding, Fresno, San Diego, Orange County) and coastal Florida (West Palm Beach-Boca Raton, Miami, Fort Myers-Cape Coral, Fort Lauderdale) are more likely to swing from boom to bust in a hurry. The Case-Shiller view would seem, at first *rougissent*, to support the view of Coe Lewis, an agent at Century 21 Award who says that people worry too much about prices. "They get paralyzed," Ms. Lewis says. "They almost overthink the process. They think there's got to be a dip. There's not going to be a dip. I'm not afraid at all of a bubble in Southern California." We wonder how well that worked out for Ms. Lewis.

## GREENSPAN GETS SMARTER AS THE BUBBLE GETS BIGGER

With the *Wall Street Journal* ahead of the pack, by early spring 2005 business analysts in the United States seemingly could not write or speak of anything other than a herd instinct in the housing market itself. Even Case and Shiller began to refer to a *national* bubble. Alan Greenspan, so early to cry wolf about Dow stock prices, joined this hunt very late in the season. At last, in response to questions following a luncheon speech on May 20, 2005, he told the Economic Club of New York: "At a minimum, there's a little froth in the market. We don't perceive that there is a national bubble, but it's hard not to see that there are a lot of local bubbles." In frothing about "local" bubbles, Greenspan appears to endorse the earlier Case-Shiller view. Besides "lather" and "fizz," however, a synonym for froth is "bubbles." The man who once claimed that bubbles cannot be found until they burst now finds bubbles all over the place, including locally. "Local" can mean "narrow" so he may have been speaking of only tiny bubbles.

While Greenspan is notorious for saying one thing and meaning another or claiming one thing but denying he meant what they say he said, he generally has recognized a financial disaster after it has happened. We have to worry then when we see the maestro going so quickly from "it can't happen" to "froth" which means bubbles. As to what is local, in the Case-Shiller study, there were so many local-bubble cities in California to make it a bubble state. California's economy is about the size of the United Kingdom's. If California and Florida were merged into the "Sunshine Boys," their economy would about equal Germany's. In a country where Treasury officials worry about how the U.K. or Germany business recession might adversely affect American interests, California and Florida are essentially countries within the U.S. As to Century 21 Award, it is a national franchise, so frothy local speeches by its agents are suspect.

As to a housing bubble, "Greenspan" was now likely to be correct, but *which* Greenspan? His inability to recognize (or at least admit to) the greatest financial bubble in world history is not encouraging. The Federal Reserve, the organization he happened to be heading at the time, issued some modest new guidelines to mortgage lenders during the same week as Greenspan's "frothy" speech. Among regulators' top concerns was the surge in popularity of interest-only loans, which allow people to pay only interest in the initial years but face the entire principal later. If there really is a bubble, however, toothlessly mouthed warnings will not stop most lenders from lending as usual. Was, in fact, Greenspan again saying one thing and doing another? He and other Fed officials denied that they were continuing to raise interest rates to slow housing asset inflation.

Once enough people believe that a bubble will continue to expand, it probably will. Once four-fifths of *Wall Street Journal* readers believe (as reported May 2005) that there is a housing bubble, it is a short step from believing that a bubble will continue and believing that not participating in it will be a lost opportunity. *Wall Street Journal* subscribers have the wealth to keep it going in California and Florida. The August 12, 2005 *Journal's* "House of the Week" was a 106-room, 11-bedroom, 13-bathroom little fix-me-up mansion for $21.5 million and it was in the Berkshires of Massachusetts, not even in California. When sky-high prices are accepted as "normal," much as Greenspan ultimately decided that Internet and tech stock prices were just what the market ordered during the early 2000s, look out below! This particular housing bubble reached a peak in September 2005, but this was not the end of the fallout, only the beginning.

## DEFINING THE BUBBLE

The existence of the bubble could have been verified. From 1895 to 1995, a 100 years epoch, nationwide house prices in the United States tracked the overall rate of inflation. On average, house prices rose at the same rate as the price of food, cars, clothes, and so on. While house prices in places like San Francisco and New York did rise far more rapidly than overall inflation, these price increases were offset by prices that trailed inflation in places like Gary, Indiana and St. Louis, Missouri.

In 1995 house prices began to outstrip the overall rate of inflation. By the summer of 2002 house prices had already outpaced inflation by 30 percent, creating more than $3 trillion of housing-bubble wealth. The question arises: Was there anything in market fundamentals — either on the demand or supply side of the market — that would explain the $3 trillion? The two main elements on the demand side are income and population. If income grows rapidly, people may want bigger and better homes, or even second homes. By the same token, a more rapidly increasing population will lead to more rapid growth in the demand for housing, especially if the growth rate is high among people in their 20s, who are forming their own households for the first time.

Neither of these factors provides an explanation for the fast run-up in house prices during this period. Income growth had been healthy during the late 1990s, but was not extraordinary. The rate of growth of median family income over the four years from 1996 to 2000 was no more rapid than the growth rate over the long boom from 1947 to 1973. Further, the country had fallen into a recession in 2001, and family income had begun to decrease. Income growth was weak through the rest of the bubble years, even though some modest gains happened in 2005 and 2006. In any case, income growth alone cannot explain the bubble in house prices during this time.

Population growth is an even less likely explanation. Though Alan Greenspan had cited immigration as a factor pushing up prices, the reality is that the inflow of immigrants in the 1990s and the following decade was a relatively minor element compared with the demographic bulge created by the baby-boom cohort. In truth, the rate of household formation was far more rapid in the 1970s and early 1980s, when the baby boomers were first forming their own households, but there was no bubble then. By the mid-1990s, the majority of the baby boomers who would ever be homeowners already owned a home. By the end of the housing bubble, the oldest baby boomers were already in their 60s.

What about supply-side fundamentals? Alan Greenspan once suggested that environmental constraints on building was one cause of the house price rises. Despite some environmental restrictions on building during the era of the housing bubble, that era was not the high point of the environmental movement. There essentially was little difference between the earlier decades and the bubble years.

Greenspan was the source of still other "reasons" for above-trend house prices. There was a limited supply of buildable land in desirable urban areas. True, land in urban areas is limited, but this condition was not new to the mid-1990s. This constraint had not been the source of a run-up in house prices over the prior hundred years. Why would it have made these prices suddenly rise nationwide in 1996?

There is a simple way to assess whether supply constraints were causing increases in house prices; look at the rate of housing construction during this period. We were building houses at a rapid pace in the 1990s and at an even more rapid pace in the first decade of the twenty-first century. The USA was building new housing units at a record rate from 2002 to 2006, when starts *averaged* 1,880,000 annually. This rate was about the five-year peak rate from 1969 to 1973. There was no supply constraint on housing during the bubble era.

Another place to look would be rental prices during the bubble years. While rental prices outpaced inflation by a small amount in the late 1990s, in the following decade they kept even with the overall rate of inflation or even trailed it slightly. This trend is still further evidence that fundamentals, the supply and demand elements, were not driving the rapid increase in house prices.

Herein we have the definition of a housing bubble. If soaring prices of houses cannot be explained by the fundamentals of demand and supply, the excess markup must constitute a bubble. The evidence was there for everyone to observe.

## GREENSPAN'S INNOCENT HYPOCRISY IN HIS ATTACK ON FANNIE AND FREDDIE

Fannie Mae and Freddie Mac were both chartered by the U.S. Congress to help finance housing for the typical family. They buy residential mortgage loans from lenders and bundle the loans into securities. Since these securities can be traded, mortgage market liquidity has been increased and interest costs lowered (enhanced "market efficiency," in Greenspanspeak). As government-sponsored enterprises (GSEs), Fannie and Freddie fall under some affordable housing goals. These mortgage purchase quotas require that no less than half of the mortgages they purchase be for low- and moderate-income households, that a fifth be set aside for those of low income, and that slightly less than a third be from geographically targeted underserved areas. In a housing bubble, finding an affordable house becomes difficult, especially as mortgage interest rates rise.

Fannie and Freddie now use derivatives in interest-rate swaps, just like commercial banks. In a typical swap, a borrower with a variable-rate loan and a borrower with a fixed-rate loan "swap" their interest-payment obligations to better match debt to assets. Fannie and Freddie use such swaps because as interest rates change, so does the likelihood that the mortgages they hold will be paid off early, before maturity. Moreover, like banks and other corporations, they issue equity so that stock can be bought and sold in these GSEs. (We will have more to say about the details of these swaps in the next chapter.)

Alan Greenspan not only is a long-time critic of Fannie and Freddie, he was — with ample backing from the Treasury and White House — to urge Congress to put severe limits on their business. The irony here blends nicely with hypocrisy. The Congress created the GSEs as *private* business enterprises. Moreover, while the Fed buys short-term securities from commercial banks to set short-term interest rates, Fannie and Freddie buy mortgages from the banks to bundle for resale and keep long-term rates lower. Except for particular goals set by the U.S. Congress, both the Fed and the GSEs are *independent.* Perhaps it is sibling rivalry: in many ways the Fed and the GSEs are similar creatures.

Their differences, however, disturbed Mr. Greenspan, as then czar of all financial markets. The Fed is cozy with banks; Fannie and Freddie compete with the mortgage business of banks. Alan Greenspan's main self-appointed task was to serve Wall Street and the wealth holders; Fannie and Freddie's main responsibility is to insure affordable housing for low- and moderate-income families. Worse, in Greenspan's view, the GSEs are "subsidized" by the "perception" that they are "too big to fail" and would be bailed out by the government. He also was concerned about Fannie and Freddie's "lack of sophistication" in handling derivatives. Worst of all, Fannie and Freddie are not fully subject to "market discipline."

As Greenspan has put it, "the existence, or even the perception, of government backing undermines the effectiveness of market discipline." This "special relationship to the government" is the root evil. Greenspan not only wanted the GSEs regulated on par with banks but also have the size of their mortgage portfolio limited. While there are some legitimate concerns with the operations of Fannie and Freddie, they should not be stones on which Greenspan grinds his free-market fundamentalist axe to serve Wall Street interests.

His hypocrisy may be innocent, but it nonetheless triumphs. Mr. Greenspan helped to create banks such as Citigroup, now too big to fail. Doubtless Citigroup will be bailed out by the Fed, because, as the smaller Citicorp, it already has been — *twice* — indirectly, along with others, in the Long – Term Capital Management bailout, and on its own mismanagement. Citigroup apparently is sufficiently sophisticated to use derivatives (though it failed to use them properly); Fannie and Freddie can't be trusted with swaps (though they have used them properly). With only ten banks controlling half of all domestic banking assets in the United States, why the great concern with the holdings of Fannie and Freddie at a time when their share of the mortgage market is declining? (Admittedly, Fannie and Freddie ended up holding half of all home mortgages by 2010.) The sincere problem seems to be this: Fannie and Freddie make it slightly more difficult for Wall Street and other financial institutions to transfer wealth to the top. Under the Greenspan Standard, Fannie and Freddie's loans are "non-conforming."

## SUMMING-UP

If there was a bubble, it was bound to burst. What would be the causes of such a calamity? The most critical consideration is the ability of speculators to make monthly payments. This ability depends on two things: income and mortgage rates. According to Federal Reserve data, the debt-to-income ratio of U.S. households reached a "Rocky Mountain high" in the fourth quarter of 2004 of 1.2:1 at very low mortgage rates. A decade earlier it had been 0.9:1. Moreover, household debt as a share of household assets also was nearing an all-time high even as the value of household assets was being inflated by rising home prices. Though it isn't the kind of leveraging known to hedge funds, households nonetheless were taking on more risk. A crisis such as the international financial crises of 1997–1998 could send interest rates soaring for those holding mortgages with adjustable rates and speed bankruptcies.

Now irony grasps us and will not let go. Alan Greenspan has been the major cheerleader for the housing boom, as he was with the dot-com and tech stocks. His good cheer was slightly muffled by the Fed's increasing short-term interest rates at a "measured pace," while encouraging the bond market players — influential in deciding mort-gage rates — to do the same. That mortgage rates declined during 12 months ending June 2005 while the fed funds rate target was being increased eight times was Greenspan's "conundrum," requiring that the fed funds rate climb continue unabated — to keep inflation-ary expectations in check, he claimed. In the August 2005 FOMC meeting, however, housing prices dominated the discussion.

There was the heightening danger that the strengthening rebound in the Dow combined with soaring house prices would produce the kind of double bubble that undid the Japanese financial system and economy in the early 1990s. Despite the creation by HedgeStreet of a "hedgelet" that allows individual investors to spec-ulate on the direction of home values in major cities, it is unlikely that new derivatives will bring stability to financial or to housing markets. Besides, like the financial bubble that led to an aftermath that led to the Fed's low interest-rate policy, the fortunes of the economy have shifted mostly to one industry. Employment in hous-ing and housing-related industries accounted for about 43 percent of the rise in private-sector payrolls between late 2001 and mid-2005, while the industry accounted for about two percentage points of the annualized GDP growth rate during 2004–2005. Without the housing boom, the GDP growth rate would have been about 1.5 percent and the official unemployment rate somewhere around 12 percent. Much of Greenspan's final legacy depended on the Fed's ability to bring high-flying houses in for a soft landing, even as he denied that the Fed was targeting housing. Would Greenspan and the Fed prick the housing bubble? By now it was a $8 trillion bubble, coming after the collapse of a $10 trillion stock bubble. On any scale the housing bust would be historic and have far-reaching implications for the global economy.

# 7

# THE ANATOMY OF THE SUBPRIME MORTGAGE BUBBLE AND COLLAPSE

*His name was George F. Babbitt, and he was nimble in the calling of selling houses for more than people could afford to pay*

Sinclair Lewis, *Babbitt* (1922); Ch. 1

The Casino Capitalism that emerged during the 1980s was an environment ripe for speculation. Speculation beset the stock market until it crashed, several times. Then, it was simply a matter of shifting the focus from the stock market to the housing market. The financial crisis of 2008–2009 had its roots not just in the subprime loans made as early as 2005 but in ideas that had hatched in 1986. Someone at Salomon Brothers created the first mortgage derivative that year.

The collateralized debt obligation (CDO), a derivative which will play an important role in our story, was invented by Michael Milken's junk bond department at Drexel Burnham in 1987. CDO became the generic name for all types of securitized assets, including mortgages. The Drexel-Burnham CDO was comprised of securitized bonds. The first mortgage-backed CDO was created at Credit Suisse in 2000 by a trader who had spent his formative years, in the 1980s and early 1990s, in the Salomon Brothers mortgage department. The CDO was just one of the instruments behind the housing bubble; we will consider others.

## THE CDO

The CDO enabled Salomon Brothers to create the mortgage bond market. A mortgage bond is not a single loan for a fixed term. A mortgage bond is a claim on the cash flows from a pool of thousands of individual home mortgages. The cash flows are problematic, as the borrowers have the right to pay off any time they pleased. To limit the uncertainty, Salomon Brothers took giant pools of home loans and carved up the payments made by homeowners into pieces, called tranches. The buyer of the first tranche was like the owner of the ground floor; he received the first wave of mortgage repayments. He also received a higher interest rate. The buyer of the second tranche — the second story — took the next wave of repayments and in exchange received the second highest interest rate, and so on. The buyer on the top floor received the lowest rate of interest but had the greatest assurance that his investment would not end before he wanted it to.

These mortgage bonds created from subprime home loans extended the logic invented to address the problem of early repayment to cope with the problem of no repayment at all. The buyer in the first tranche, the first floor, would be exposed not to repayments but to actual losses. That buyer took the first losses until his investment was entirely wiped out, whereupon the losses hit the guy on the second floor. And so on. In the boom years of 2005 and 2006, about four-fifths of the securities in CDOs were mortgage-backed. Often about 10 percent of the supporting assets were subprime.

To fully understand the bubble, we need to know more about the other innovations and instruments that made it possible.

## THE BLACK-SHOLES MODEL AND
## THE ORIGIN OF DERIVATIVES

The Black-Sholes financial model had a lot to do with what followed. A formula for asset pricing is its most important feature. Fischer Black and Myron Scholes, two finance professors at the University of California at Berkeley, developed the options-pricing model. Myron

Scholes shared a Nobel Prize with Robert C. Merton for "a new method to determine the value of derivatives" in 1997. The model is based on the idea that a trader can evade all market risk by taking a *short position* in the market and increasing that position as the market falls. The steepness of the decline of the market was presumed not to matter. Most employee stock-ownership plans use Black-Scholes as their guide. For example, instead of buying a put option from a Wall Street broker — an option to sell at a set price, limiting potential losses — on the S&P 500, portfolio managers can short the S&P 500 as it falls, and, according to the model, be free of all market risk. It seemed to be such a good theory that everyone bought into it; the Black-Scholes model eventually was the only thing not being sold short. No longer simply a model, Black-Scholes became the paradigm for financial risk avoidance.

For those paying close attention, the Black-Scholes model failed its own test during the stock market crash of 1987. On Black Monday of the crash, there were essentially only sellers of stocks, no buyers. There were Wall Street broker-dealers on the other side of the market who had to be betting that the decline in the market would quickly end; otherwise they would have no profits from taking the bet that the market would eventually reverse. In a free fall, broker-dealers eventually refuse to take that bet and the short-sellers have no one left to sell to. If the market keeps falling, the short sellers have to use loans to buy back their own stock at prices that are continuing to fall. The problem was aggravated when the major brokerage houses such as Merrill Lynch began to short stocks for their own protection. Without brokers to support the market, it collapsed. This debacle led to a massive restructuring of Wall Street and financial markets around the world.

Financial instruments had to be invented to provide insurance to the insurers. If banks were lending to brokers who were going bust, the loans could not be serviced and the banks would go under. In the aftermath of the 1987 crash there arose the need to insure the insurers. As luck would have it, there was a surplus of long-term bonds in American banks. American banks could then make money by borrowing at low long-term interest rates and lending at high short-term rates. The borrowers were consumers buying automobiles and using lines of credit from equity in their homes. Such lines of credit were derivatives — loans derived from the underlying market value of the home as an asset. Additional consumer credit came from unsecured credit-card debt.

The bonds could be sold, more often than not to Asian commercial and investment banks to raise capital to issue low-interest mortgages and associated lines of credit. In order to keep this game going, commercial banks had to create their own derivatives. That is, a mortgage on the bank's balance sheet is not directly transferable to a credit card customer. The mortgages were bundled into "securities" that were then resold for cash. A market developed in which the buyers of these new derivatives became known as hedge funds.

This whole scheme was such a good idea for the commercial banks that they decided not to keep the buying and selling of derivatives on their balance sheets; they were off-balance-sheet accounts. The growing hedge funds, financed by rich people (with minimum holdings in the $10 million range), were entirely unregulated. No one seemed to know what these funds were doing because their balance sheets were not required to be public. They had no capital requirements. With the private commercial banks keeping derivatives off their balance sheets, their capital reserves gave a false sense of security. To this day the Black-Scholes formula assures the market players that securities (including derivatives) are priced just right, with no need for further regulation.

## THE ROLE OF THE SUBPRIME MORTGAGE

Black-Scholes had to have securities to price and Casino Capitalism needed new chips with which to speculate. The rise of the subprime mortgage market provided new mortgages to package as securities. This market for subprime mortgages evolved from the skewed income distribution in the country. With the rich getting richer and the poor getting poorer, the American Dream of home ownership depended on very special circumstances favoring the lower income class. Ultimately, new chips were supplied for the many players in the casino. In other words, the *income distribution* is the key to understanding what happened.

As house prices rose to levels increasingly out of line with the fundamentals of the housing market — including family incomes, which were not rising — fewer families could afford to buy a home. Still, home sales and home ownership rates were hitting record levels, thanks to the collapse of lending standards and the spread of subprime mortgages, including Alt-As. The George Babbitts of the USA were selling houses like crazy. Because of the attitudes spawned by Casino Capitalism the explosion in nonprime mortgages did not send off warning signals of a serious housing bubble.

Subprime mortgages are riskier than standard mortgages and therefore carry higher interest rates. Typically interest rates on subprime mortgages are about two percentage points higher than prime mortgages, but sometimes as much as four percentage points higher. Just two or four percentage points add significantly to already low interest rates. Those who qualify for subprimes typically have poor credit records due to past defaults or irregular work histories; for whatever reasons, they have failed to qualify for a prime mortgage. Through the 1990s and the beginning of the following decade, subprime loans constituted only six to eight percent of the mortgage market. This share suddenly exploded to 25 percent by 2006. What regulators there were presumed that this was just Casino Capitalism operating the way it should.

The regulators who missed the subprime explosion should not have missed the growth in Alt-A loans. But they did. Alt-A loans are typically given to borrowers who have good credit records but cannot fully document their income or assets. They are often small business owners, who see substantial yearly fluctuations in their income. Besides, Alt-A borrowers may not be able to fully document their income because they do not fully report it, to avoid paying income taxes. Prior to 2002, the Alt-A market constituted a mere one or two percent of the mortgage market. This share had jumped to 15 percent by 2006.

Being subprime, Alt-A mortgages typically carry interest rates that are higher than prime mortgages. One might think that borrowers would have a substantial incentive to go though old tax forms if they were, indeed, honestly reporting their income. On a $400,000 mortgage (many Alt-A loans were attached to fairly expensive homes in bubble markets), such documentation could save the borrower $4,000 to $8,000 a year in interest. The truth is less forgivable. Alt-A mortgages increased during this period because more people were lying about their income on mortgage applications, something that would only add to the instability in the mortgage market.

There was another characteristic of these mortgages that made matters even worse. The vast majority of the subprime mortgages issued were adjustable-rate mortgages (ARMs), mortgages with interest rates that could be expected to rise in the future. The typical subprime mortgage had the interest rate fixed at a relatively low rate for the first two years, then reset to a higher rate in subsequent years, based on market rates at the time. Often the rate was reset at four percentage points or more above the initial low "teaser" rate.

What was characteristic of subprimes generally was characteristic of Alt-A loans. However, there were some differences. The Alt-A loans were more typically ARMs, but often with low rates for the first four to five years of the mortgage. Toward the peak of the bubble, lenders were issuing "interest-only" mortgages, which allowed borrowers to pay only interest for this initial period. Borrowers would only have to start paying down the principal after the reset date. Banks also developed "option ARMs," which allowed borrowers to vary the amount of their monthly payment during the initial period. These loans generally did not even require that the payment cover the monthly interest on the mortgage. Such "negative amortization" loans allowed the size of the mortgage to grow each month, and the borrower didn't have to start paying down the mortgage until after the reset.

By 2002 the subprime industry had virtually died. Some $30 billion was a big year for subprime lending in the mid-1990s. In 2000 there had been $130 billion in subprime mortgage lending, and 55 billion dollars' worth of those loans had been repackaged as mortgage bonds. In 2005, at the peak in home sales, though not home prices, there would be $625 billion in subprime mortgage loans,

$507 billion of which found its way into mortgage bonds! Even as interest rates began to rise, subprime lending was booming. Worse, back in 1996, 65 percent of subprime loans had been fixed-rate but by 2005, 75 percent of subprime loans were some form of floating-rate scheme, with a fixed rate usually for the first two years only.

The subprime lending companies were growing rapidly. They were using strange accounting which could mask the fact that they had no real earnings, just illusory, accounting-driven, ones. It was essentially a Ponzi scheme: The fiction of profitable enterprises required more and more capital to create more and more subprime loans. The Federal Reserve and the banking system was providing all the liquidity that was needed and usually at very favorable interest rates. By early 2005 all the big Wall Street investment banks were players in the subprime game. Bear Stearns, Merrill Lynch, Goldman Sachs, and Morgan Stanley all had subprime holdings. The major commerical banks also held subprimes on their balance sheets. As the subprime market grew, in fact, every financial company was, one way or another, exposed to it, as it surpassed the equity market.

Why were the banks not concerned? Banks paid little attention to their borrowers' ability to repay loans because the banks had resold the loans as mortgage bonds in the secondary market almost as soon as they were issued. This secondary market exploded. Private issuers of mortgage-backed securities — such as Merrill Lynch and Citigroup — were willing to package almost any mortgage into a mortgage-backed security. The risks were no longer held by the issuer of the mortgage. Still, all retained some small fraction of the loans they originated.

Then, there were Fannie Mae and Freddie Mac as issuers of mortgage-backed securities. Fannie and Freddie began entering the nonprime market in 2005, after losing almost half of their market share to private issuers of mortgage-backed securities. They entered the market in response to competitive pressures from the investment banks. Often, Fannie Mae and Freddie Mac had the left-overs: the banks held on to the best, even when it was the "best" of subprime mortgages.

It was a system that worked fine as long as the bubble continued to expand. Borrowers facing trouble paying their mortgages could always refinance. Many homeowners refinanced multiple times during the bubble. If a mortgage became unaffordable, it was simply a matter of taking out a new mortgage with a new two-year teaser-rate period. And, it was supposed that housing prices would continue to rise forever, a belief in something which could not possibly be true for a number of reasons. Borrowers were enjoying the fantasy.

As early as 2004, you could clearly see the decline in lending standards. The very bottom of the standards even had a name: the *interest-only negative-amortizing adjustable-rate subprime mortgage*. The home buyer was given the option of paying nothing at all, and rolling whatever interest she owed the bank into a higher principal balance. It was easy to select the most likely person for such a loan — one with no income. Still, a few of these loans were taken on by the rich. The year 2004 was bracketed by 2003 and 2005 on two sides of the market. In 2003 borrowers had already lost restraint; by early 2005 lenders had, too.

## THE CREDIT DEFAULT SWAP

Something was missing in this growing stack of cards. You couldn't short houses like you can short stocks. You couldn't bet explicitly against subprime mortgages; mortgages simply had no room for a dim view. The answer to the no-shorting problem was found in the credit default swap. This swap turned out to be the joker in the dark. The original credit default swap was an insurance policy, typically on a corporate bond, with semiannual premium payments and a fixed term. For instance, you might pay $300,000 a year to buy a ten-year credit default swap on $100 million in General Electric bonds. The most you could lose was $3 million: $300,000 a year for ten years. The most you could make was $100 million, if General Electric defaulted on its debt any time in the next ten years and bond-holders recovered nothing. It was a zero-sum bet. If you made $100 million, the person who had sold you the credit default swap lost $100 million.

In the beginning, the credit default swap was a tool for hedging. Very quickly, however, the new derivatives became tools for speculation, more playing chips for the casino. A lot of people wanted to make bets on the likelihood of GE's defaulting altogether. The same thing was to happen with subprime mortgage bonds. If one wanted to make side bets on subprime mortgage bonds, the only way to do it would be to buy a credit default swap.

Michael Burry, a stock investor who had recently immersed himself in the bond market, was one of the first to see that betting against subprime mortgage bonds could be done with credit default swaps. There was one problem; there was no such thing as a credit default swap *on a subprime mortgage bond*. He would need to prod the big Wall Street firms to create them. When Michael Burry started conversations with Wall Street firms in the beginning of 2005, only Deutsche Bank and Goldman Sachs had any real interest in continuing the conversation. Within three years, however, credit default swaps on subprime mortgage bonds would become a trillion-dollar market and precipitate hundreds of billions of dollars' worth of losses inside big Wall Street firms. The year 2008 would be the pinnacle year.

Earlier, Michael Burry had founded Scion Capital, a small hedge fund for investors worth $15 million. The success of Scion Capital is related by Michael Lewis.

> In his first full year, 2001, the S&P 500 fell 11.88 percent, Scion was up 55 percent. The next year, the S&P 500 fell again, by 22.1 percent, and yet Scion was up again: 16 percent. The next year, 2003, the stock market finally turned around and rose 28.69 percent, but Mike Burry beat it again — his investments rose by 50 percent. By the end of 2004, Mike Burry was managing $600 million and turning money away.[1]

By the middle of 2005, over a period in which the broad stock market index had fallen by 6.84 percent, Burry's fund was up 242 percent. Meanwhile, Burry had one eye on the real estate market. Stock prices were not doing well but house prices in San Jose, the bubble's epicenter, were still rising. By May 2003 he concluded that

---

[1] Michael Lewis, *The Big Short* (New York and London: W.W. Norton & Company, 2010), p. 42.

the real estate bubble was being driven ever higher by irrational behavior of mortgage lenders and the extension of easier and easier credit. He felt that a large portion of current housing demand at current prices would disappear if only people became convinced that prices were no longer rising. The collateral damage would be of great magnitude.

In early 2005 Burry set out to bet against the subprime mortgage bond market. The first big problem he encountered was that the Wall street investment banks that might sell him credit default swaps didn't share his sense of urgency. The time to place the bet was *now*, before the U.S. housing market woke up and was restored to sanity. Still, it did not take Wall Street long to catch on; soon it was reshaping its business in a way that left the new derivative smack at the center of the Wall Street universe. The dealers, led by Deutsche Bank and Goldman Sachs, came up with the pay-as-you-go credit default swap. The buyer of the swap — the buyer of insurance — would be paid off not all at once, if and when the entire pool of mortgages went bust, but incrementally, as individual homeowners went into default.

Mike Burry did his first subprime mortgage deals on May 19, 2005. He purchased $60 million in credit default swaps from Deutsche Bank — $10 million each on six different bonds. He went looking for the bonds backed by the worst of the home loans. From the point of view of Deutsche Bank, all subprime mortgage bonds were the same. The price of insurance was driven by the ratings placed on the bond by the rating agencies, Moody's and Standard & Poor's. He might pay 20 basis points (0.20 percent) on a triple-A-rated tranche. (A basis point is one-hundredth of one percentage point.) He was after, however, the triple-B-rated tranches — the ones that would be worth zero if the underlying mortgage pool experienced a loss of just 7 percent. Goldman Sachs e-mailed him a long list of "crappy" mortgage bonds to choose from. In a few weeks Burry bought several hundred million dollars in credit default swaps from half a dozen banks, in chunks of $5 million. He found one mortgage pool that was 100 percent floating-rate *negative-amortizing mortgages*. By the end of July he owned credit default swaps on $750 million in subprime mortgage bonds.

The story of Mike Burry highlights the happenings of 2005. In November subprime loans were going bad at an alarming rate. The *Wall Street Journal* published an article explaining how the new wave of adjustable-rate mortgages were defaulting, in their first nine months, at rates never before seen. It seemed that lower-middle-class America was tapped out. Now Wall Street firms were no longer selling credit default swaps, they were buying. Over a three-year period housing prices had risen far more rapidly than they had over the previous 30; housing prices generally were still rising but some home prices had ceased to rise and the loans against them were now going sour at amazing rates. While the subprime mortgage market was generating half a trillion dollars' worth of new loans a year, the circle of people redistributing the risk that the entire market would collapse was tiny.

During these years Alan Greenspan was still assuring everyone that home prices were not prone to national bubbles *or* major deflations. Again, these forces were closing in on the year 2008.

## THE COLLAPSE

Some institution had to be betting against people like Mike Burry.[2] The party on the other side of his bet was the triple-A-rated insurance company AIG, American International Group, Inc. Or, rather, a unit of AIG called AIG FP. AIG FP was created in 1987 by refugees from Michael Milken's bond department at Drexel Burnham. AIG was selling credit default swaps on triple-A-rated subprime bonds for a mere 0.12 percent a year. Goldman Sachs created a bunch of multibillion-dollar deals that transferred to AIG the responsibility for all future losses from $20 billion in triple-B-rated subprime mortgage bonds. The Goldman traders had booked profits on somewhere between $1.5 billion and $3 billion worth of bonds. In the process, Goldman Sachs created the *synthetic* subprime mortgage bond-backed CDO or collateralized debt obligation.

---

[2] For a much more detailed account of the Mike Burry story see Lewis, *The Big Short, ibid.*, especially pp. 26–84.

The ordinary CDO was being reconfigured to disguise the risk of subprime mortgage loans. Goldman Sachs gathered 100 different mortgage bonds — usually, the riskiest, lower floors of the original structure — and used them to erect an entirely new tower of bonds. The triple-B-rated bonds were harder to sell than the triple-A-rated ones, up on the safe, upper floors of the building. Still, the triple-B-rated bond floor was pronounced 80 percent triple-A by the rating agencies.

The rating agencies were being paid large fees by Goldman Sachs and other Wall Street firms for each deal they rated. As it turns out, the CDO was a credit laundering service for the residents of Lower Middle Class America: for Wall Street it was a machine that turned lead into gold. Fortunes were being made on Wall Street.

That home prices would never fall increasingly looked like a bad bet. By early 2006 AIG FP stopped insuring any more deals. AIG sold no more credit default swaps to Wall Street but did nothing to offset the $50 billion worth of swaps that it had already sold. Others were betting against shares of companies, such as New Century and IndyMac Bank, which originated subprime loans, along with companies that built the houses bought with the loans, such as Toll Brothers (a popular stock).

In May 2006 Standard & Poor's announced that it was changing the model used to rate subprime mortgage bonds. With this fear of new and better ratings, the creation of subprime bonds shot up dramatically. By now, Wall Street firms knew that the bonds they'd been creating had been overrated.

Home prices also were back in the news. One measure of sanity in housing prices is the ratio of median home price to income. In the United States that ratio has been around 3:1; by late 2004, it had risen nationally, to 4:1. It was nearly as high in some other countries. But that is not all. In Los Angeles it was 10:1 and in Miami, 8.5:1. And the buyers were speculators. The number of For Sale signs began rising in mid-2005 and has yet to stop. The broad-based quarterly index of the U.S. Census has home prices peaking in the second quarter of 2007. Even in the face of a collapsing mortgage market, speculators took home prices still higher after 2005. This is a measure of the extent of the bubble. Irrational exuberance had morphed into mania.

In Table 7.1 the U.S. Census index is based on actual purchases. The annualized percentage changes in the index provides a dramatic view of the bubble and bust. There are steady increases throughout but some acceleration in the advances beginning in the year 2000 as the players began to shift out of Nasdaq and into houses. However, the really drastic changes on the upside come in 2004 and continues until the first quarter of 2006. Prices then slow their increase but do not turn negative until the fourth quarter of 2007. Thereafter, the floor falls out from under the housing market; the collapse reaches its nadir in the second quarter of 2009 but the negative percentage changes continue into 2010. When prices declined, the bubble was deflated and the percentage price decline was 21 percent (in whole numbers) by the second quarter of 2007. (By some measures, house prices resumed their decline in early November 2010.) If we mark the start of the bubble in the first quarter of 2000 and the end in the second quarter of 2007, there was a 60.6 percent increase in national housing prices.

Mortgage default rates were not uniform, but varied by state. The default rate in Georgia was five times higher than that in Florida. Indiana had a 25 percent default rate; California, only five percent. This would set the stage for a third round of defaults in 2010, wherein California and Florida would not be spared.

Firms on Wall Street were looking for the *best shorts* — the bonds ultimately backed by mortgages most likely to default. They had several characteristics. One, the underlying loans were heavily concentrated in the "sand states" of California, Florida, Nevada, and Arizona. There is where house prices had risen fastest and so would crash fastest in a bust. Two, the loans were made by the more dubious mortgage lenders such as Long Beach Savings, wholly owned by Washington Mutual. Three, the pools would have a higher than average number of low-documented or no-documents loans, loans more likely to be fraudulent. Southern California especially was notorious for 30-year payment option ARMs, or adjustable-rate mortgages. Michael Lewis reports that "in Bakersfield, California, a Mexican

**Table 7.1:**  USA Housing Price Index and Percentage Changes

| Year | Quarter | Seasonally-Adjusted Purchase-Only Price Index (1991Q1 = 100) | Percent Change, Previous Four Quarters | Year | Quarter | Seasonally-Adjusted Purchase-Only Price Index (1991Q1 = 100) | Percent Change, Previous Four Quarters |
|---|---|---|---|---|---|---|---|
| 1997 | 1 | 117 | 2.75 | 2004 | 1 | 182 | 8.04 |
|      | 2 | 118 | 2.93 |      | 2 | 185 | 8.5 |
|      | 3 | 119 | 3.03 |      | 3 | 190 | 8.96 |
|      | 4 | 120 | 3.45 |      | 4 | 194 | 9.3 |
| 1998 | 1 | 122 | 4.03 | 2005 | 1 | 199 | 9.27 |
|      | 2 | 123 | 4.46 |      | 2 | 203 | 9.61 |
|      | 3 | 125 | 5.06 |      | 3 | 208 | 9.53 |
|      | 4 | 127 | 5.6  |      | 4 | 213 | 9.35 |
| 1999 | 1 | 129 | 5.78 | 2006 | 1 | 216 | 8.74 |
|      | 2 | 131 | 5.93 |      | 2 | 217 | 6.95 |
|      | 3 | 133 | 6.08 |      | 3 | 218 | 4.93 |
|      | 4 | 135 | 6.03 |      | 4 | 220 | 3.59 |
| 2000 | 1 | 137 | 6.36 | 2007 | 1 | 222 | 2.78 |
|      | 2 | 139 | 6.57 |      | 2 | 222 | 2.16 |
|      | 3 | 142 | 6.7  |      | 3 | 220 | 0.89 |
|      | 4 | 144 | 6.91 |      | 4 | 218 | -1.22 |

(Continued)

Table 7.1: (Continued)

| Year | Quarter | Seasonally-Adjusted Purchase-Only Price Index (1991Q1 = 100) | Percent Change, Previous Four Quarters | Year | Quarter | Seasonally-Adjusted Purchase-Only Price Index (1991Q1 = 100) | Percent Change, Previous Four Quarters |
|---|---|---|---|---|---|---|---|
| 2001 | 1 | 147 | 6.97 | 2008 | 1 | 214 | -3.66 |
|  | 2 | 149 | 6.99 |  | 2 | 210 | -5.48 |
|  | 3 | 151 | 6.94 |  | 3 | 205 | -6.8 |
|  | 4 | 154 | 6.77 |  | 4 | 200 | -8.29 |
| 2002 | 1 | 156 | 6.6 | 2009 | 1 | 199 | -6.98 |
|  | 2 | 159 | 6.76 |  | 2 | 197 | -5.92 |
|  | 3 | 162 | 7.17 |  | 3 | 197 | -3.85 |
|  | 4 | 165 | 7.63 |  | 4 | 197 | -1.45 |
| 2003 | 1 | 168 | 7.68 | 2010 | 1 | 193 | -3.17 |
|  | 2 | 171 | 7.43 |  | 2 | 194 | -1.6 |
|  | 3 | 174 | 7.44 |  |  |  |  |
|  | 4 | 178 | 7.57 |  |  |  |  |

Source: U.S. Census.

Note: The percentage changes in the table are based on the raw data, whereas the index numbers are expressed as whole numbers.

strawberry picker with an income of $14,000 and no English was lent every penny he needed to buy a house for $724,000."[3]

There were other signs of the debacle to come. On November 29, 2006 the index of subprime mortgage bonds (called the ABX) would post its first interest-rate shortfall. Borrowers were failing to make interest payments sufficient to pay off the riskiest subprime bonds. Underlying mortgage loans were going sour, while the prices of the bonds backed by the loans stayed stable because of CDOs on the other side of the market. The CDO was essentially a pile of triple-B-rated mortgage bonds. They were still being rated triple-A, double-A, or A. In 2005 the main buyer of the triple-A-rated tranche of subprime CDOs had been AIG. But AIG exited the market thereafter.

From mid-2005 until early 2007, there had been a growing disconnect between the price of subprime mortgage bonds and the value of the loans underpinning them. However, in late January 2007 the ABX index made up of the prices of bonds began to fall. It fell steadily but then rapidly — by early June, the index of triple-B-rated subprime bonds was closing in the high 60s, which meant that the bonds had lost more than 30 percent of their original value. Nonetheless, the CDOs, which were created out of these triple-B-rated subprime bonds did not collapse. Indeed, Merrill Lynch and Citigroup created and sold $50 billion in new CDOs.

The collapse of Bear Stearns, a CDO firm, began on June 14, 2007. It declared that it had lost money on bets on subprime mortgage securities and it was being forced to dump $3.8 billion of these bets before closing the fund. (We will visit Bear Stearns more than once.) Then, on February 8, 2007, HSBC, a British bank, announced that it was taking a big, surprising loss on its portfolio of subprime mortgage loans. It had entered the U.S. subprime business in 2003, when it bought Household Finance, a giant consumer lender. By now the subprime mortgage bond market was in an uninterrupted decline. When those in the marketplace stopped buying

---

[3] *Ibid.*, p. 97.

subprime mortgage bonds and CDOs backed by subprime mortgage bonds, the Wall Street investment banks were in trouble. In July 2007, Merrill Lynch announced a decline in revenues from mortgage trading due to losses in subprime bonds. Ben Bernanke, the Fed chairman, sought to sooth the markets on July 19, 2007 when he told the U.S. Senate that he saw no more than $100 billion in losses in the subprime mortgage market. A few days later, investors in the collapsed Bear Stearns hedge funds were informed that their $1.6 billion in triple-A-rated subprime-backed CDOs had not merely lost some value, they were worthless. Subprime loans continued to default in record numbers. Financial institutions were less steady every day. A fund run by Goldman Sachs took a huge loss in subprime and had rapidly turned from betting on the subprime mortgage market *to betting against it*. The Casino had turned against its clientele.

One by one the giant Wall Street firms left the market. J.P. Morgan had abandoned the market by the late fall of 2006. Deutsche Bank was next, to be followed by Goldman. The defaults mounted, the bonds universally crashed, and the CDOs composed of the bonds followed. Morgan Stanley lost more than $9 billion.

Meanwhile, money was being minted on the other side of the market. Some $205 million in credit default swaps, which cost about a million dollars to buy, were suddenly worth a bit more than $60 million. The total losses on U.S.-originated subprime-related assets was about a trillion dollars. Suddenly, that amount of money simply vanished. Most Wall Street firms split the losses. On September 22, 2008 Lehman Brothers filed for bankruptcy. On the same day Merrill Lynch, after $55.2 billion in losses on subprime bond-backed CDOs, sold itself to Bank of America. (We will revisit this duo.) The next day the Federal Reserve announced that it had lent $85 billion to the aforementioned insurance company AIG, to pay off the losses on the subprime credit default swaps AIG had sold to Wall Street banks — the largest of which was the $13.9 billion AIG owed to Goldman Sachs. Goldman Sachs had transferred more than $20 billion in subprime mortgage bond risk into AIG. With a trillion dollar balance sheet, AIG was simply too big to fail. Merrill Lynch admitted to losses of over $50 billion. At Citigroup it was another $60 billion. Morgan Stanley's $9 billion hit began to pale. The stocks of Morgan Stanley and Goldman Sachs were tanking; only the U.S. government could save them.

Once more, the year 2008 would be pivotal. In early October 2008 the U.S. government stepped in to absorb all the losses in the financial system and prevent any big Wall Street firm from failing. Treasury Secretary Henry Paulson had persuaded the U.S. Congress to hand over some $700 billion to buy subprime mortgage assets from banks. The congressional bill was dubbed TARP or the Troubled Asset Relief Program. Paulson provided billions of dollars to Citigroup, Morgan Stanley, Goldman Sachs, and a few others. Moreover, the $13 billion AIG owed to Goldman Sachs, as a result of its bet on subprime mortgage loans, was paid off by the U.S. government — 100 cents on the dollar.

These fantastic payments not only prevented Wall Street firms from failing but spared them from recognizing the losses in their subprime mortgage portfolios. Citigroup returned in November for another $20 billion from TARP and a guarantee for $306 billion of Citigroup assets or nearly two percent of U.S. gross domestic product. The $700 billion was not enough and the Federal Reserve began buying subprime mortgage bonds directly from the banks. By early 2009 the risks and losses associated with more than a trillion dollars' worth of poor investments were transferred from giant Wall Street firms and into the Federal Reserve. The American financial system and by extension, the global system, had been saved but the price tag was high. For the first time, the Federal Reserve was buying subprime mortgage bonds, putting them on its balance sheets.

## COLLAPSES AROUND THE WORLD

While some countries only experienced a steady rise in housing prices, others saw bubbles even more extensive than the ones that happened in some regions of the USA. The run up in housing prices happened in many countries beginning later than in the USA, but with declines starting sometime in 2008.[4] Some countries, especially former communist countries, saw an unprecedented rise in housing prices followed by an even steeper bust. In Estonia price changes between the lowest and highest levels in the decade of the 2000s reached some 600 percent. In Singapore, Dubai, Latvia, Iceland, and the U.K., price declines following dramatic price bubbles range between 19 and 50 percent as of the first quarter of 2009. Australia, although seeing a slight dip in prices at the end of 2008, was beginning to worry about a potential housing bubble in 2009. At about the same time Singapore was experiencing the beginning of a drop.

The data trends show that local home prices, affected by the performance of the local economy and even varying considerably within a country, are increasingly influenced by international variables. Foreign buyers, especially rich ones, consider the benefits of purchasing homes abroad. Those markets more susceptible to global economic conditions and fluctuations find maintaining affordable property prices for local residents to be challenging. Where bubbles exist, demographic trends, incomes, and urbanization do not fully explain the outcomes. However, increases in credit and liquidity and the demand for assets add fuel to the expanding bubbles. Even though their timing may be different, the causes of bubbles remain universal.

Table 7.2 summarizes the findings from the National Association of Realtors (NAR). The NAR used official data wherever it was available, a major exception being the United States; all data sources are provided in an Appendix. The countries chosen were largely selected based on available data from public sources, generally from the Internet. The use of an index potentially accounts for changes in currency rates and in consumer price indexes. Most of the country data are based on real prices (adjusted by a consumer price index), the exception being the United States.

---

[4] The Research Division of the National Association of Realtors (NAR) conducted an extensive study of recent historical housing prices. The study is located at www.REALTOR. org/research and contains 17 nations, including the United States. The discussion in this section draws upon the NAR study. My analysis of the data differs in some cases from theirs.

**Table 7.2:**   House Price Indexes, Selected Nations

| Change in House Price Index since Q1 2000 | | | |
|---|---|---|---|
| | Q4 2008 | Q1 2009 | Price Peak |
| United States | 21.8% | | 2006-Q2 |
| Australia | 114.0% | | 2008-Q1 |
| Austria | 28.4% | | 2008-Q4 |
| Columbia | | 76.3% | 2008-Q4 |
| Denmark | | 69.1% | 2007-Q2 |
| France | 104.5% | | 2007-Q4 |
| Ireland | | 75.5% | 2007-Q2 |
| Malta | | 69.1% | 2006-Q2 |
| Netherlands | 56.0% | | 2008-Q3 |
| New Zealand | | 98.5% | 2007-Q4 |
| Norway | | 64.5% | 2008-Q2 |
| Singapore | 1.1% | | 2008-Q1 |
| Sweden | 87.1% | | 2008-Q3 |
| Switzerland | 27.8% | | 2009-Q1 |
| Estonia | 322.0% | | 2007-Q3 |
| Iceland | 135.0% | | 2008-Q1 |
| Thailand | 27.9% | | 2009-Q1 |
| United Kingdom | 90.4% | | 2007-Q3 |

*Source*: National Association of Realtors, "Housing Price Indexes: A World Wide Overview of Real Estate Prices in Recent Years," p. 9.

A Composite House Price Index was developed for the countries in Table 7.2. This index is based on the weighted individual country indexes, using the 2007 countries' populations. Since the United States has the largest population among the 17 countries, it accounts for 50 percent of the composite index. As a result, the composite price index mimics to a considerable extent the path of prices for the United States.

In Table 7.2 the bubble is measured from the first quarter of 2000 as the base year (Year 2000 = 100). Moreover, the ending date for the bubbles are selected as either the fourth quarter of 2008 or the first quarter of 2009. What is notable are the sizes of the bubbles in the other 16 countries compared with the U.S., the exception being Singapore, where its bubble was just getting underway. Estonia has the biggest bubble in the sample with 322 percent, followed by Iceland, 135 percent, and Australia, with 114 percent. After that, France is 104.5 percent, and Sweden with 87.1 percent. The bubbles ending in the first quarter of 2009 are uniformly large, led by New Zealand and followed by Iceland. We should note that the price peaks for the bubbles did not necessarily coincide with the somewhat arbitrary ending dates. But, as in the United States, price increases did not turn negative right away. The bubbles were often enduring.

The NAR percentage increase of 21.8 percent greatly understates the U.S. bubble compared with U.S. Census data (see above). This results partly because the Census peak comes much earlier than that for the National Association of Realtors (which is based on their own data collection). Moreover, median prices and a base year of 2000 = 100 was used in the NAR survey compared with the Census with purchase prices and a base year of 1991, first quarter = 100. Because of its importance for the financial and banking crisis, we will return to the housing bubble-collapse and consider the Case-Shiller Index in Chapter 9.

Do the lags and leads of the peaks versus the selected ending dates for the bubbles tell us anything about cause and effect? That is, did the U.S. bubble leak over into the global economy or was the country's bubble independently generated? The peak came for the U.S. bubble first, which provides only one criterion for cause to effect. The peaks for the other 16 countries came during the Money and Banking Panic in the United States to be considered in Chapter 9. This too was the time of the unraveling of the subprime mortgages and CDOs, which made the effects of the bubble much worse. The banks in the United States had counter-parties in the sweet 16, the exception possibly being Estonia. Subprime mortgages were common in the United Kingdom and its 90.4 percent bubble may have been generated independently of the United States.

Alan Greenspan had not only been the cheerleader for subprime lending, he had facilitated the bubble early on with aggressively easy monetary policy. Thus far we have seen what this process did for the bond market, the giant Wall Street firms, and the housing market. The American bubble in mortgages and house prices preceded most of the bubbles abroad. Later, we will consider other causes and effects. Next, we consider the implications for Main Street USA where its homeowners reside.

# 8

# THE FALLOUT FROM
# THE HOUSING COLLAPSE

On February 14, 2008 Ben Bernanke told the Senate Banking Committee that the serious housing slump and a credit crisis triggered by rising defaults in subprime mortgages had greatly strained the economy. "The outlook for the economy has worsened in recent months and the downside risks to growth have increased," Bernanke told the committee. "To date, the largest economic effects of the financial turmoil appear to have been on the housing market, which, as you know, had deteriorated significantly over the past two years or so." He still did not predict a full-blown recession, only sluggish growth. Some economists said that he had underestimated the coming calamity. The Dow Jones industrials fell 175 points the next day, as if to highlight Bernanke's remarks.

## IN THE BEGINNING

We will now summarize a turning point in the housing crisis. Weighing heavily on the stock market that day in February was Bear Stearns, the venerable investment bank, which lost nearly half its market value in a matter of minutes. On the verge of a collapse that could have shaken the very foundations of the U.S. financial system, Bear Stearns was bailed out by a rival and the Federal Reserve. JPMorgan and the Federal Reserve rushed to pump new money into the Wall Street firm. JPMorgan and the central bank agreed to extend loans for 28 days to Bear Stearns, then the nation's fifth-largest investment bank and the one hit hardest by the subprime mortgage mess.

Two hedge funds managed by Bear Stearns had failed during the prior summer, setting off a credit crisis that swept up banks and brokerages around the globe. Now Bear Stearns itself was endangered. In backing up JPMorgan, the Fed had dusted off a rarely used Depression-era provision to provide loans to investment banks. This represented a major shift in Federal Reserve policy. Bernanke also said that he was ready to step in to fight an erosion of confidence in the nation's largest financial institutions.

The JPMorgan deal was valued at $236.2 million or initially $2 a share for Bear Stearns. At their peak, the shares had traded at $159.36. While the Fed had agreed to fund up to $30 billion of Bear Stearns' less liquid assets, the deal did not go through. A combination of risky bets on securities tied to subprime mortgages and loans given to customers with poor credit histories had crippled Bear Stearns. JPMorgan's attempted acquisition of Bear Stearns represented roughly one percent of what the investment bank had been worth just 16 days prior. As it turned out, the $2 a share offering did not stick.

Conditions in early spring 2008 foreshadowed dark prospects for the American and global economies. In March nervous employers in the U.S. slashed 80,000 jobs, enough to vacate a small city. With the most jobs lost in five years, the national unemployment rate climbed to 5.1 percent, modest only in retrospect. Job losses were nearing a quarter-million for the year in just three months. It had been the third month in a row that total U.S. employment had shrunk; the sharp sustained increase was a sign of tremendous economic stress. Even Ben Bernanke used the word "recession," acknowledging the possibility.

In a rare weekend move, the Federal Reserve took bold action on a Sunday evening (March 16) to provide cash to financially squeezed Wall Street investment houses. Moreover, the central bank cut its lending rate to financial institutions to 3.25 percent from 3.50 percent, effective immediately, and created another lending facility for big investment banks to secure short-term loans. The new lending facility was available to the the big Wall Street firms on St. Patrick's Day. The investment houses needing immediate help included Goldman Sachs, Lehman Brothers, and Morgan Stanley. The CEO at

Goldman Sachs was Lloyd C. Blankfein; at Lehman Brothers, Jasjit S. ("Jesse") Bhattal; and John J. Mack at Morgan Stanley.

The Fed slashed its federal funds rate a remarkable three-quarters of a point on March 18, capping its most aggressive two months of action in a quarter-century. The Fed had now cut the federal funds rate by three-fourths of a percentage point twice in 2008, the first coming at an emergency meeting on January 22, only to be followed by a half-point cut at a regularly scheduled meeting on January 30. These rapid-fire rate cuts comprised the most aggressive credit easing since mid-1982, when Paul Volcker was trying to move the nation out of the deepest recession since the Great Depression. Now, with the federal funds rate at a mere 2.25 percent, the real interest rate (adjusted for CPI inflation) was below zero and heading even lower. Soon, at a regularly scheduled meeting on March 30, 2008, the fed funds rate was trimmed to 2.00 percent. Bernanke knew that the Federal Reserve was running out of bullets.

The housing crisis could not have come at a worse time in terms of national politics. Not only was George W. Bush a lame duck president, his popularity was at all time lows. Still, President Bush proposed an ambitious plan for the Federal Reserve to take on the unwieldy role of the cop in charge of financial market stability. Other regulatory agencies would see their influence diminished.

The consumer price index (CPI), which had gone up on only 2.8 percent in 2007, was now headed for an annual rate of four percent. The real federal funds rate was headed for −1.75 percent. The real rate is important because banks expect to have loans repaid in dollars that are not depreciating. Even more troubling was the source of the inflation. Food prices had risen four percent in 2007 compared with an average 2.5 percent annual rate in the prior 15 years. The price of a barrel of oil was heading toward US$120 and the price of gasoline to US$4 per gallon. With a falling international value of the U.S. dollar, U.S. exports were soaring, putting additional pressure on the price of basics. While significant, the inflation was to be temporary.

The markets for food and oil are global and so are the interdependencies. Wheat mills across the world were using words like "rationing" and "shortages." To explain the temporary but troubling rise in the price of a loaf of bread required the following: dairy prices driven higher by food conglomerates buying up milk supplies, rising demand from newly industrializing economies, and a weak dollar. The rise in food and fuel costs led wage earners to expect higher nominal wages. The rising price of jet fuel had led to several bankrupt airlines in an already stressed and concentrated industry. The crisis in transportation was epitomized by the merger of the two largest U.S. airlines, Delta and Northwest airlines. Another sign of the times: Ford Motor Company sold its storied Jaguar and Land Rover business to India's Tata Motors at a substantial loss. At the same time Tata Motors announced plans to build a US$2,500 car, the cheapest in the world. These stresses and strains were restructuring key elements of the global economy.

The U.S. housing industry was in worse shape and with foreclosures there was further dampening consumer demand for durable goods. In March 2008 sales of new homes plunged to the slowest pace in more than 16 years. Worse still, the median price of new homes in March compared with the prior year fell at the fastest clip in 38 years. Sales of new homes dropped by 8.5 percent to a seasonally-adjusted annual rate of 526,000 units, the slowest sales pace since October 1981, according to Commerce Department figures. According to a Realty/Trac Inc. report, the number of U.S. homes heading toward foreclosure more than doubled in the first quarter-year from the year before. The median price of a home sold in March dropped by 13.3 percent, compared with March 2007, this the largest year-over-year price drop since a 14.6 percent plunge in July 1970.

Foreclosures comprised the size of small city during the first three quarters of 2006, but escalated thereafter. The rise in foreclosures was especially steep during 2007, then showing an increase in the first quarter of 2008 of 23 percent over the previous quarter. Thus, by spring 2008 the foreclosures would equal a *major* city. Moody's Economy.com estimated that one in about four USA families with mortgages had zero or negative equity in the first quarter of 2008; they already owed more than the current value of their homes and were "underwater." This translated into 2.3 million foreclosures in 2008. By early 2009 some 12.2 million homeowners would be underwater. According to the U.S. Census, there were about 75 million homeowners in America. The latest estimates suggest that some 6.4 million homes are at risk of sinking into foreclosure by the end of 2012. That is a number without precedent. There was a plague on most houses.

Congress passed Bush's tax rebate bill that would have temporarily beneficial results. Some $50 billion of the economic stimulus payments were sent out by the end of May 2008, slightly less than half of the $106.7 billion scheduled for 2008. The immediate effect was to increase retail sales by about one percent in May. Without the tax rebate package, the U.S. would have had relatively flat growth over the middle of the year. The results were nonetheless temporary and all eyes turned to monetary policy as the source of continuing stimulus. A surge in oil prices past US$140 a barrel and warnings of trouble in financial, automotive and high-tech industries sent the Dow down 358 points on June 26. In particular General Motors was being hurt by the fallout of the prolonged housing slump and the nearly year-old credit crisis. Citigroup, headed by Vikram S. Pandit as chief executive, fell sharply after an analyst placed a "sell" rating on the stock and warned investors to expect less from the brokerage sector in the uneasy economic climate.

Housing had boomed for five years, but now was in a prolonged slump. Prices were being depressed by the continued huge inventory of unsold homes, a backlog from rising mortgage defaults that were dumping more homes on an already overbuilt market. Meanwhile, AutoNation Inc., the nations' largest auto retailer, said that decelerating vehicle sales in Florida, California and other key states were the result of these sagging home prices. AutoNation saw no light at the end of the tunnel until 2009, if then. Even Wendy's hamburgers were in trouble, not unrelated to the housing crisis. Triarc Companies, the owner of Arby's and its roast beef sandwiches, bought Wendy's, after Wendy's stock had fallen from highs of over $40 a share in summer 2007 to a buyout price of around $26 a share. Homeowners were dining in to save money. With minority stock financing from Warren Buffett, candy maker Mars Inc. on April 28, 2008 offered to buy confectioner Wm. Wrigley Jr. Co. for an estimated $223 billion in cash, making it the largest confectioner in the world.

Our concerns come full circle to those commercial banks holding mortgages on homes that homeowners cannot afford. The Babbits of real estate had done all too well. Moreover, there were all those derivatives that were off the twin balance sheets of banks and hedge funds. Then, there were the brokerage firms that had sold puts and calls to the hedge funds. The round-robin continues as the commercial banks lent to troubled brokerage firms to keep them afloat. They were all in a life raft that had sprung more than one leak.

There was the fast-moving decline of IndyMac Bank, a mortgage lender that was one of the nation's largest savings and loans. It illustrated how wide and deep the problems of the U.S. banking system had become. IndyMac did a lot of business in Alt-A mortgages, which are described as just below qualifications for a prime mortgage, but better than for a normal subprime mortgage. The U.S. government seized IndyMac Bank around mid-July 2008. More likely than the kind of exodus of depositors that quickly sank IndyMac is what some bankers are describing as a slow-motion "walk on the bank," which could cripple financial institutions already weakened by credit problems. IndyMac had Depression-like lines of people waiting to withdraw their money from the bank, the largest regulated thrift to fail.

Treasury Secretary Henry Paulson sought to reassure an anxious public that the banking system was sound, while also bracing people for more troubled times ahead. He testified before the House Financial Services Committee on July 10. "The three big issues we're facing right now are, first, the housing correction which is at the heart of the slowdown; secondly, turmoil of the capital markets; and thirdly, the high oil prices, which are going to prolong the slowdown," he said. "But remember, our economy has got very strong long-term fundamentals, solid fundamentals." The latter echoed comments coming from President Herbert Hoover and his secretaries during the Great Depression. Democratic leaders, including presidential candidate Barack Obama, were pushing for a second, smaller economic stimulus. Paulson said he did not want to speculate about the idea.

## INNOVATIONS IN HOUSING

Scary stories began to circulate among mortgage brokers. One in particular should have raised the eyebrows of the regulatory authorities. There was bad underwriting, fraudulent income documentation, and even equity lines equaling 125 percent of the equity that persons had in their home. The ATM machine had gotten larger. These practices were becoming standard operating procedures.

The lending business was becoming a dangerous game of hot potato. Lenders were increasingly reluctant to hold onto the riskier mortgages. Meanwhile, Greenspan was extolling the virtues of equity financing. In a classic bait and switch tactic, beginning in early 2004, Greenspan began to raise the fed funds rate. During the next two years Greenspan more than quadrupled this key rate in a serious of 17 hikes, from one percent to 4.5 percent. This meant that adjustable mortgage rates, earlier highly recommended by Greenspan, rose sharply. Mortgage holders had unexpected increases in their rates, and higher monthly bills to pay. Unfortunately, subprime borrowing accounted for 20 percent or more of the total mortgage lending for 2004 to 2006. This compares with a mere three percent in 1997.

One of the industry's innovations was the aforementioned Alt-A Mortgage. These are the nonprime mortgages without standard documentation such as income and credit references, often referred to as "liar's loans." Alt-A mortgages soared more or less in tandem with equity lines of credit. While Alt-A mortgage debt was about three percent of total mortgage debt in 2003, it averaged about 15 percent during 2005–2007. Meantime, home equity loans soared from an average of about five percent of total mortgage debt in 2001–2003 to about 15 percent in 2006–2007. The housing bubble approached a peak in 2005, leaving all these subprime mortgages, liar's loans, and equity lines of credit hanging out to dry. The housing ATM alone was responsible for a large share of GDP growth during 2000–2005. Other innovations in the form of derivatives would follow.

Unlike the stock market bubble, the real estate bubble of 2000–2005 was fueled by debt. Then from 2004 to 2007 banks and mortgage companies were making trillions of dollars of ultra-liberal adjustable rate mortgage loans to millions of Americans who had little to no chance of servicing these loans to maturity. By counting on rising real estate prices to paste over this problem, this lending spasm turned the U.S. housing market into a system of Ponzi finance, as defined by Post Keynesian Hyman Minsky. Ever rising house prices would shore up the mortgages before the truth was revealed, or so it was thought.

## THE SUBPRIME MORTGAGE MESS

By August 2008, the nation's struggling housing market, already awash in subprime foreclosures, was getting hit with a second wave of losses as homeowners with liar loans began to default in record numbers. In California, Florida, Nevada and Arizona, the loans were threatening to drag out the mortgage crisis for another two years. A broker who signed up a borrower for a liar loan could gain as much as $15,000 in fees for a $300,000 loan; traditional lending is far less lucrative, netting brokers around $2,000 to $4,000 in fees for a fixed-rate loan. Those writing the loans were not among the best and brightest. Many of the lenders that specialized in such loans had gone under, including American Home Mortgage, Bear Stearns and IndyMac Bank. More lenders, particularly commercial banks, would suffer the same fate.

Fannie Mae and Freddie Mac, the nation's largest buyers and backers of mortgages, lost a combined $3.1 billion between April and June of 2008. (The stocks of Fannie Mae and Freddie Mac reached amazing lows.) Roughly half of these losses came from up-ended liar loans. The total expected losses on liar loans was around $100 billion on top of $400 billion in expected losses from other subprime loans. The lies had real world consequences.

Underlying the mortgage credit explosion was the use of the options and futures markets. These markets expanded with the advent of the aforementioned Black-Scholes formula, the most famous equation in the history of finance. With currently known variables such as a risk-free interest rate, the term of the option, the price and volatility of the stock, and the strike price of the option, the Black-Scholes formula can be solved for the price of the option. This is a remarkably useful but overused pricing tool for portfolio managers. With it, a portfolio of cash and options or futures can be made to behave just like a stock portfolio. As noted, however, the Black-Scholes formula provides a misreading of the market when the entire market is at risk.

One way to hedge a stock portfolio from a market fall is to sell stock index futures. The futures are packaged as indexes like the S&P 100 and are traded on the Chicago Mercantile Exchange (the Merc). Of course, if stocks rise, money will be lost on the futures, but if stocks fall, the hedge works so that futures profits offset the market loss.

Portfolio insurance sounds like a magical way of covering from potential losses. However, it only works in "normal" markets. When the strategy is adopted for the entire market, it leads to disaster as it did with the stock market crash of 1987 and, later, the failure of the hedge fund, Long-Term Capital Management (LTCM). LTCM was founded by John Meriwether, a well-known trader at Salomon and included as partners Myron Scholes and Robert Merton, who won Nobel Prizes in economics in 1997, and David Mullins, a former vice chairman of the Fed. Myron Scholes was half of the Black-Scholes formula.[1]

When it opened for business in 1994, LTCM raised $1.25 billion from its first investment offerings. The business, however, was not financed entirely from within. Other firms hoped to learn from Meriwether's trading strategies. Among the firms lining up to provide leverage loans on very generous terms, requiring little or no collateral, and demanding almost no information on LTCM's positions were Merrill Lynch and Goldman Sachs. Meanwhile, LTCM began to trade in arenas in which it had little experience,

---

[1] The original Black-Scholes formula was named for an article published by Scholes and Fischer Black in the *Journal of Political Economy* in 1973. Black died in 1995 which accounts for him not being one of the recipients of the Nobel Prize. Scholes and Black acknowledged the importance of Merton's prior work leading to the formula.

like currency trading and equity arbitrage (betting on takeovers, even as they greatly increased leverage).

Currency collapses throughout Asia in mid-1998 did not help LTCM's cause. Then Russia began to have trouble financing its external debt. LTCM entered the Russian bond market. Unfortunately, the Russians soon defaulted on their bonds. This was the final straw for LTCM. The Russians would not even pay in rubles. The President of the New York Federal Reserve Bank, William McDonough (with Alan Greenspan's blessing) intervened. With considerable arm-twisting some 20 major commercial and investment banks agreed to a $3.65 billion bailout of LTCM. Greenspan helped by lowering the fed funds rate. Thus the Fed and these Wall Street firms prevented a global meltdown. Long after this experience, in 2003 Greenspan told an investment conference that derivative markets' participants were keenly aware of the counterparty credit risks associated with derivatives and take various measures to mitigate those risks. This clearly had not been the case with the LTCM catastrophe; Greenspan was a slow learner.

## COMPLICATIONS FROM DERIVATIVES

Wall Street configured residential mortgage portfolios into structured bonds through collateralized mortgage obligations (CMOs). An entire portfolio of mortgages could be dedicated to support the issuance of a family of bonds. The bonds were tiered in horizontal slices, or tranches, and portfolio cash flows were preferentially directed to the top tranches. Wall Street pushed the tranching technology to an extreme and triggered a serious mortgage market crash in 1994. As the market slowly recovered, more conservatively structured residential mortgage-backed securities (RMBS) replaced many of the CMOs in most big investor portfolios.

Following the RMBSs, the commercial mortgage-backed securities (CMBS) entered stage right. Unlike the residential mortgages, commercial mortgages do not lend themselves to pooling. To solve this problem, rating agencies were used to construct the pool. The financials, management, tenant history, maintenance records, and mortgage details were collected by banks. Then, rating agencies used proprietary models to estimate default risk and negotiate the pool structure. For example, a CMBS might have five or six tranches, and might include 140 buildings with face-value mortgages in the $10 million range and upward. These served to broaden the investor base for such mortgages and tightened interest spreads. Several other financial innovations were to follow.

The rating agencies played a big role. As long as the documentation of credit was done with the rating agencies, anything could be securitized. Businesses begin to sell asset-backed securities (ABS) to finance equipment, fleets of vehicles, and other things of value. General Electric, for example, became an early ABS issuer. Furthermore, investment banks created collateralized bond obligations (CBOs), and commercial banks issued collateralized loan obligations (CLOs). As noted earlier, collateralized debt obligations (CDOs) became the generic name for all types of securitized assets, including the old-fashioned mortgages. In most cases a trust, technically independent of the parent, would be created to purchase the assets, a purchase financed by selling securitized paper, usually with a tranched structure. Banks continued to conduct these transactions off their balance sheets.

It got still more complicated. New credit derivatives such as the credit default swap were invented. Suppose a U.S. bank is under-exposed to credits in Brazil. It used to be that this could be fixed by buying some Brazilian bank branches or partnering with a local bank. A credit default swap cuts through this process. For a fee, the U.S. bank can guarantee against any losses on a loan portfolio held by the Brazilian bank and can receive interest and fees on those loans. The Brazilian bank will continue to service the loans, so its local customers will see no change, but the Brazilian bank will have purchased insurance for its risk portfolio, freeing up regulatory capital for business expansion. The notional value of credit default swaps grew from $1 trillion in 2001 to $454 trillion by mid-2007.

Meanwhile, the credit agencies were doing quite well. Between 2002 and 2006, Moody's doubled its revenue and more than tripled its stock price. Their main customers were the big commercial banks and investment banks, and the agencies slanted their ratings to please these clients. Despite the high ratings for bonds, especially, their default rates were rising.

Leverage was compounded. There were even CDOs of CDOs. Risky tranches of a number of CDOs were collected and used to support a new CDO, with a range of high-to-low risk-rated tranches. Among all this mess was the highly inflated ratings for bonds.

Events in the fall of 2007 led to an evolving slow-motion crisis in the banking industry. The top banks had committed to some $300 billion to $400 billion in bridges for private equity deals that were still being completed when the subprime debacle hit. CDO financing stopped, and the banks were in trouble; the CDOs had played a critical role in maintaining bank liquidity. Moreover, the rates on commercial paper, used by the banks for short-term liquidity, suddenly spiked up nearly 20 percent in early September. Among the banks in trouble were the giants Citibank and J.P. Morgan (later, JPMorgan Chase). In October the big banks and investment banks reported some $20 billion in losses, with $11 billion of that at Citibank and Merrill Lynch, mostly in subprime-based CDOs. Within a few weeks the banks revised their losses to more than $45 billion. Again, some $20 billion was at Citibank and Merrill Lynch.

We can begin to see how home mortgages led to a banking crisis. Investment bankers created mortgage bonds by pooling thousands of home loans or home-equity lines of credit. You might think that mortgage bonds made up of thousands of home loans would provide safety through diversity. It didn't happen that way. These bonds become so toxic that they poisoned banks and threatened the entire economy.

Look under the hood of one of these diversified bonds and you can understand why the banks were in trouble. The mortgage bond holds other mortgage bonds made up of the riskiest portions of other bonds, some of which are themselves a collection of other poorly rated mortgage bonds. In a rising real estate market, such risks are deemed acceptable. When first issued, the mortgage bond might have been rated AAA. But when things unwind, it is a different story as any default gets compounded by the chain of linked bonds. While say

4.4 percent of typical loans tied to the mortgage bond are in default, nearly 59 percent of the investments are now worthless. The mortgage bond has become a toxic asset.

The banks come back into the picture. Banks hold tens of billions of dollars in mortgage bonds, and as the bonds fall in value or are wiped out completely, they erase precious capital the banks need to survive. Secretary of Treasury Timothy Geithner said that he wants to start a public-private partnership to buy up such toxic assets. Geithner and others believe that rescue banks for these bonds will save the commercial banks. To pull that off, the bond has to be priced to sell. Once again, the Black-Scholes formula comes back into play. The price has to be right. A look at Jupiter High Grade V, one of these mortgage bonds, illustrates how difficult setting the price would be. Jupiter owns 223 other mortgage bonds. One of those bonds is Mantoloking, which in turn owns 126 other bonds. Mantoloking's mortgage bonds own hundreds of other mortgage bonds. Those mortgage bonds are then all made up of thousands of actual loans, some of which may be current, while others may have expired.

A Goldman Sachs report estimates that most investment banks believe bonds like Jupiter are worth 40 percent less than what was paid for them, or 50 cents for every dollar invested. But because so many of Jupiter's bonds have gone bad, you could just as easily guess that it is worth 41 cents on the dollar. Given where loan defaults are headed, the best part of the bond could be worth as little as 5 cents. If some entity, be it the Treasury or the Federal Reserve, buys these assets, there will be very little new capital on either balance sheet. And, all of this traces back to the foreclosure crisis.

The various mortgage transactions involved commercial banks. The overall effect was found in bank failures. By May 22, 2008 some 36 banks had been taken over by the FDIC, which arranged for a merger of the failing bank with a "healthier" bank where possible. All FDIC checking accounts are insured up to $250,000. Since the inception of FDIC during the Great Depression, no depositor has lost money unless their account exceeded the insurance limit. Although there were only three failures in all of 2007, many more banks were distressed throughout 2008. The largest bank failure by far was that of the aforementioned savings and loan IndyMac Bank, which was seized by regulators on July 11 with about $32 billion in assets and deposits of $19 billion. On August 22, 2008 federal regulators shut down Columbian Bank and Trust Company in Topeka, Kansas. The Federal Deposit Insurance Corporation (FDIC) was appointed receiver of Columbian Bank, which had $752 million in assets and $622 million in deposits as of June 30. It was the ninth failure in 2008 of an FDIC-insured bank. Later banks seized were Strategic Capital Bank and Citizens National Bank, both in Illinois. The closure of Strategic Capital Bank is expected to cost the FDIC $173 million, while Citizen National Bank's closure will cost about $106 million. The banking crisis worsened in 2009, but did not end then.

The most recent cases contrast with the about $46 million in uninsured deposits at Columbian bank that exceeded the insurance limit. Concern continues to grow over the solvency of some banks amid the housing slump and the steep slide in the mortgage market. Banks are being subjected to tumbling home prices, rising foreclosures, and tighter credit conditions, afflicting both large and small banks across the USA. The FDIC had been adding to the staff of examiners to handle the expected failures and planned to raise insurance premiums paid by banks and thrifts to replenish its reserve fund after the huge payout to IndyMac.

Late in July 2008 Merrill Lynch announced plans to write down another $5.7 billion tied to bad mortgage debt, raising fears that other banks and financial firms will follow. Merrill Lynch said it would sell repackaged mortgage-backed securities for just $7 billion, only a few weeks after they had been valued at $31 billion.

In response, the Federal Reserve extended emergency loans to Wall Street firms, a practice continued in 2009. As financial companies have racked up multibillion dollar losses on sour mortgage investments and credit problems spread to other areas, firms have hoarded cash and clamped down on lending. That has crimped spending by people and businesses, which in turn has weighed on the national economy, a vicious cycle the Fed wants desperately to break.

Concern continues to grow over the solvency of some banks amid the housing slump and the steep slide in the mortgage market.

Banks are being subjected to rising foreclosures and tighter credit conditions, afflicting both large and small banks across the USA. The FDIC and its counterpart for savings and loans planned to raise insurance premiums paid by banks and thrifts to replenish its reserve funds after their huge payout to IndyMac and other banks.

## PROBLEMS GO GLOBAL

Seigniorage refers to the ability of a government to debase its currency. After the American dollar's status as the world's reserve currency was established by the Bretton Woods agreement after World War II, international seigniorage refers to the persistent overvaluation of the dollar as a reserve currency. The status of a reserve currency is always tenuous for it depends on the country's running trade deficits, though not too large. In recent years the USA has exceeded the limits to this precarious balancing act.

The trade account deteriorated steadily through the 1980s and 1990s, before tilting into free fall about 1999. The trade deficit in 2006 was over US$750 billion, and the total current account deficit topped US$800 billion. What is most important, the accumulated deficit for 2000 to 2006 was about US$4 trillion. By the end of 2006 the net investment position of the USA was US$2.5 billion in favor of foreigners. But, the most important number is that US$4 trillion. All these dollars floating around led to a depreciation in the dollar as the reserve currency. Now central banks and treasuries are increasingly nervous about holding more dollars, dollars that are depreciating.

Big, emerging countries such as China, Pakistan and India follow an export-led growth plan. This means that they have to accept the reserve currency in payment. As ever, there are nonetheless limits. If the reserve currency comes under too much pressure, central banks in these countries will shift to a basket of currencies in which to hold reserves. The danger is the major oil producing countries will do the same. According to U.S. Treasury estimates, total accumulated surpluses, in all reserve currencies, within the control of governments, has risen to US$7.6 trillion or about 15 percent of global GDP, or more than 60 percent of global savings. Some 50 percent of the oil exporter surpluses are owned by just three countries. As oil prices rise, these surpluses rise as well. Except for Norway, the oil exporting surplus countries are not Western-styled democracies.

As a reaction to the mounting surpluses, the surplus countries are setting up sovereign wealth funds (SWFs). The SWF is a private investment fund set up outside official reserves and free of the investment limitations that apply to official reserves. The oldest SWF is Singapore's Temasek Holdings, a US$100 billion fund created to invest the state's excess reserves. It claims an 18 percent annual return since it inception 30 years ago, and its bonds have a triple-A rating. At least 25 surplus countries have established SWFs with investable funds estimated at US$3 trillion in 2007. The SWFs of Kuwait, Dubai, Abu Dhabi, and Qatar are also quite active. Incidentally, the SWFs tend to exert upward pressure on long-term interest rates in the USA.

One big question mark concerns the price of oil. According to Goldman Sachs, speculators account for about 42 percent of all oil trading on Nymex; index investors, 11 percent; and oil producers and other companies make up the balance. Commodity index funds had an estimated US$250 billion in assets by summertime 2008 compared with just US$13 billion at the end of 2003. How much have hedge funds and proprietary trading desks of big banks been betting on crude? Nobody knows except that the figure is huge. On Wall Street, commodities trading that includes oil has proved to be substantial and is a real profits machine.

To those such as Alan Greenspan who claimed that bubbles cannot be identified until they burst, the housing crash provided all the evidence that was needed. The housing collapse would have repercussions for the real economy. But, the most immediate adverse effects were felt in the banks holding all those mortgages and associated CDOs and other derivatives. We have summarized some of the early effects on commercial banks; we go on to consider the effects throughout the financial system. And, if there were adverse effects on banks here and abroad, there had to be effects on the money market (the money supply and interest rates). We next turn to these adversities.

# 9

# THE GREAT MONEY AND BANKING PANIC

On December 9, 1985, the cover of *Business Week* featured John Gutfreund, the CEO of Salomon Brothers and "The King of Wall Street." While Merrill Lynch is the best-known Wall Street house and Goldman Sachs is the best-managed, Salomon Brothers is the firm most feared by its competitors. It is the prototype of the thoroughly modern investment bank. Salomon was the epitome of the new breed of Wall Street investment banks, built around a risk-taking bond trading operation powered by "quants" recruited from academic research institutions and filled with financial engineers designing new products. Some four years later, Michael Lewis's *Liar's Poker* would set its status as the paradigmatic bank of the 1980s, the same decade that produced Oliver Stone's *Wall Street* movie, with Gordon Gekko's famous "greed is good" speech.

That was then. If the financial crisis of 2008–2009 produced a king of Wall Street, it would most likely be Jamie Dimon, CEO of JPMorgan Chase. (Lloyd Blankfein of Goldman Sachs would be the other likely contender.) JPMorgan Chase had over $2 trillion in assets, not counting positions recorded off its balance sheet, such as derivatives; it had $155 billion in balance sheet equity; and it earned $4.1 billion in operating profits in the second quarter of 2009. In comparison, the 1985 Salomon Brothers, after converting to 2009 dollars, only had $122 billion in assets, $5 billion in equity, and $2 billion in operating profits for an entire year. Goldman Sachs had $890 billion in assets.

## CHANGES IN BANKING AND FINANCE

A lot changed during the last quarter-century. For one thing, there was a wave of mergers that created fewer and fewer but larger and larger financial institutions. JPMorgan Chase emerged out of the mergers of Chemical Bank, Manufacturers Hanover, Chase Manhattan, J.P. Morgan, Bank One, and First Chicago, to be followed by the acquisitions of Bear Stearns and Washington Mutual in 2008. Salomon was acquired by Travelers, which then merged with Citicorp into Citigroup.

Besides that, the financial sector got bigger and bigger. In 1978, all commercial banks together held $1.2 trillion of assets. By the end of 2007, the commercial banks had grown to $1.8 trillion in assets. But there was more. Investment banks, including Salomon, grew from $33 billion in assets, or 1.4 percent of GDP, to $3.1 trillion in assets, or 2.2 percent of GDP. Asset-backed securities such as collateralized debt obligations (CDOs), which barely existed in 1978, accounted for another $4.5 trillion in assets in 2007, or 32 percent of GDP. The debt held by the financial sector grew from $2.9 trillion, or 125 percent of GDP, in 1978 to over $36 trillion in 2007, or 259 percent of GDP. The financial sector had grown in importance; every dollar of GDP required $2.59 in financial debt. The USA was leveraged.

At the risk of some repetition, we are reminded that the asset expansion of the financial sector vastly outran that growth in households and nonfinancial companies. Most of the growth in the sector was due to the increasing financialization of the economy, the conversion of one dollar of lending to the real economy into many dollars of financial transactions. Again, in 1978 the financial sector borrowed $13 in the credit markets for every $100 borrowed by the real economy; by 2007, that had grown to $51. These figures exclude the off-balance sheet derivatives. Globally, over-the-counter derivatives, which essentially did not exist in 1978, grew to over $33 trillion in market value — over twice the U.S. GDP — by the end of 2008. A great portion of these derivatives was held by U.S. financial institutions, the world leaders in the business.

From 1978 to 2007 the financial sector grew from 3.5 percent to 5.9 percent of the economy, while its share of corporate profits climbed much faster. While from the 1930s until around 1980, financial sector profits grew at roughly the same rate as profits in the nonfinancial sector, from 1980 until 2005, financial sector profits grew by 800 percent, adjusted for inflation, while nonfinancial sector profits grew by only 250 percent. Although the sector's profits plummeted at the peak of the financial crisis, they quickly rebounded; by the third quarter of 2009, financial sector profits were over six times their 1980 level, while nonfinancial sector profits were little more than double those of 1980. (We highlighted these data in Figure 5.1).

Bankers' salaries and bonuses grew alongside these gigantic profits. In 1978, average per-person compensation in the banking sector was $13,163 (in 1978 dollars), essentially the same as in the private sector overall. After 1982, banking pay took off, until by 2007, the average banker was making over two times as much as the average private sector employee. Early on, the comic poet Ogden Nash put it in the title of a poem — "Bankers Are Just Like Anybody Else, Except Richer." In comparison though, the money in hedge funds was obscene. In 2007 five fund managers earned at least $1 billion each, led by John Paulson, who made $3.7 billion from betting against the housing market and the mortgage-backed securities built on top of it.

Along with all this growth came greatly diminished regulation. The deregulation trend begun in the administration of Jimmy Carter was transformed into a crusade by Ronald Reagan. The financial services industry had broken free from the constraints placed on it by the Great Depression. The result was an out-of-balance financial system that still enjoyed the full backing of the federal government. This free-market ideology extended to the derivatives markets where the Black-Scholes formula was being used to calculate the prices of financial derivatives.

In 1982 the Garn-St. Germain Depository Institutions Act lifted many regulations on the savings and loan industry, allowing them to expand into new businesses, engage in commercial lending and invest in junk bonds. The bill also authorized state-chartered banks to offer mortgages with adjustable rates. At the same time Lewis Ranieri, one of the legendary traders at Salomon Brothers, worked directly with Reagan officials to create a new market for mortgage-backed securities. A new bill, the Secondary Mortgage Market Enhancement Act of 1984, which Ranieri helped create and defend, cleared away state regulations that had hampered Salomon's earlier efforts to create its own mortgage-backed securities out of Bank of America mortgages. The new market for private mortgage-backed securities also helped commercial banks and S&Ls to pass on the risk of their fixed rate mortgages to investors in these new securities. These new laws were good for investment banks and their fees. Still, 2,000 banks failed between 1985 and 1992. Only 79 banks had failed during all of the 1970s.

## INCREASES IN THE USE OF DERIVATIVES

By buying mortgages, guaranteeing their principal payments, and turning them into mortgage-backed securities, Fannie Mae and Freddie Mac provided funding for banks to make more mortgages and absorbed some of the risk of the market. Besides, securitization created many new ways for banks to make profits. Securitization created a new market for banks' loans, boosting volume. In turn, investment banks had three new ways to make money. They exacted fees from each securitization they created; they earned fees from selling the new mortgage-backed securities to investors; and they earned by trading these securities for profits. The volume of private mortgage-backed securities (excluding those issued by Ginnie Mae, Fannie Mae, and Freddie Mac) grew from $11 billion in 1984 to over $200 billion in 1994 to close to $3 trillion in 2007.

Salomon Brothers also pioneered arbitrage trading. Traders could make certain money by finding two securities that should but did not have the same value; buying one, selling the other, and waiting for their prices to converge. Or, the same goal could be achieved by buying the interest payments and the final principal payment on a 30-year bond separately while selling the whole 30-year bond (including interest and principal) for a higher price. Arbitrage trading soon spread to other investment banks. The popularity of arbitrage fueled the rapid growth of hedge funds which grew from less then $30 billion in assets in 1990 to over $1.2 trillion in 2005, and then on to $2 trillion by 2008.

On the coattails of high-yield debt, securitization, and arbitrage trading came the modern derivatives market. This revolution began with that invention of the interest rate swap by Salomon Brothers in 1981. Interest rate swaps allow companies to exchange fixed rate payments for floating rate payments, or vice-versa, "swapping" interest rate risks between the two parties. In a similar way, currency swaps allow companies to swap currency risks by exchanging different currencies for combinations of currencies. The two kinds of swaps can be combined into one. By mid-2008, the market for over-the-counter interest rate swaps had grown to over US$350 trillion in face value (the amount on which interest is calculated) and over US$8 trillion in gross market value.

The credit default swap played an important role in the financial crisis. It is a form of insurance on debt; the buyer of the swap pays a fixed premium to the seller, who agrees to pay off the debt if the debtor fails to do so. Typically the debt is a bond or a similar fixed income security, and the debtor is the issuer of the bond. These credit default swaps were popularized by JPMorgan in the late 1990s. This explosion of new products provided vast new profit-making possibilities for financial institutions.

Banks not only got bigger, they got broader with the help of derivatives and commercial paper; they began to look matronly. We should not lose sight of the fact that the traditional role of commercial banks is to raise money for corporations. In 1978, Bankers Trust began placing commercial paper (short-term debt) issued by corporations with investors. The Federal Reserve opened up another loophole in 1985, allowing commercial banks to set up affiliated companies (through a bank holding company) to deal in specific securities that were otherwise off-limits to commercial banks. Over the next decade, Alan Greenspan expanded the loophole, which began with government bonds, mortgage-backed securities, and commercial paper, to include corporate bonds and equities. Commercial banks were taking on the functions of investment banks, which had been prohibited by the Glass-Steagall Act. At the same time, investment banks encroached on the business of commercial banks. For example, Merrill Lynch introduced the cash management account (CMA), a money market account with check-writing privileges. The major commercial banks used acquisitions not only to become larger, but also to move into investment banking. What was once a divide between commercial banks and investment banks became a divide among mega-banks. These mega-banks became the new Wall Street.

## MORE DEREGULATION

The mega-banks and their operations were aided and abetted by further deregulation, as the final dismantling of the regulatory system constructed in the 1930s was completed in the 1990s. Derivatives now enter the picture. The Riegle-Neal Act of 1994 mostly eliminated restrictions on interstate banking, allowing bank holding companies to acquire banks in any state and allowing banks to open branches in new states. The Gramm-Leach-Bliley Act of 1999 demolished the remaining barriers separating commercial and investment banking by allowing holding companies to own subsidiaries engaged in both businesses as well as insurance. At the same time the government refused to regulate derivatives. It was thought that market forces would be sufficient to prevent fraud and excessive risk-taking. The rapid growth of the derivatives market was proof that they were socially beneficial; this was the view of Alan Greenspan.

Greenspan was not the only one to celebrate financial innovation. In 2006, even as he warned about potential risk management challenges from derivatives, Timothy Geithner (then New York Fed president) said of the wave of financial innovations,

> These developments provide substantial benefits to the financial system. Financial institutions are able to measure and manage risk much more effectively. Risks are spread more widely, across a more diverse group of financial intermediaries, within and across countries.

These changes have contributed to a substantial improvement in the financial strength of the core financial intermediaries and in the overall flexibility and resilience of the financial system in the United States.[1]

In April 2009, *during* the financial crisis, Ben Bernanke, Greenspan's successor, said, "Financial innovation has improved access to credit, reduced costs, and increased choice. We should not attempt to impose restrictions on credit providers so onerous that they prevent the development of new products and services in the future."[2] Derivatives would do everything except prevent war as we know it.

## HOW THE U.S. HOUSING BUBBLE BURST IN THE FACES OF BANKS

This is an opportune time to summarize the causes of the bubble. Next, we will look at U.S. housing prices over long historical time. In this context, the U.S. led much of the rest of the global economy. Then, we will consider it as part of the banking crisis.

A multitude of forces led to the housing inflation. The increased availability of mortgage loans combined with lower initial monthly payments increased home-buyers' ability to pay and pushed prices upward. Since borrowers could always refinance when their mortgages became unaffordable, making mortgage-backed securities and CDOs more attractive to investors and to the investment banks that created them, prices could continue to climb. The higher prices also induced existing homeowners to take out home equity loans, which provided more raw material for asset-backed securities and CDOs. At the same time, lower risk reduced the price of credit default swaps on mortgage-backed debt, making CDOs and synthetic CDOs easier to

---

[1] Timothy F. Geithner, "Risk Management Challenges in the U.S. Financial System" (lecture, Global Association of Risk Professionals, 7th Annual Risk Management Convention and Exhibition, New York, February 26, 2008).

[2] Ben S. Bernanke, "Financial Innovation and Consumer Protection" (lecture, Federal Reserve System's Sixth Biennial Community Affairs Research Conference, Washington, D.C., April 17, 2009).

create. The enhanced Wall Street demand for mortgages to feed the securitization pipeline funneled cheap money to mortgage lenders. By the early 2000s subprime lending became a larger and larger share of the market, not only in the USA but in much of the rest of the world.

Despite the ability to pass risk along, some banks kept some of the risk anyway. They used financial innovation in the form of structured investment vehicles (SIVs), which were used to raise money by issuing commercial paper and investing it in longer-term, higher-yielding assets. Citigroup, for example, used SIVs to buy over $80 billion in assets by July 2007. These SIVs allowed banks to invest in their own structured securities without having to hold capital against them. Thus, the SIVs enabled banks to take on more risks with the same amount of financial capital — that is, as long as housing prices soared. When things did go bad in 2007 and 2008, many banks, including Citigroup, bailed out of their SIVs, incurring billions of dollars of losses.

Historical housing data from Robert Shiller are displayed in Figure 9.1. We can see from Figure 9.1 how real U.S. housing prices fell off a cliff, beginning around 2006. Once again, a picture is worth a thousand words. Before that, as noted, mortgages were already in

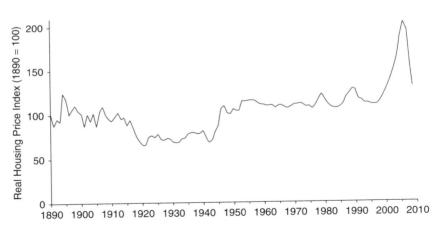

*Source*: Reprinted in Johnson and Kwak, *13 Bankers, op. cit.*, p. 130.

*Note*: Data were originally used in Robert Shiller, *Irrational Exuberance* (Princeton: Princeton University Press, 2000).

**Figure 9.1:**    Real U.S. Housing Prices, 1890–2009.

trouble by 2005, as the housing boom approached its peak, a peak not reached, according to U.S. census purchase prices, until the second quarter of 2007. The picture is made more dramatic by the inclusion of data from 1890 through the estimated value in 2010. Those who report that U.S. housing prices "doubled" are using the Schiller Index with 1890 as the base year. The Shiller and (later) Standard-Poor's Case-Shiller index is based on a sample of 20 cities and metropolitan areas. The index may be a more accurate view of the real estate bubble in the U.S. After all, the bubbles were in particular cities. Still, one thing is clear: speculators in housing were reluctant to leave the market, irrespective of their locale.

Robert Shiller has a good track record in calling bubbles. Just before the stock market crashed in 2000, he warned about the prospects for Nasdaq stocks. Just before housing prices dropped in 2006, he again called the turn. There are many housing indexes that bear Shiller's name, but we will consider one more in Figure 9.2. The bubble actually peaks in the second quarter, but there is very little

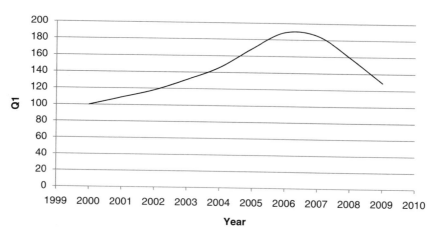

Source: Wikipedia at http://en.wikipedia.org/wiki/Case-Shiller_index, November 2, 2010, p. 4. The original index appears at http://www2.standardandpoors.com/spf/pdf/index/csnational_value_052619.xis. There is a fee for accessing the original indexes.

**Figure 9.2:**   First Quarter Standard & Poors-Shiller Index Values (Rounded to the Nearest Whole Number).

difference between each of the four quarters of 2006. According to our version, we have an 89 percent bubble, if the year 2000 is used as the base. This is only slightly different from the annual data results and is not wildly different from the broader U.S. Census index of Chapter 7.

Home sales picked up after 2009 in response to the U.S. Treasury's home-buyers tax credit, only to fall eight percent in September 2010. With foreclosures rising again, the housing slump probably is not over. Shiller, for one, sees home prices as more important than the foreclosure crisis. On November 2, 2010, he said, "...if home prices drop further, homeowners will fall further underwater and lending institutions' balance sheets will become more distressed. That could bring on another phase of the crisis."[3] He is referring to a second wave and possibly a third wave of foreclosures. Still, I would argue that more foreclosures would add to any future decline in housing prices. Later, we will assess the consequences of the housing collapse on the overall economy.

## THE BANKS WERE NEXT

In 2006 borrowers unable to refinance their mortgages began defaulting in sharply rising numbers. In 2007 the mountain of assets based on housing values began to crumble as increasing defaults torpedoed the prices of mortgage-backed securities and CDOs. The avalanche almost brought down the global financial system in 2008. Yet, big, risk-loving banks had become crucial to the USA economy and to our way of life.

The nine banks sitting on this mountain of crumbling assets were too big to fail. On October 13, 2008, with their stock prices in decline and the short-term viability of their firms in doubt, the heads of nine major banks — Bank of America, Bank of New York Mellon,

---

[3] Jennifer Schonberger, "Robert Shiller Sees More Housing Pain Ahead," Kiplinger at http://www.kiplinger.com/columns/dekaser-practical-economics/archives/robert-shiller, p. 2.

Citigroup, Goldman Sachs, JPMorgan Chase, Merrill Lynch, Morgan Stanley, State Street, and Wells Fargo — arrived at the Treasury for a meeting with then Treasury Secretary Henry Paulson. The government was stepping in to protect the massive USA financial system and, by extension, the global economy.

The October 13th deal was structured as a purchase of preferred shares, which meant that the Treasury loaned the banks money, at an initial five percent annual interest rate, that never had to be repaid. The purchases meant that the government now owned part of the banks. The banks in turn received virtually free money. At the meeting, the government began guaranteeing debt issued by the banks, allowing them to raise money by selling bonds to private investors who now knew that the government would guarantee their investments. Meanwhile, Lehman Brothers went bankrupt, Bear Stearns and Merrill Lynch were sold, and Goldman Sachs and Morgan Stanley fled into the safety of bank holding company status, which gave them enhanced access to emergency lending from the Federal Reserve.

The banks were facing a liquidity crisis and needed more capital. In March 2008 Bear Stearns, the weakest of the big five investment banks, collapsed. The cause? Bear Stearns was brought down by a modern-day bank run. It was more exposed to structured mortgage-backed securities than its rivals. The Fed first attempted to lend Bear Stearns money by using JPMorgan Chase as an intermediary; as an investment bank, Bear was not eligible for direct loans from the Fed. As noted earlier, this failed to bolster confidence and Paulson, Bernanke, and Geithner attempted to broker the sale of Bear to JPMorgan for a miserly $2 per share. JPMorgan refused to go along even with this bargain price without government help. The New York Fed agreed to assume all the losses on $30 billion of Bear's illiquid securities. The deal was renegotiated to a purchase price of $10 per share. It was a coup for JPMorgan, which was paying for Bear Stearns approximately what its building was worth. To prevent the other investment banks from the same fate as Bear Stearns, the Federal Reserve immediately created the Primary Dealer Credit Facility, which would allow investment banks for the first time to borrow money *directly* from the Fed. It was a dramatic expansion of the safety net for the investment banks.

No one knew the value of toxic assets setting on major banks' balance sheets, or how much they would lose if they were forced to sell. The banks were taking major write-downs. In 2007, Citigroup took $29 billion in write-downs, Merrill Lynch $25 billion, Lehman $13 billion, Bank of America $1 billion, and Morgan Stanley $10 billion. In 2008, Citigroup took another $53 billion in write-downs, Merrill $39 billion, Bank of America $29 billion, Lehman $14 billion, JPMorgan Chase $10 billion, and Morgan Stanley $10 billion. If some of the major banks were to acknowledge the true decline in the value of their assets, they might be insolvent.

Next, Fannie Mae and Freddie Mac came under pressure. Their balance sheets were heavily exposed to the housing market, and falling housing prices were tearing a hole in those balance sheets, threatening their survival. In July 2008, Paulson obtained the right to back up Fannie and Freddie with taxpayer money. This was not enough. On September 7, Fannie and Freddie were taken over by the government, placed in a conservatorship (the equivalent of bankruptcy). In exchange for keeping Freddie and Fannie in operation, the government got a controlling ownership share and the right to manage them. The federal government had taken over two pillars of the financial system because they too were too big to fail.

Next, Lehman Brothers was short of cash. Over that famous weekend of September 12–14, Paulson and Geithner cast about for a buyer.[4] No taxpayer money was to be used this time. When a plan for Barclays to acquire Lehman fell through on Sunday, the backup plan was bankruptcy early on Monday morning. The demise of Lehman triggered a chain reaction that ripped the financial markets. The aforementioned American International Group (AIG), struggling with its derivatives, faced downgrades by all three major credit rating

---

[4] A book by a Wall Street TV reporter is devoted to this hectic weekend. For a detailed account of the personalities, the many phone calls, the conflicts of the Wall Street CEOs with each other and with Fed and government officials, see Maria Bartiromo (with Catherine Whitney) *The Weekend That Changed Wall Street* (New York: Penguin, 2010).

agencies. These downgrades, in turn, could force it into bankruptcy. On Tuesday, the Fed stepped in with a $85 billion credit line to keep AIG afloat. If the insurer defaulted on its hundreds of billions of dollars in credit default swaps, its counter-parties would suffer devastating losses or at the least, fear of such losses would end liquidity in world financial markets.

Tuesday was an especially busy day. The Reserve Primary Fund, one of the largest money market funds, announced that it would "break the buck"; because of losses on Lehman debt, it could not return one dollar for each dollar put in by investors. Money flooded out of the money market funds, forcing the Treasury to create a new program of insurance for those funds. The continued flight of money market funds dried up demand for the commercial paper used by corporations to manage their cash, raising the specter of major corporations unable to make payroll. The Fed was forced to establish a program to buy commercial paper from issuing corporations, lending money not just to banks, but directly to nonfinancial companies.

The mighty continued to fall. Washington Mutual collapsed as depositors pulled out their money, thus far the largest bank failure in U.S. history. Wachovia, on the brink of failure, was acquired by Wells Fargo. Running out of cash, banks stopped lending. Money moved toward the safety of U.S. Treasury bills and stayed there. There was a liquidity trap. Overnight lending rates were near zero and could go no lower, no matter how fast the money supply was increased. In any event, the money supply was not increasing because banks were not lending and therefore were not creating any new demand deposits (a large part of the money supply) as "inside" money.

## FISCAL POLICY IS INVOKED

The Treasury and Federal Reserve remained in crisis mode. On September 18, Paulson and Bernanke had asked Congress for that $700 billion for the express purpose of buying toxic securities. Congress responded by passing the Emergency Economic Stabilization Act on October 3. Now the Troubled Asset Relief

Program (TARP) had $700 billion to buy "troubled assets" from financial institutions. Never before had so much taxpayer money been designated to save an industry from the consequences of its own misdeeds.

But there was a great deal at stake. With panic seizing the financial markets, a sudden evaporation of credit, coupled with rapid deleveraging by financial institutions and corporations everywhere, we would have had a second Great Depression. The immediate threat was a panic-induced bank run, but the underlying issue was the toxic securities held by banks that were plummeting in value. Liquidating those assets at current market prices meant insolvency for many financial institutions, most of them being giants.

Over the course of the financial crisis, the principal economic policymakers had to become increasingly inventive. As noted, the original purpose of TARP was to buy toxic assets from financial institutions — transferring risk from banks to the federal government. But if the Treasury paid enough to solve the banks' problems, that would constitute a massive subsidy from the taxpayer. Instead, the government chose to recapitalize banks by giving them cash for preferred shares. For every $100 committed by Treasury at the October 13th meeting, only $22 was a subsidy to the banking sector, but it clearly was still a subsidy.

In November 2008 Citigroup was struggling to fend off concerns about its viability. The government announced a second bailout package. Besides another $20 billion investment the government agreed to guarantee a $305 billion pool of Citigroup assets against declines in value. In return the government received additional preferred stock. A similar asset guarantee was provided to Bank of America in January, in exchange for agreeing to complete the acquisition of Merrill Lynch in December. The government guaranteed a $118 billion pool of assets in exchange for $4 billion in preferred stock of Bank of America.

Meanwhile, the AIG bailout greatly benefited the major banks. The banks had purchased credit default swaps from AIG to insure $62 billion in CDOs. The AIG bailout financed a new entity (Maiden Lane III) to buy CDOs so that AIG could then settle the credit default swaps. Maiden Lane III paid $30 billion at the market price to buy the CDOs from the banks, and AIG, under instructions from the New York Fed, then paid the banks $32 billion to retire the credit default swaps. As a result, the banks received 100 cents on the dollar in this backdoor bailout.

The megabanks now faced even less competition. Bear Stearns, Lehman Brothers, Merrill Lynch, Washington Mutual, and Wachovia had all vanished, and an entire class of nonbank mortgage lenders had evaporated with the housing bubble. The banks now had a number of options. Banks could raise money at low interest rates from depositors virtually for free; they could borrow cheaply from each other at the near zero fed funds rate; they could borrow cheaply at the Fed's discount window; they could sell bonds at low interest rates; they could swap their asset-backed securities for cash with the Fed; they could sell their mortgages to Fannie and Freddie, which could in turn sell debt to the Fed; and on and on. Despite all this aid to the banks, every type of bank loan became harder to get in every quarter of 2008, 2009, and through the first three quarters of 2010. Still, the overall strategy brought the financial system back from the brink of ruin; it did so without stimulating much lending to the real economy.

## CONSEQUENCES

The financial crisis of 2008–2009 that really got under way in late 2007 left the big banks even bigger. Bank of America absorbed Countrywide and Merrill Lynch and saw its assets grow from $1.7 trillion at the end of 2007 to $2.3 trillion in September 2009. JPMorgan Chase absorbed Bear Stearns and Washington Mutual and grew from $1.6 trillion to $2.0 trillion. Wells Fargo absorbed Wachovia and grew from $600 billion to $1.2 trillion. By mid-2009, Bank of America, JPMorgan Chase, Wells Fargo, and Citigroup controlled half the market for new mortgages and two-thirds of the market for new credit cards. The United States has had a rule since 1994 that prohibits any single bank from holding more than ten percent of total retail deposits. In 2009 this rule had to be waived for JPMorgan Chase, Bank of America, and Wells Fargo. Derivatives became more concentrated; at the end of June 2009, five banks had over 95 percent of the market for derivatives contracts traded by U.S. banks, led by JPMorgan Chase.[5]

By 2010 there are at least six banks that are too big to fail — Bank of America, Citigroup, Goldman Sachs, JPMorgan Chase, Morgan Stanley, and Wells Fargo. "Too big to fail" creates three major problems for society. First, these institutions have to be bailed out by the government when they do come to the brink of failure. Second, giant financial institutions have a strong incentive to take excess risk, since the government will bail them out in an emergency (moral hazard). Third, giant financial institutions are bad for competition, and this is bad for the economy. Even during the financial crisis, the large banks could pay 0.78 percentage points less for money than small banks.

Not surprisingly, small banks are continuing to fail. This is where the next phase of the crisis could hit. In 2009, 140 U.S. banks failed, the most since deposit insurance was introduced in the 1930s. As of October 29, 2010, 139 banks (mostly small ones) had failed, a pace well in advance of that of 2009. The closings in 2010 included 29 in Georgia, 23 in Illinois, 20 in California and 18 in Florida. Week after week, banks are failing — in Norcross, Georgia; Springfield, Illinois; San Clemente, California; and Fort Myers, Florida. The failures in the bubble states of Arizona and Nevada were modest in 2010, but massive in 2008–2009 and could be large again. There were mounting losses on loans in the toughest economic climate since the 1930s. These failures have sapped billions of dollars out of the FDIC fund, which fell into the red during 2009. Its deficit stood at $20.7 billion as of March 31, 2010.

Why are failures of small banks important? After all, giant corporations such as IBM and Microsoft depend on the large banks, those already bailed out. Some 64 percent of the loans of small banks are to USA small businesses, which in turn create about 65 percent of all new jobs and employ about half of the private sector workforce.

---

[5] These shares are based on data from the Office of the Comptroller of the Currency. See Johnson and Kwak, *13 Bankers, op. cit.*, p. 180.

Worse, the FDIC has 829 banks at risk of failure (as of October 29, 2010), most of them small ones. These are likely to fail unless the climate in business changes very soon.[6]

*Time* magazine has provided the story of one community bank that destroyed a Georgia town's faith in government, the economy and itself. It is a microcosm of what we might expect soon across small town America.[7] The Community Bank & Trust (CBT) headquarters is in Cornelia, Georgia. Behind Daniel Bell of the Federal Deposit Insurance Corporation (FDIC) on January 29, 2010, a team of 25 experts swooped down on CBT, taking control of the coded Federal Reserve tokens that allow access to payment systems and seized the terminal on which interbank transfers are made. The FDIC knew that the balance sheet of CBT was a mess. Though Community Bank had thrived in flush times, its practices led to hundreds of residential and commercial foreclosures in the local economy (and may produce thousands more). Both homes and businesses underwritten by CBT have been foreclosed in 2010, 1,500 loans are in serious trouble, and at least 2,700 were so poorly documented that no one is sure whether they should be foreclosed or not. In other words, CBT is part of the mortgage mess which is driven by subprime mortgages, including liar's loans. All this despite the bank having been well-managed for many years.

Although the FDIC had the option of taking over the bank and running it, it decided to find a buyer. The buyer is South Carolina Bank and Trust (SCBT) based in Columbia. SCBT itself had been stabilized with the help of TARP funds in 2009, and made the best of five competing bids for CBT. For taking on nearly all of CBT's assets and liabilities, SCBT was given $158 million with the agreement to cover 20 percent of losses on outstanding residential and commercial loans up to $233 million and to cover five percent on loans above

---

[6] The FDIC data and information is from the FDIC website. For a complete list of bank names of failures, go to http://www.fdic.gov/bank/individual/failed/banklist.html.

[7] Massimo Calabresi, "Death of a Small-Town Bank," *Time*, September 1, 2010, pp. 57–60.

that amount. The new owners proceeded to close ten branch offices, declined to rehire 120 employees and began an investigation of the old bank's 10,822 loans. While they moved 1,500 to a special asset group, they foreclosed on 224 loans originally worth $49 million, 35 residential, the rest commercial.

Not everyone was happy with what the FDIC did. "Cornelians believe SCBT is foreclosing on the bad loans so rapidly that it is taking the local economy down the tubes."[8] CBT had foreclosed on just 2.14 percent of its business loans and 1.75 percent of its residential mortgages, all of which were more than 100 days delinquent. The problem is the shift of faith from CBT to SCBT. It is a problem facing small bank after small bank. This lack of confidence overlooks some basic facts. SCBT can get reimbursement on losses from the FDIC whether or not it forecloses on delinquent loans. Moreover, if SCBT keeps its losses on CBT's loans under $233 million, the FDIC will write a check to SCBT for 50 percent of the difference. This gives SCBT a reason to keep loans that can produce interest income. CBT is a small bank but the process is still complicated. Attempting to reassure Cornelians, SCBT kept the CBT name. If other small banks fail in the same way, and the FDIC assures us they will, the USA faces the crisis of failing banks along with failing confidence in those that survive.

## U.S. BANK CREDIT AND THE STOCK MARKET

Most Americans live in a small circle as either debtors or creditors; some are stock holders. We can summarize the effect on two financial indicators that the Federal Reserve watches closely. One is bank credit, the other is stock market price indexes. This is not to say that these are the only financial indicators of the Fed, but they comprise parts of the financial outcomes. The relevant bank credit can be divided between commercial/ industrial loans and real estate loans (mostly mortgages). The percent change (year over year) in the level of bank credit

---

[8] *Ibid.*, p. 60.

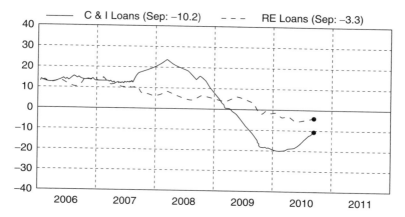

*Note*: C & I Loans equals Commercial and Industrial Loans. RE loans equals Real Estate Loans
*Source*: Haver Analytics, Federal Reserve Board of Governors website.

**Figure 9.3:** Bank Credit: Percent Change Over Year–Ago Level.

is shown in Figure 9.3. Both measures began to slump slightly in 2006, with real estate credit falling in 2007 and taking a steep descent in 2008 and 2009. Late in 2009 the percentage changes turn negative and remain so through the latest available data. The decline for real estate loans in September 2010 is –3.3 percent.

The credit crunch measured by commercial and industrial loan activity did not hit until early 2008, that pivotal year. The divergence of the two types of credit reveals much about the institutions of banking compared with overall mortgage credit. The banking system proved to be more vulnerable than the mortgage lenders. Commercial banks are purely private, especially during this time of virtually no regulation. Despite the Federal Reserve's best efforts, commercial and industrial credit fell sharply after early 2008 and accelerated in 2009. By September 2010, despite having leveled off early in the year, C & I loans declined 10.2 percent from their level a year earlier. In contrast, the mortgage industry experienced slower downward changes. The mortgage market was cushioned by the presence of Fannie Mae and Freddie Mac, despite all their problems. This is not to deny the severe repercussions of the subprime debacle.

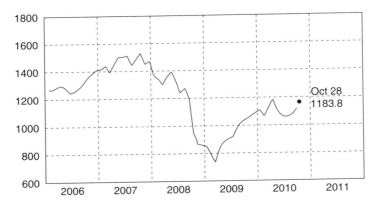

*Source*: Haver Analytics, Federal Reserve Board of Governors website.

**Figure 9.4:**   Stock Market Index: Standard & Poor's 500 Composite.

As we already know, there is more than one stock market price index. The one favored by the general public and the media is the Dow industrials, which is a blue chip indicator. A broader index and the one apparently favored by the Fed is Standard & Poor's 500 Composite index. Its behavior during the Great Recession is displayed in Figure 9.4. After peaking in late 2007 near 1600, the S & P 500 stairsteps its way downward and then falls off a cliff around mid-2008. It reached its near-term bottom in early in 2009, only to begin a recovery punctuated by three dips. It had recovered to 1183.8 by October 28, 2010. Although the stock market is considered a leading indicator for the overall economy, at the present time it is driven by the presence of very low rates of interest, especially short-term.

During the Great Money and Banking Panic, besides the FDIC the Federal Reserve was often at the center of action. While the FDIC may have prevented a massive run on commercial banks, the Fed has so far prevented the money and banking crisis from bringing the economy into a second Great Depression. It served to ease the credit crunch and the stock market decline. In this process the Fed took on additional powers, powers not granted by any institution but itself. At the same time its powers over the American economy greatly expanded. Since the Fed is closely allied with American and foreign financial institutions, its new powers without a countervail raise new questions about its expanded role in a democratic society. We next turn to consider its expanded powers and role in today's economy.

# 10

# THE UNCONVENTIONAL USE
# OF MONETARY POLICY

## THE FEDERAL RESERVE AT INCEPTION

In the United States monetary policy is conducted by the Federal
Reserve System, often referred to, as I have, as simply "the Fed." The
impetus for the congressional act establishing the Federal Reserve was
the Panic of 1907. In the fall of 1907 stock prices were falling and a
number of prominent brokerage houses already had closed their
doors. Bank managers instructed their tellers to count out with-
drawals slowly, as the banks were facing runs on their assets.
New York City was a week or two away from declaring bankruptcy.
It was the Panic of 1907 and the nation turned to 70-year-old
J. Pierpont Morgan to save the day. He was viewed as the lender of
last resort, and to this day a giant bank bears his name.

J.P. Morgan had ended "ruinous competition" by overseeing
mergers and consolidations. He merged companies that had been
rivals to create giants such as General Electric and U.S. Steel.
Between 1894 and 1904, more than 1,800 companies were merged,
acquired, and consolidated into a mere 93. However, all was not
calm in the financial markets. For one thing, there was considerable
speculation in copper financed by various financial institutions. The
Bear Stearns of the day, Knickerbocker Trust Company, had lent
heavily to the copper speculators. When the word got out, depositors descended on its offices to withdraw money, the sort of bank
run that was more probable before the establishment of the FDIC.
Then, on October 18, 1907 the National Bank of Commerce said it

would no longer act as the intermediary between Knickerbocker and the clearinghouse. On Monday, October 21, after paying out $8 million in less than four hours, Knickerbocker had run out of cash. Benjamin Strong, a young deputy of J.P. Morgan's, was sent to inspect the bank's books. Strong concluded that the trust company was insolvent. The panic spread to the Trust Company of New York.

Financial conditions were so dire that J.P. Morgan called the Secretary of the Treasury, George B. Cortelyou, and summoned him to New York. Cortelyou went post haste; it was a measure of the power held by Morgan. At Morgan's direction, Cortelyou offered to deposit $25 million of government money in New York City banks. This offer was made in a late-night October 1907 meeting with the heads of New York's biggest banks. It was clear that rescuing the Trust Company of New York was crucial. As before, Benjamin Strong was sent to look over the Trust Company's books and told to report back by noon. Later, Morgan told the bankers that the Trust Company was the place to stop the trouble. Meanwhile, 1,200 depositors had gathered at the Trust Company's offices to withdraw their deposits. Morgan had tried to persuade other trust companies and banks to raise the money the Trust Company needed to avoid collapse. That effort failed and Morgan next instructed the Trust Company's president to bring his most valuable securities to Morgan's office. Morgan gathered together $3 million in collateral. The next day Morgan convinced the other banks to come up with $10 million.

Contrary to Morgan's belief, this did not end the crisis. Concerns shifted to New York City, the New York Stock Exchange, a major brokerage firm, banks outside New York, and, eventually, steel, rail, and coal companies. Morgan pushed on. In November, the Treasury issued $150 million in bonds and permitted banks to use the securities to create new currency. At the time paper currency printed by banks circulated alongside government-printed greenbacks. The economy suffered a yearlong recession, but a depression was avoided. Unemployment went from 2.8 percent to eight percent and some 240 banks failed. J.P. Morgan had prevailed.

Some congressmen and senators, Senator Nelson Aldrich among them, surmised that something had to be done, for the nation may not always have Pierpont Morgan around to meet the next banking crises. The Bank of England had been around since 1694, and the "lender of last resort" role for central banks was codified by British journalist and economist Walter Bagehot in his remarkable 1873 book, *Lombard Street*. Bagehot advised that in a panic, a central bank should lend freely on good collateral and charge a high interest rate to discourage overuse. Perhaps it was time, suggested Senator Aldrich, that the United States had such a central bank.

Congress created the National Monetary Commission, chaired by Senator Aldrich, to address this issue. Aldrich arranged a week-long secret meeting in November 1910 at Jekyll Island, Georgia, a resort owned by John D. Rockefeller and J.P. Morgan, to design a new central bank for the United States. A handful of bankers convened at Jekyll Island, among them Benjamin Strong, the Morgan lieutenant. They agreed to back a version of a plan based on one crafted by investment banker Paul Warburg, who later was a member of the Federal Reserve Board. The resultant 24-volume report released in January 1911 called for a National Reserve Association with branches spread throughout the country that would issue currency and make loans to member banks. The association would be controlled by a board of directors dominated, of course, by bankers.

There was fervent opposition to the plan by William Jennings Bryan, who proclaimed that their plan would leave bankers in complete control of national finances. It was a view notable most of all for its accuracy. But President Woodrow Wilson had promised speedy and sweeping financial reform while standing on a Democratic Party platform that rejected the Aldrich proposal. Just after Christmas 1912, the incoming chairman of the House Committee on Banking and Finance, Carter Glass of Virginia, and his economic adviser, H. Parker Willis, came to Wilson to lay out an alternative. They proposed 20 or more privately controlled regional banks that would issue currency and lend to other banks, a plan crafted to dilute New York's dominance and avoid the creation of a central bank in Washington. Wilson, however, insisted on an appointed board to oversee the regional banks. Eventually Glass agreed to Wilson's government-controlled board. Wilson signed the Federal Reserve Act on December 23, 1913; it was the most significant achievement of his first year in office.

The Federal Reserve Act provided for a weak Federal Reserve Board in Washington, chaired by the secretary of the Treasury and including the comptroller of the currency and five others to be appointed by the president. Also mandated were up to 12 regional or "district" Fed banks, each to be owned by the private banks in their districts, each to be run by a governor. It was a classic American compromise between centralization and decentralization that provided no clear division of responsibilities between the board in Washington and the regional Fed banks. This lack of clear responsibilities proved troublesome before and during the Great Depression. Benjamin Strong had campaigned against this compromise legislation as too decentralized and too fragmented. Still, and with some reluctance, he became president of the Federal Reserve Bank of New York, the most powerful player in the system to this day. Strong regarded the 12 reserve banks as 11 too many.

Benjamin Strong was among the few who understood central banking. The Great Depression might have been avoided had Strong not died in October 1928, a year before the crash. The Fed's original sin was to tighten credit and raise interest rates in 1928 and 1929, in what was a misguided attack on speculation in the stock market at a time when the deeper problem was a weakening overall economy and the absence of inflation — indeed, the threat of deflation. The Fed tightened credit again in 1931 at precisely the wrong moment. This monetary policy led to a deflation of about ten percent a year and a greatly increased value of debts, which therefore led to more defaults and bankruptcies. The credit squeeze helped to convert the severe but not unprecedented downturn of 1929–1930 into a depression. Nearly half the banks that existed in 1929 had collapsed or been merged into other banks by the end of 1933.

As noted in Chapter 2, during 1929–1932 the failure of the Fed to bail out commercial banks contributed to the greatness of the Great Depression. By the time that Franklin Delano Roosevelt entered the White House in 1933, thousands of banks had gone under and many more were facing potential runs on their checking and saving deposits. F.D.R. declared a bank holiday; when the banks reopened, he gave the Fed broader power to bail out those that still survived. Soon thereafter, the Glass-Steagall Act established the aforementioned federal deposit insurance, removing the threat to depositors. The banking system was stabilized, but the Fed was still free to make mistakes such as its raising interest rates in 1936–1937 out of fear, of all things, of "inflation." The cost of protection for the commercial banks was regulation.

The debacle of the 1930s led to new financial reforms, some of which altered the Federal Reserve. The Banking Act of 1933, better known as the Glass-Steagall Act, reduced the riskiness of the financial system. In the Act commercial banks were protected from failure. Investment banks and brokerages were not. As noted earlier, the Glass-Steagall Act separated commercial banking from investment banking to prevent commercial banks from being "infected" by the risky activities of investment banks. Commercial banks were protected from panic-induced bank runs by the Federal Deposit Insurance Corporation (FDIC), but accepted tight federal regulation in return. The FDIC guaranteed deposit accounts up to an amount that has changed over the years.

There were changes at the Federal Reserve. The hand of presidential appointees was strengthened and the relative power of the regional banks weakened. Regulation Q, a provision of the Banking Act of 1933, allowed the Federal Reserve to set ceilings on savings account interest rates. The effect was to limit competition for customers' deposits while guaranteeing banks a cheap source of funds. Limits were placed on opening branches and on expanding across state lines, and investment banks were prohibited from taking deposits. In short, commercial banks offered a narrow range of financial products and made their money from the spread between the low interest rate they paid depositors and the higher rate they charged borrowers.

The overall consequence was the safest banking system that the United States has known in its history. As noted in the previous chapter, these safeguards were to be undone over time, mostly at the urging of private bankers.

## BEN BERNANKE AT THE FED

In February 2006 Ben Bernanke replaced Alan Greenspan as head of the Federal Reserve. A year later the Great Money and Banking Panic would begin. It was as if Bernanke had been trained to understand the unfolding debacle. Bernanke built on the pioneering work of monetarists Milton Friedman and Anna Schwartz, the scholars who blamed the Federal Reserve for the disaster of the 1930s. Bernanke elaborated on that thesis, showing how the consequent collapse of the banking system deepened the depression. All this is consistent with our depiction of the Great Depression in Chapter 2.

Bernanke's research on the Great Depression was the lens through which he would later view the Great Panic. Beginning with an article published in 1983 in the *American Economic Review* and in subsequent publications, Bernanke emphasized the role of banking in the economy. The widespread banking panics of the 1930s caused many bankers to shut their doors to would-be borrowers. The bankers, facing the risk of runs by their depositors, wanted to keep their balance sheets as liquid as possible. These actions inhibited consumer spending and capital investment and made the Depression worse. The Federal Reserve failed to reverse these developments and Bernanke was determined to prevent this from happening on his watch.

In his analysis of the Fed's mistakes during the 1930s, Bernanke cited the Fed's misreading of interest rates as a gauge to the availability of credit. Bankers and others rush to the security of the safest securities, especially the debt of the U.S. Treasury, at times of panic and uncertainty. This has the effect of pushing down the interest rate that the Treasury has to pay to borrow money. It is important to compare this safe interest rate with the rates that consumers and businesses have to pay to borrow, if they can borrow at all. The gap between the rates the Treasury pays on super-safe borrowing and the rates that ordinary borrowers pay is known as "the spread." It is a measure of financial distress. Bernanke found that the gap between medium-grade Baa corporate bonds and super-safe U.S. Treasury bonds widened from 2.5 percentage points in 1929 to 1930 to nearly eight percentage points in mid-1932. It was more than double the spread recorded during the deep recession of 1920–1922. Bernanke also noticed that the same spread widened sharply from about 1.6 percentage points in December 2006 to over six percentage points in December 2008.

In the end, Bernanke revolutionized monetary policy by a stunning series of interventions into the financial system. Even his use of conventional monetary policy was radical. Beyond this, Bernanke directed a massive expansion of the Federal Reserve's power over the economy. As explained earlier, some of these monetary policies infringed on the traditional fiscal powers of the executive and congressional branches of government. That is, the Fed exercised the power to spend federal funds. The Bernanke Fed assumed various powers, implied and otherwise, to swap safe government bonds for toxic assets and, more radically, to purchase toxic assets and hold them on its balance sheet. This was an end run around Congress. It is important to understand why, given the size and power of the financial community, these radical measures were necessary.

## THE SPECTER OF DEFLATION

Bernanke recognized deflation as a characteristic of the Great Depression. In this respect the recession that accompanied the Great Panic was different from the other post-WWII recessions. Prices not only moderated but in some instances declined for the first time in 50 or 60 years. *The New York Times* reported in the fall of 2008 how the recurrence of deflation "gives economists chills." Come spring Bernanke explained, "We are currently being very aggressive because we are trying to avoid...deflation."

Deflation can deter consumers from spending on big-ticket items such as a car or a house because they expect their prices to be lower in the future. Producers facing falling prices for their products are likely to postpone investment in new plant and equipment until prospects brighten. These acts of postponing spending slow economic growth and can lead to economic decline. Debt burden increases with the deflation in the value of liabilities. Debt-deflation is characteristic of depressions compared with garden-variety recessions. From October 1929 to March 1933, while debtors frantically reduced the nominal value of their debts by 20 percent, deflation actually increased their remaining debt burden by 40 percent. Deflation creates a problem: the dollars being used to pay off the debt are worth less than when you incurred the debt. Debtors — households, firms, banks, and others — see their borrowing costs rise above and beyond what they originally anticipated. Anyone who owes money has much more difficulty making good on his debt or, alternatively, refinancing it on less onerous terms. Financial panic only adds to the problem.

A litany of problems emerge during deflation. Business investors shun risky assets, seeking the shelter of liquid and safe assets such as cash and government bonds. Households hoard cash; worse, so do banks and they refuse to lend it. The cycle is destructive. As credit contracts, more and more people default, feeding the original cycle of deflation, debt deflation, and further defaults. Only the central bank is in a position to do anything about deflation; it is the only source of reflation. The price indexes used by the Federal Reserve are presented in Figure 10.1.

These figures require some explanation. The overall consumer price index (CPI) is the one familiar to newspaper readers. The U.S. Bureau of Labor Statistics (BLS) compiles the index from the prices of 80,000 items that represent a cross-section of goods and services purchases by urban households.[1] Similar indexes are used abroad. The core CPI is based on the consumption of goods and services except food and energy. This is related to core personal consumption expenditures or expenditures excluding food and energy

---

[1] The businesses chosen in the BLS survey are the types frequented by a sample of 14,500 families. The CPI includes sales taxes so that a value added tax would add (as a one-time adjustment) to the index when collected. The CPI does not include the value of homes nor stocks and bonds. Historical data are available at the BLS website as well as a complete list of items in the index.

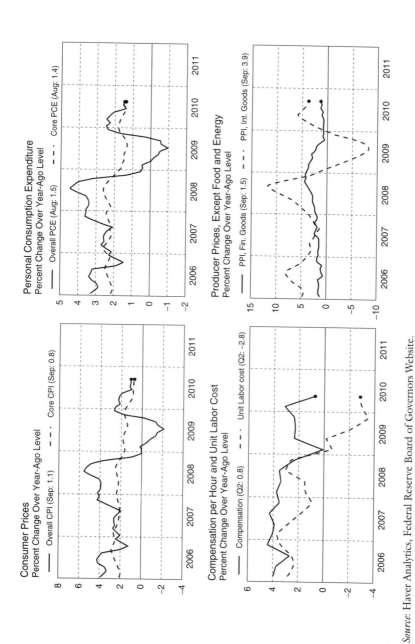

*Source:* Haver Analytics, Federal Reserve Board of Governors Website.

*Note:* Unit Labor Cost and Compensation are from the Nonfarm Business Sector.

**Figure 10.1:** U.S. Price and Cost Indicators.

(Core PCE). Food and energy items are subject to market forces since their raw materials are traded worldwide as commodities. There is a futures market for such things as cattle and oil, where prices fluctuate by the minute. While food supplies are subject to weather variations, oil supplies often come from politically unstable areas.[2] World oil prices did decline sharply in 2008, during the worst recession since the Great Depression. Overall personal consumption expenditures (Overall PCE) are driven by discretionary spending for durables such as autos, which is characteristic of an advanced economy. Following sharp dips in 2006 and 2007, percentage changes in overall consumption expenditures dropped off a cliff after mid-2008 and turned negative in 2009.

The effects of core and overall consumer spending is shadowed by the two consumer price indexes. The Core CPI changes descended gradually, but nonetheless approached a zero inflation rate. The Overall CPI percentage changes, reflecting the effects of discretionary spending, plunged into negative territory in 2009 (deflation), bounced up temporarily, only to fall again in the second and third quarters of 2010. In addition to consumer expenditures, unit labor costs, which are determined by compensation per hour (wages and benefits) and the choice of plant and equipment, contribute to inflation (see Chapter 4). Compensation took a sharp dip in 2005, was slow to grow in 2007, and began to plunge in 2008, only to bounce back some in 2009, level off, and plunge again in early 2010. Compensation rose only 0.8 percent in the second quarter of 2010. Unit labor cost inflation turned negative (deflationary) because employers were conserving labor by using plant and equipment more intensively. Unit labor costs *declined* nearly four percent in 2009 and 2.8 percent in the second quarter of 2010. This action reflects the high levels of unemployment that are continuing.

---

[2] The presence of OPEC can moderate energy price changes on which the USA remains dependent. However, the massive oil reserves of Saudi Arabia dominate price negotiations. OPEC did not have the will or the power to maintain prices during the Great Recession at least from mid-2008 on. If global growth resumes or oil shipments are destroyed, oil prices will rise.

Producer prices reflect the input-output side of the economy (see Chapter 4). Intermediate inputs are used to produce finished producer goods. This gives us two producer price indexes, the PPI for finished producer goods and the PPI for intermediate goods. Producer durable goods include equipment used in final production. Machine tools used in automotive and appliance production are of this type. The intermediate producer goods are the "raw materials" for producer durable goods. The PPI for intermediate goods inflation and deflation mimics the overall personal consumption expenditure index behavior. Though producers of equipment can economize on intermediate inputs, finished goods producers can resist price declines for awhile even during the worst of times. Still, even they caved in and moved to a near-zero inflation rate as manufacturers capital goods nosedived beginning in 2008, continuing in 2009, and laying low into the first three quarters of 2010.

Before the Great Recession, this kind of price deflation had not happened since the 1930s.

## LIQUIDITY TRAPS

The liquidity trap is feared by the monetary authorities even more than deflation, because they can sometimes do something about deflation while being powerless in fighting the liquidity trap with conventional monetary policy. In a financial crisis, cutting interest rates to zero may not be enough to restore confidence and incite banks to lend money to one another. Banks are so mutually distrustful that they will hoard any liquid assets such as cash rather than lend it out. The banks are willing to lend only at an interest rate below zero, an impossible monetary policy target.

Conventional monetary policy consists of open market operations. Open market operations involves the buying and selling of government Treasury bills by, in the United States, the Federal Open Market Committee of the Federal Reserve (FOMC). The FOMC is comprised of the seven members of the Board of Governors of the Fed plus five of the regional bank presidents. Four of the five Federal Reserve Bank presidents serve on a rotating basis, whereas one, the president of the Federal Reserve Bank of New York, is a permanent member of the committee. Bernanke, as chair of the committee, attempts to arrive at a consensus before a vote is taken. When the FOMC buys or sells short-term government securities, it adds or subtracts from the nation's money supply. In doing so, it changes the federal funds rate, the interest rate banks charge each other for overnight loans for funds on deposit at the Federal Reserve. In normal times other interest rates charged by banks and mortgage lenders are set by a fixed markup from the federal funds rate.

When this conventional policy was exercised during the Great Recession, it worked like this. The Fed bought, say, $10 billion of short-term government debt. The Fed writes a check for the Treasuries, creating a deposit of $10 billion, which comprises a $10 billion increase in the money supply. The purpose of increasing the money supply is to lower the target for the federal funds rate. It was eventually lowered to zero. The private commercial banks can use the money from the Fed to make loans at some markup from the federal funds rate. During normal times the increase in bank lending would lead to increases in consumer and producer spending, stimulating the GDP and employment. This takes place, it is emphasized, only during normal times.

This was the first action taken by the central banks during the Great Panic. By late 2008 and early 2009 the Federal Reserve, the Bank of England, the Bank of Japan, the Swiss National Bank, the Bank of Israel, the Bank of Canada, and the European Central Bank had pushed interest rates to near zero. This conventional policy was swift and somewhat coordinated. However, these interest rate cuts did little to stimulate loans, much less consumption, investment, or capital expenditures. Rather than a fixed markup on the central banks' short term interest rates, the private banks increased the spread between their rates and the central bank rates. The private banks rationed credit because of their uncertainty regarding the stability of their deposits and the goodness of their loans. Monetary policy was like pushing on a string and there was no favorable effect on deflation.

There are several ways of measuring the spread between risk-free rates and other interest rates, including the difference between the federal funds rate and the prime loan rate to corporations. A popular measure is the TED spread or the difference between the interest rate on the short-term government debt of the United States and the three-month LIBOR, the interest rate that banks charge one another for three-month loans. During normal times, the TED spread is around 30 basis points, reflecting that the market considers bank-to-bank loans as only slightly riskier than loans to the government.

At the height of the Great Panic, the TED spread was 465 basis points, because the banks no longer trusted one another enough to lend money on a three-month basis, except at very high rates. Risk-averse holders of cash bought the longer-term debt of the U.S. Government. The cost of borrowing for banks was driven up as the cost of borrowing for the U.S. Government went down. It was worse than this. The rates of many other kinds of short-term loans and of variable-rate mortgages are pegged in part to the LIBOR; this meant higher lending rates for private firms and households. It also meant less credit availability.

As noted more than once, the main conventional tool of the Federal Reserve was the use of the federal funds rate. Figure 10.2 shows the results during the Great Recession: this is the effective rate or the rate actually charged banks by each other for the use of funds (bank reserves). From above five percent in 2007, the effective fed funds rate quickly dropped to two percent by mid-2008 and thereafter plunged to near zero. In fighting the Great Recession, the Federal Reserve contributed to the conditions of the liquidity trap. Though Keynes did not name it, the liquidity trap has become Keynesian. The pure trap cannot exist because the money supply cannot be infinite in supply even with a rapidly expanding demand for money. A decline in bank reserves (behind demand deposits) is a necessary but not sufficient condition for a decline in the money supply. Since commercial and industrial loans actually fell during the Great Recession, the money supply remained stagnant and in fact was considered virtually irrelevant by Ben Bernanke and the Board of Governors.

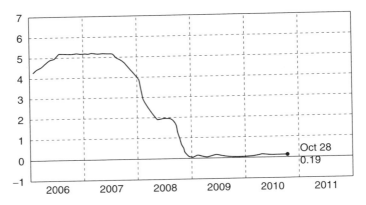

*Source*: Haver Analytics, Federal Reserve Board of Governors Website.

**Figure 10.2:**   Federal Funds Rate (Effective).

The three-month Treasury bill, a short-term interest rate, closely tracks the federal funds rate. In this sense, to the extent the commercial bank interest rates are a markup removed from the Treasury bill rate, the Fed has control over short-term rates. Its control over longer-term interest rates is more problematic. The bond market players perceive more risk in the long-term end of the bond market; moreover, the bondholders are extremely inflation-sensitive and their expectation of inflation (not necessarily based on reality) can drive long-term bond rates upward. This is why quantitative easing was deployed by the Federal Open Market Committee (FOMC). The results can be seen in Figure 10.3. As noted, the three-month Treasury bill rate closely followed the path of the fed funds rate. However, the long-term rate (the ten-year Treasury yield) did not. The long-term rate is based on the biased inflationary expectations of the bondholders. It did slowly come down, thanks in large part to quantitative easing, the purchase of long-term Treasuries by the FOMC. The sharp dip in the long-term yield in late 2008 was due to aggressive quantitative easing.

Moreover new "liquidity" facilities made low-cost loans available to anyone who needed them. Rather than relying on the federal funds rate, the Fed moved directly into the markets. The Fed became the lender of last resort across the entire spectrum of finance.

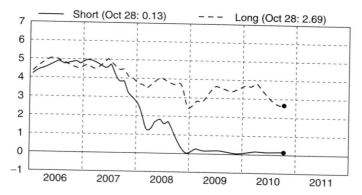

*Source*: Haver Analytics, Federal Reserve Board of Governors Website.

**Figure 10.3:** Short-Term and Long-Term Interest Rates: 3-Month Treasury Bill Rate, 10-Year Treasury Yield.

The first action was to make the use of the discount window at the Fed banks more attractive. The Fed lowered the discount rate to conform with the federal funds rate and by March 2008, banks could borrow for up to 90 days with almost no penalty. Next, as the crisis continued, the Fed set up the Term Auction Facility (TAF) that targeted depository institutions. The TAF gave depository institutions another means of securing ready cash for periods much longer than overnight. Next, as the crisis continued, the Federal Reserve established the Primary Dealer Credit Facility (PDCF), which made overnight loans to "primary dealers," the banks and broker dealers with whom the Fed trades when it conducts open market operations. The Term Securities Lending Facility (TSLF) made loans of medium-term maturity to the same group, in exchange for illiquid securities held by such institutions. For the first time since the Great Depression, the Fed used its emergency powers to lend to *non-depository* institutions, as the new facilities multiplied. There followed the Commercial Paper Funding Facility (CPFF), the Money Market Investor Funding Facility (MMIFF), and the Asset-Backed Commercial Paper Money Market Mutual Fund Liquidity Fund (ABCPMMMFLF), better known as AMLF.

This multitude of new lending facilities operated in different ways and had different objectives. Sometime financial institutions would borrow directly from the Fed. At other times, the financial institutions would swap illiquid assets (asset-backed securities, corporate bonds, commercial paper) for super-safe and liquid government debt. In still other times, the facilities directly or indirectly financed the purchase of illiquid shorter debt. Whatever, the aim was to inject liquidity into markets that showed signs of trouble and stress. In this unprecedented intervention, the Federal Reserve accepted as collateral only "higher-quality debt."

The effects were eventually felt. At the end of 2008, in the aftermath of the Lehman collapse, the Fed and other central banks flooded the financial markets with hundreds of billions of dollars' worth of liquidity, and the spreads between short-term market rates and safe government assets started to decline. In this process, the central banks had gone from simply lender of last resort to lender of first, last, and only resort. The Fed even lent money to corporations via the CPFF. It also provided liquidity support or low-cost lines of credit to a host of institutions considered too big to fail; these included AIG, Fannie Mae and Freddie Mac, and Citigroup. Central bankers in Europe followed the Bernanke example.

The Fed waded into the financial system and began buying long-term government debt — ten-year (see above) and 30-year Treasury bonds. As the bonds were purchased, cash flowed to the banks that sold them. Hopefully, the banks would be tempted to lend the extra cash. The policy was announced in March 2009, and went hand in hand with the massive purchases of other assets. On the same day that it bought $300 billion in long-term Treasury bonds, the Fed also bought a trillion dollars' worth of mortgage-backed securities and $55 billion worth of agency debt. The Fed also announced that it would commit a trillion dollars to the Term Asset-Backed Securities Loan Facility (TADLF), to support the private securitization of credit card debt and auto loans. By broadening the range of assets it purchased, the Fed sought to stimulate the markets for various kinds of long-term debt. Its purchases at Fannie Mae and Freddie Mac gave the agencies breathing room to guarantee more mortgages or bundles of mortgages.

The balance sheet of the Federal Reserve was transformed. In 2007, the Federal Reserve held approximately $900 billion of assets, consisting mostly of U.S. Government debt. By the summer of 2009, the balance sheet had ballooned to about $2.3 trillion, with the overwhelming majority of assets being those esoteric items acquired during the crisis. The Fannie Mae and Freddie Mac debt was fairly safe, but those assets derived from home mortgages, credit card debt, and auto loans were suspect. Most suspect of all were the collateralized debt obligations (CDOs) and other potentially toxic assets acquired during the bailout of Bear Stearns and AIG.

At the end of November 2009 the overnight fed funds rate target was 0.0 percent to 0.25 percent, where it still stood in early November 2010 (see the effective rates above). The prime rate charged the best business borrowers was marked up to 3.25 percent. Other borrowers, including some home buyers and many credit card holders, had interest rates marked up from the prime rate. Meanwhile, Bernanke and other Fed officials were saying that few asset classes were overvalued. Besides, if they were to raise interest rates to prevent a future bubble, this could kill or slow any economic recovery. And, besides that, Bernanke was arguing that it was better to strengthen financial institutions to weather the inevitable. Still, the Fed was reluctant to commit to a policy of leaning against future bubbles.

The at-best mixed outcome for lending can be seen in Figure 10.4. After taking a dip in the third quarter of 2006, total net borrowing by nonfinancial corporations rallyed, only to begin a descent in the fourth quarter of 2007, going into negative territory in the third and fourth quarters of 2009. What happened to net loans and mortgages was more dramatic. They afflicted the private banks as well and Fannie Mae and Freddie Mac. After a sharp decline in the third quarter of 2006, there too was a rally, only to be followed by negative numbers in the fourth quarter of 2008, all of 2009, and the first quarter of 2010. The worst was −$374 billion in the third quarter of 2009. Loans and mortgages, which comprised a large part of a credit crunch, still were −$143 billion in the first quarter of 2010. Net borrowing of commercial paper, the lifeblood of day-to-day activity of

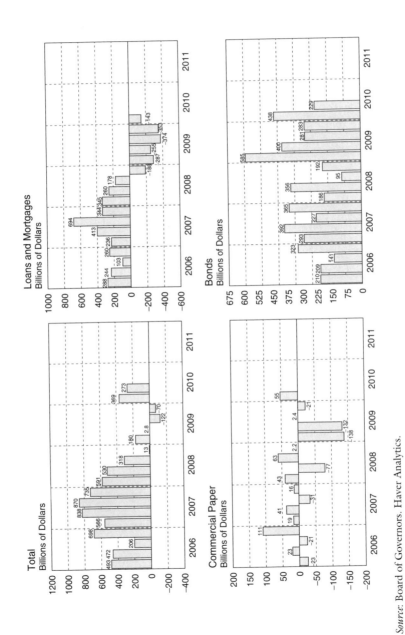

*Source:* Board of Governors. Haver Analytics.

*Note:* Equity issues are not included.

**Figure 10.4:** Net Borrowing by U.S. Nonfinancial Corporations.

nonfinancial corporations, dried up during the Great Recession. Commercial paper borrowings were either negative or close to it during 12 quarters beginning in 2006 and continuing though the fourth quarter of 2009. There was a recovery to $55 billion in the first quarter of 2010. Throughout the Great Recession, the most consistent borrowing took place in the bond market where historically low interest rates prevailed. In contrast, very little funding from equity finance or the stock markets took place. The bondholding class was not much disturbed.

Little noticed was the aforementioned fact that some of the monetary policies went beyond managing the money supply to fiscal policy. The Fed was subsidizing the operations of the financial system, potentially incurring losses that could ultimately fall on the shoulders of the Treasury. The policies were affecting the government's power to tax and spend, normally the prerogative of the legislative branch. For the first time since the Great Depression, the Fed was buying long-term bonds or engaging in quantitative easing, an idea borrowed from Japan, when it was faced with a similar problem (and is again). When the time comes to sell it, the Fed may even lose money on its long-term bonds, potentially requiring a transfer of funds from the Treasury. This would reverse the historical flow of surpluses from the Fed to the Treasury. A fundamental question lingers: Will overdependence on the Federal Reserve continue?

## THE GLOBAL DIMENSION

The Bank of England in Great Britain was caught in a liquidity trap as well. Moreover, also following the Fed's lead, it had cut its benchmark rates close to zero, the lowest since its founding in 1694. It also created liquidity facilities similar to those devised by the Fed. As in the USA, these actions failed to halt debt deflation. In March 2009 it bought some 150 billion pounds worth of government debt and corporate bonds. Later, the European Central Bank bought €60 billion of "covered bonds," a form of mortgage debt. All these were unprecedented actions.

During the crisis the emerging countries looked to the International Monetary Fund (IMF) for assistance. The IMF provided support in two forms. It extended its traditional lifeline, a Stand-By Arrangement (SBA), to 14 countries, with Hungary, Ukraine, and Pakistan among the biggest recipients. This support was contingent on the adoption of economic reforms. The IMF extended Flexible Credit Lines (FCLs) to Mexico, Poland, and Colombia. Unlike the SBAs, the FCLs served as precautionary lines of credit. In these unconventional lines, pledges were made but money was not immediately disbursed. The inscrutable Chinese stood alone, and above the fray.

By the summer of 2009, the IMF had authorized over US$50 billion in SBAs and US$78 billion in FCLs. These actions were supplemented by the Federal Reserve. While the Federal Reserve limits its loans directly to private financial institutions outside the United States, it can lend unlimited dollars to foreign central banks, who can in turn lend them to the private foreign institutions on an as needed basis. The Fed receives an equivalent sum of whatever currency is involved. Great quantities of dollars went from the Federal Reserve to the European Central Bank, the Swiss National Bank, and the Bank of England, as well as to the central banks of Sweden, Denmark, and Norway. These swap lines of credit totaled half a trillion dollars by late 2008; they did not start to decline until the spring of 2009. All in all, the global economy still declined 0.6 percent in 2009. Obviously, some countries such as Brazil and Argentina escaped the disaster, at least so far.

## CONCLUSIONS

In 2008–2009 the Fed faced the same conditions that had prevailed during the Great Depression — deflation and a liquidity trap. Great Britain and many European countries were enduring the same conditions. In order to avoid a second Great Depression, an innovative monetary policy was required. The actions taken included both conventional and unconventional monetary policy. Looked at broadly, these actions constituted a massive and unprecedented intervention in financial systems.

Four kinds of tools were deployed by Bernanke and to a lesser extent, some other central bankers. The traditional policy was the provision of short-term liquidity as lender of last resort to commercial banks. Beyond this, non-depository institutions such as brokerages and investment banks, and even foreign central banks were lent dollars by the Fed. Still more unconventional was the creation of special facilities that purchased or financed the purchase of specific kinds of short-term debt such as commercial paper. Finally, the Fed began to play a role as investor of last resort. It intervened in markets for long-term debt such as asset-backed securities and long-term government debt. By subsidizing financial institutions of all stripes, the Fed took on a fiscal policy role, one normally reserved for the legislative authorities and the President of the United States. The Federal Reserve began to operate as a fourth branch of government.

The Great Panic was bound to have adverse effects on output and employment in the real economy. Next, we return to the basics industry. There we find unusual challenges facing conventional Keynesian fiscal policy.

# 11

# THE DEEP DECLINE IN OUTPUT AND EMPLOYMENT

## THE ECONOMIC CRISIS OF SUMMER 2008

The turmoil in housing and banking had to affect the real economy and the stock market. On August 29, 2008 stocks fell as the U.S. Government said personal incomes fell in July by the largest amount in nearly three years, while consumer spending slowed. The Dow Jones industrial index was down more than 170 points, while a disappointing profits report from computer maker Dell Inc. weighed on the technology-heavy Nasdaq composite index. This downbeat news about consumers came after several days of sizable gains in stocks and on the final session before the long Labor Day weekend. Personal incomes had fallen by 0.7 percent in July, well beyond the drop of 0.1 percent that analysts had predicted. Consumer spending rose a modest 0.2 percent, well below the 0.6-percent increase seen in June, while real spending fell by 0.4 percent in July. This was quickly followed by unexpected declines in August.

Overseas markets dropped sharply the day after the Labor Day weekend. This was quickly followed on September 4th by a plunging Dow Jones, down more than 340 points after retailers and the government added to the mountain of bad economic news and devastated hopes of a year-end recovery. Broader indexes also tumbled. The Standard & Poor's 500 Index fell 2.99 percent, and the Nasdaq composite index dropped 74.69 or 3.20 percent, to 2,259.04. These declines came on the heels of sharp sell-offs in Asia and the Middle East, and was followed on September 5, 2008 by still more declines in Asian and Japanese markets.

As the USA economy continued to falter, concern was building about a second wave of mortgage defaults flooding the market through 2010. In August the unemployment rate reached 6.1 percent, the highest in five years. Unemployment and/or a drop in income comprise the main reason for falling behind on mortgages and loss of homes. Meanwhile, the 11th bank failure of the year occurred.

The source of trouble in the mortgage market had shifted from subprime loans made to borrowers with bad credit to homeowners who had solid credit but took out exotic loans with ballooning monthly payments. Early in September it was announced that four million American homeowners with a mortgage, a record nine percent, were either behind on their payments or were in foreclosure at the end of June. As the overall economy declined and with home prices continuing to fall, there was a second wave of mortgage defaults flooding the market through 2010.

It was on September 7, 2008 that the Bush administration took over the troubled mortgage giants, Fannie Mae and Freddie Mac. It was an attempt to stabilize the housing market turmoil that continues to threaten financial markets, the overall economy, and even the global economy. President Bush said that the historic takeover was required to keep mortgage financiers from failing, a risk he called "unacceptable" for an economy battered by housing and credit crises. This was another step in the direction of a new New Deal.

As noted earlier, Fannie Mae and Freddie Mac were placed into a government conservatorship to be run by the Federal Housing Finance Agency, a new creature of Congress. The Treasury Department said it immediately would be issued $100 billion in senior preferred stock, paying ten percent interest, from each company. Eventually the Treasury could be required to put up as much as $100 billion for each company if funds were needed to keep the companies afloat as losses mount. Out of necessity, the government was now in the housing mortgage business.

The Dow industrials enjoyed a 350 point jump the next day, while other indexes were up modestly. The tech-heavy Nasdaq lagged, as usual.

# THE CRISIS DEEPENS

Economic problems spread from the housing and banking sectors to industry even as the credit crisis deepened. The Institute for Supply Management announced that its reading for the nation's manufacturers fell to 49.9 in August from 50 in July. A reading below 50 signals contraction. This was only the beginning of a long slide. General Motors reported a $15.5 billion second-quarter loss, the third-worst quarterly performance in its nearly 100-year history. Through the first half of the year, it used up more than $7 billion in cash, including $3.6 billion from April through June. Thus began a long sales slump in the auto industry. Because of a lack of financing, auto sales continued to slump in September. Ford sales were down 34 percent from the year before, followed by Chrysler down 33 percent and GM down 16 percent. GM sales were buoyed temporarily by its pricing vehicles at employee rates. Auto sales were to drop by three million for the year 2008.

Meanwhile, troubles in the financial sector worsened. Lehman Brothers, in a desperate bid to survive, announced plans to sell a majority stake in its prized investment management business and said a sale of the entire company was possible. Lehman, battling the nation's worst financial crisis since the Great Depression, also said it would spin off a troubled real estate unit and slash its dividend. A failed plan to rescue Lehman Brothers was followed by more seismic shocks from Wall Street, including a government-brokered takeover of Merrill Lynch by the Bank of America. A global consortium of banks, working with government officials in New York, announced a $70 billion pool of funds to lend to troubled financial companies. The aim was to prevent a worldwide panic on stock and other financial exchanges. Seven banks and three investment companies — Bank of America, Barclays, Citibank, Credit Suisse, Deutsche Bank, UBS, JPMorgan Chase, Merrill Lynch, Morgan Stanley, and Goldman Sachs — each agreed to provide $7 billion to help enhance liquidity and mitigate the unprecedented volatility and other challenges affecting global equity and debt markets. In the midst of this wheeling and dealing, Bank of America acquired Merrill Lynch for $29 a share.

Bank of America has the most deposits of any U.S. Bank, while Merrill Lynch is the world's largest brokerage. The wall between commercial banks and security sellers came tumbling down. Earlier Washington Mutual, the nation's largest thrift, was seized by the Federal Deposit Insurance Corp. Soon thereafter, JPMorgan Chase bought WaMu for $1.9 billion, and said it planned to write down WaMu's loan portfolio by approximately $31 billion. This was the second time in six months that JPMorgan Chase had taken over a major financial institution crippled by bad bets in the mortgage market.

The Bush administration fashioned the aforementioned $700 billion TARP-expansion proposal to buy a mountain of bad mortgage debt in an effort to unfreeze the nation's credit markets. Congressional leaders endorsed the plan's main thrust, saying passage might occur in a matter of days. This was the "mother of all bailouts" that would cost $1 trillion when the cost of the government takeovers of Fannie, Freddie and AIG are included.

The stunning makeover of Wall Street sent stocks falling precipitously on September 16. The shakeup of the financial industry took out two storied names from the stock lists: Lehman Brothers and Merrill Lynch. The Dow fell 504. Worse was to come. On September 29 the Dow Jones industrial average lost 777 points. The Dow Jones Wilshire 5000 Composite Index recorded a paper loss of $1 trillion across the market for the day, a first. A House vote had rejected the Bush administration's $700 billion plan to buy up bad debt and shore up the financial industry, but it was a vote soon to be reversed during the calamity. Faced with the biggest financial debacle since the Great Depression, Ben Bernanke repeated a warning of dire economic consequences if the bailout was not enacted and if credit woes persist. Neither businesses nor consumers would be able to borrow money.

The Fed had been moving on several new fronts. On September 21 the Federal Reserve granted a request by the country's last two major investment banks, Goldman Sachs and Morgan Stanley, to change their status to bank holding companies. The change in status allows them to create commercial banks that will be able to take deposits, bolstering the resources of both institutions. As commercial banks, Goldman Sachs and Morgan Stanley will have permanent access to emergency loans from the Fed, the same privilege that other commercial banks enjoy. Meanwhile, the central bank provided increased funding support to the two institutions during the transition period.

Soon came the realization that the financial and economic crisis was global. In a rare coordinated move, the Federal Reserve and other major central banks from around the world slashed interest rates on October 8, 2008 to prevent a global economic meltdown. The Fed reduced its fed funds rate from two percent to 1.5 percent. In Europe, which also has been hard hit by the financial crisis, the Bank of England cut its bank rate by half a point to 4.5 percent and the European Central Bank sliced its rate by half a point to 3.75 percent. The central banks of China, Canada, Sweden and Switzerland also cut rates. The Bank of Japan said it strongly supported the actions.

The erosion of confidence had spread to consumers in the USA. Consumer spending, which is 70 percent of GDP, dropped a sharp 0.3 percent in September. A survey by the University of Michigan showed consumer confidence in October fell to 57.6, the biggest one-month drop in the survey's history (dating to 1978). The cuts in spending for durable goods such as automobiles were especially sharp. Soon the nation's personal saving rate would reach historic highs as consumers further retrenched. The damage to consumer confidence would prove to be long-lasting. This condition is heightened by unemployment. The number of out-of-work Americans continuing to draw unemployment benefits surged to a 25-year high in late October. An extension of unemployment benefits was included in the Congressional stimulus package. Unemployment benefits had been established during the Great Depression.

It was increasingly clear that the American automobile industry was being trampled by the economic downturn and the crisis in the financial markets. Despite a request by the automakers for an additional $50 billion in loans from Congress to help them survive tough economic conditions and pay for health care obligations for retirees, the Bush administration refused to broaden the $700 billion financial bailout to include producers of products other than financial instruments. Bush was favoring the nonbasic financial sector at a risk to the basic manufacturing sector. Any money would be in addition to $25 billion in loans that Congress passed in September to help retool auto plants to build more fuel-efficient vehicles. The heart of the USA manufacturing sector and the jobs of tens of thousands of American workers were at risk. President-elect Barack Obama said his transition team would explore policy options to help the auto industry. In a sign of the times, General Motors ended an endorsement deal with Tiger Woods, who had attracted younger buyers to the Buick brand.

A $14 billion rescue package for the nation's imperiled auto industry sped to approval in the Democrat-dominated U.S. House on December 10. The legislation would provide money within days to cash-starved General Motors and Chrysler. Ford said it had enough money to stay afloat, but would also be eligible for federal aid. On January 2, 2009 the U.S. Treasury supplied Chrysler with a $4 billion loan that was necessary to keep it operating. This was an initial loan for a company that generally pays its suppliers $7 billion every 45 days. This followed a similar transfer of $4 billion from Treasury to General Motors, the first tranche of a $9.4 billion loan.

The National Bureau of Economic Research, the caller of such things, had concluded on December 1, 2008 that the country had been suffering through a recession since December 2007. Everyone knew this except perhaps Wall Street where the news sent the Dow industrials down 680 points the next day. The Institute for Supply Management reported that the index of manufacturing sank to 36.2 in November, a 26-year low. The unemployment rate in October zoomed to 6.5 percent, a 14-year high. The news was worse in Japan. Output at that nation's manufacturers tumbled 8.1 percent in November, the largest drop since Tokyo began measuring such data in 1953. Japan's automakers and others slashed production to cope with slowing global demand (including falling imports from the USA and Europe). The jobless rate jumped and household spending fell. The contraction in China's steel production, a global bellwether for heavy industry, deepened in November, driving the nation's factory output to its worst performance on record.

Meanwhile, in the USA, median household income, adjusted for inflation, fell 3.6 percent during 2008 to $50,303, the steepest year-over-year drop in 40 years. The poverty rate, at 13.2 percent, was the highest since 1997. About 700,000 more people did not have health insurance in 2008 than the year before.

The income distribution barely changed. The best-off five percent of households got 21.5 percent of all income, up from 21.2 percent in 2007. Half of all income went to the top fifth of American households. According to the U.S. Census, about 54 million people were living under 125 percent of the poverty line, about three million more than in 2007. The number of "deep poor" — people whose earnings put them at less than half the poverty line — increased by 1.5 million to 17 million people.

One would have to go back to 1933 to find a year with a more troubled economy. The housing and credit crisis had spread to the industrial economy. The automobile industry remains the core of the manufacturing sector. The same could be said for Europe and Japan, which were experiencing similar conditions.

On December 16, 2008, the Federal Reserve used its last measure of conventional monetary policy. It was entering a new era, lowering its benchmark interest rate virtually to zero and declaring that it will now fight the recession by pumping out vast amounts of money to businesses and consumers through an expanding array of new lending programs. The Federal Open Market Committee (FOMC) added: "The committee anticipates that weak economic conditions are likely to warrant exceptionally low levels of the federal funds rate for some time." The private banks were continuing to hoard cash instead of lending. Wall Street and the Dow industrials roared their approval of the Fed's actions.

The Troubled Assets Relief Program (TARP), the $700 billion bailout, originally had three purposes. First the financial crisis began with falling home prices and fears of rampant mortgage defaults — fears that came true. Those fears depressed the value of securities based on mortgages, making them "troubled." Foreclosures are painful and costly events that destroy real estate values and force fire sales of homes — which depress prices further. It was (and is) hard to see a way out of this mess without seriously reducing foreclosures. Congress had directed the Treasury secretary to use TARP funds to get mortgages refinanced. But Secretary John Paulson did not.

Second came the mortgage-related securities. There were several rationales for buying troubled mortgage-backed securities. For one thing, panic had virtually shut down the markets for these securities — markets that must be restarted to restore the system of mortgage finance. For another, one source of that panic was that nobody knew what the securities were worth, the Black-Scholes formula notwithstanding. Finally, many mortgages are buried in complex securities. Buying the securities would allow the government to refinance the underlying mortgages. Buying mortgage-backed securities helps the government acquire mortgages to refinance: refinancing mortgagers to avert foreclosures enhances the values of these securities, bolstering the finances of banks.

Third came the recapitalizing of banks. The Congress gave the Secretary catch-all authority to buy "any other financial instrument," which offered the flexibility to respond to unforeseen circumstances, such as an auto bailout, for example. But the TARP funds were used exclusively for recapitalizing banks and other financial institutions. Treasury bought preferred stock with no control rights. And there were no public-purpose quid pro quos, such as a minimal lending requirement. So banks just sat on the capital, or used it to make acquisitions (which does not create any new capital). Paulson bent over backward to make the terms attractive to banks. He contended that wide participation was essential and even forced money on several bankers who did not want it.

This was the way that the first $350 billion was spent. The remaining $350 billion was left to the discretion of the Obama administration.

Under the direction of Ben Bernanke, the Federal Reserve Bank of New York began to do what TARP had failed to do. On January 5, 2009 the New York Fed began buying mortgage-backed securities in an effort to bolster the battered housing market. The program allows the Fed to spend $500 billion to buy mortgage-backed securities guaranteed by mortgage giants Fannie Mae and Freddie Mac and an additional $100 billion to directly purchase mortgages held by Fannie, Freddie and the Federal Home Loan Banks.

Problems were mounting on the employment front. A staggering 2.6 million jobs disappeared in 2008, the most since World War II, and the pain was only getting worse with 11 million people out of work and searching. The unemployment rate hit a 26-year high of 7.2 percent in December and was headed even higher. Employers also were cutting workers' hours and forcing some to go part-time. Boeing Co., the world's second-largest airplane maker, announced plans to cut 4,500 workers from its payroll. The Dow Jones industrial average slumped in sympathetic reaction. On January 14 telecommunications equipment maker Nortel Networks Corp. filed for bankruptcy protection, becoming the first major technology company to take that step in this global downturn. The Dow quickly gave up 248 points the next day, the stock market keeping its promise of volatility.

## THE KEYNESIAN FISCAL STIMULUS

With deflation and a liquidity trap hampering conventional monetary policy, the conditions cried out for some kind of Keynesian fiscal stimulus. Indeed, President-elect Barack Obama was hoping that a massive stimulus package would jolt the economy back to life. House leaders on January 15 proposed $825 billion of federal spending and tax cuts. This constituted the first serious pure fiscal stimulus of the Great Recession. A day later the Bush administration agreed to provide Bank of America with an additional $20 billion in support from the TARP funds. The administration, the Federal Reserve and the Federal Deposit Insurance Corp. also agreed to participate in a program to provide guarantees against losses on approximately $118 billion in various types of loans and securities backed by residential and commercial real estate loans. The bulk of these holdings were assumed by Bank of America when it acquired Merrill Lynch & Co. in the deal that closed earlier in the year.

The second $350 billion of TARP funds were released by Congress only following assurances that a healthy portion of it would be spent to try to reduce foreclosures, rather than directly aid banks. Lawmakers prepared to spend up to $100 billion on a sweeping foreclosure prevention plan pushed by President-elect Barack Obama. Four states — California, Florida, Nevada and Arizona — were generating about half of all foreclosures filings nationwide. But until the foreclosure disaster is solved, unemployment will continue to remain high and will affect communities that have no foreclosures.

On January 21 President Barack Obama took the oath of office and appealed for "hope over fear." The ascendance of the first black man to the presidency of the United States was heralded as marking a new era of tolerance and possibility. He was welcomed into a world of warfare, deep recession and fear. Boeing, Pfizer, Home Depot and other U.S. corporate titans announced tens of thousands of job cuts during the same week. The mass layoffs were continuing.

The recession was picking up speed. Chrysler's U.S. vehicle sales plunged 55 percent in January 2009, while General Motors' tumbled 49 percent and Ford's dropped 40 percent, starting 2009 at an abysmal pace for the whole auto industry as lower sales to fleet buyers such as rental car companies weighed down the results. The foreign producers did little better with Toyota's sales diving 32 percent for the month, Nissan's dropping 30 percent and Honda's falling 28 percent, putting the overall industry on track for its fourth straight month in which U.S. sales plunged 30 percent or more. Tens of thousands of new layoffs were announced by companies including Ford Motor Co., Eastman Kodak Co., Black & Decker Corp., Boeing Co., Pfizer Inc., Caterpillar Inc., Home Depot Inc. and Target Corp. Everybody was trying to figure out how to survive.

In a major victory for President Barack Obama, Democrats muscled a huge, $787 billion stimulus bill through Congress one day before Valentines's day in hopes of combating the worst economic crisis since the Great Depression. Republican opposition was nearly unanimous. The bill included tax relief for 95 percent of all Americans, much of the relief in the form of a break of $400 for individuals and $800 for couples.[1] It was one of the biggest packages for economic

---

[1] This was perhaps the most invisible tax cut in history. It was immediately offset by a decline in employment and incomes as well as by massive increases in local and state taxes, which we will deal with in more detail in Chapter 14.

recovery in the nation's history. Soon thereafter President Obama threw a $75 billion lifeline to millions of Americans on the brink of foreclosure. Furthermore, the government pledged support to mortgage giants Fannie Mae and Freddie Mac, doubled the promised amount to $400 billion, as part of an effort to encourage them to refinance loans that are "under water" — those in which homes' market values have sunk below the amount the owners still owe. The administration was loosening refinancing restrictions for many borrowers and providing incentives for lenders in hopes that the two sides would work together to modify loans. But no one was (or is) required to participate. Wall Street was unimpressed as the Dow closed at a five-year low on February 19, this despite commercial banks and investment firms borrowing more and more from the Federal Reserve's emergency lending program. The nation's banks had lost $26.2 billion in the final quarter of 2008, the first quarterly deficit in 18 years, as the housing and credit crises escalated.

## THE CRISIS IN THE AUTOMOTIVE INDUSTRY AND OBAMA'S RESPONSE

Meanwhile, the American auto industry was on life support. In late March 2009. President Obama delivered an ultimatum to General Motors and Chrysler, telling them to adopt radical changes in short order or face bankruptcy — a move that came after a series of somber discussions in which he concluded that a controlled bankruptcy might be the best way to reorganize the two ailing auto giants.

In the end, the president threw the companies a short lifeline. He gave GM 60 days and Chrysler one month to avert bankruptcy and restructure on their own. Clearly Chrysler was not viable as a stand-alone company. It was given until April 30 to complete a merger with Fiat or face a cutoff of taxpayer help. If the merger is successful, the administration will consider giving Chrysler $6 billion in additional taxpayer aid. In essentially taking command of General Motors and telling Chrysler to merge with a foreign competitor or cease to exist, Mr. Obama was saying that economic conditions were sufficiently dire to justify a new level of government involvement in the management of corporate America. As to GM, the company's lender of last resort, the government, will have the final say on every significant decision until the company is turned back out into the marketplace.

Finally, the Obama administration offered a bailout for the owners of gas-guzzling, rust-bucket, heap-of-junk, rattletrap pieces of clunkers. This was part of the plan to save General Motors and Chrysler from collapse. Those trading in a clunker would be required to buy a new fuel-efficient car. Similar incentive programs overseas have lifted automobile sales despite the awful global economy. In Germany, an offer of about US$3,290 for trade-ins helped to increase February car sales there by 21.5 percent from a year earlier. The final U.S. measure would offer up to $4,500 for the trade-in of gas guzzlers up to seven years old, $3,000 for cars that are eight to ten years old and $2,500 for cars older than that. The plan is not limited to cars assembled in North America. In California, a statewide program has been in effect for about a decade, and it was expanded. Drivers whose vehicle fails a smog check are entitled to have their car scrapped and paid $1,000 in return. The payment is increased to $1,500 for low-income drivers. The state prepared a new version of the program with the goal of scraping an additional 60,000 vehicles a year.

President Obama forced Chrysler into federal bankruptcy protection the last day of April so it could pursue a life-saving alliance with the Italian automaker Fiat, in yet another extraordinary intervention into private industry by the federal government. The plan would allow the United Automobile Workers, through their retirement plan, to take control of Chrysler, with Fiat and the United States as junior partners. The government would lend about $8 billion more to the company, on top of the $4 billion its already provided. It was a stark moment, and one unseen in modern times, as the fledgling president deepened his involvement in a struggling but iconic American company. A "pillar" of the industrial economy, Chrysler had invented the minivan and owns the jeep brand.

By mid-May the auto companies were struggling to lower costs. GM had targeted 1,100 dealerships to be closed for "underperforming." The cuts are part of a larger GM plan to drop 2,600 of its 6,200 dealerships as the automaker tries to restructure to become profitable again. The moves will cause the loss of thousands of jobs and untold dollars in tax revenue. In addition to the dealership cuts, GM is providing updates to about 470 Saturn, Hummer and Saab dealerships on the status of those brands, which it plans to sell. Chrysler is looking to break 789 dealership agreements.

The picture of the automotive industry is clouded by its further integration into the global economy. Moreover, imports and exports do not necessarily capture the complexity. In order to avoid expected higher U.S. tariffs, manufacturers in Japan, Germany, the U.K., and South Korea located production plants in the United States. GM has plants abroad, but recently the Chinese has begun buying shares of GM stock. This may mean that GM will be producing some of its cars in China or vice versa.

Meanwhile, problems persisted in the banking industry. In early May regulators completed an examination of the U.S.'s 19 largest financial institutions in a "stress test." The Federal Reserve directed at least seven of the nation's biggest banks to bolster their capital levels by $57 billion. Regulators told Bank of America it must take steps to address a roughly $34 billion capital shortfall, the biggest gap among its peers. Citigroup needs to find $5 billion; Wells Fargo & Co., $15 billion; Morgan Stanley, $1.5 billion; and GMAC, $11.5 billion. Regions Financial Corp. and State Street Corp. of Boston also are in need of more capital. Many should be able to add to their capital without tapping TARP. These banks are too large to allow failure. In an era of low interest rates the banking industry will be challenged to make a lot of money, and that is a dilemma for keeping banks solvent and getting them lending. On average about two banks a week were going bankrupt. This is a trend that will continue for small banks.

On the regulator front, the battle lines are being drawn in the US$684 trillion derivatives market, as Wall Street tries to pre-empt new laws that could drain a big source of banks' profits. Earlier in May, the U.S. proposed giving the Securities and Exchange Commission and the Commodity Futures Trading Commission authority to mandate centralized clearing of certain derivatives, impose new trade-reporting requirements, and force trading of "standardized" contracts onto exchanges or electronic platforms that will make prices more transparent. Wall Street banks with large derivative-trading businesses have been outwardly supportive of greater regulatory oversight but behind the scenes, there has been hand-wringing over the details of certain proposals and the industry's role in shaping new rules.

The industry is detailing plans to expand central clearing of credit-default swaps to investment funds and other market participants. It also will propose that customized credit derivatives like those that nearly brought down American International Group (AIG) be reported to a trade-information warehouse run by Depository Trust & Clearing Corp (DTCC). Meanwhile DTCC moved to have its warehouse overseen by the Federal Reserve as it seeks to align itself with regulators' goals. The days of conducting standardized derivative trades over the phone may well be numbered. For credit-default swaps, information about intraday trades and prices has long been controlled by a handful of larger banks that handle most trades and earn bigger profits from every transaction they facilitate if prices are not easily accessible.

General Motors was in bankruptcy court at the end of May. It plans to push through restructuring that will cost taxpayers billions of dollars more than previously envisioned, turning what once was one of the most profitable companies in the world into a government ward. As part of the revised plan, the U.S. would provide GM with at least $30 billion in financing to carry it through and out of bankruptcy, on top of the $20 billion in loans the government already has given the company. It also agreed to turn the loans into a 72.5 percent ownership stake in GM — a bet that could cost taxpayers dearly if the automaker fails to recover. The filing set in train an unprecedented experiment in U.S. industrial policy in which the government, from the White House to Congress, will seek to remake an icon of American business while not appearing to bore too deeply into its day-to-day operations. Amid a nearly 40 percent drop in new-car sales since January, no revival is likely without a substantial return of buyers.

After a 42-day stay in bankruptcy court cleansed the company of much of its debt and labor costs, Chrysler was reborn June 10 under a new Italian parent. But it cannot shake the shadows of its past: It is not selling enough cars, its fleet is tilted to trucks and SUVs, and help is more than a year away. Cars designed by its new owner, Italy's Fiat, will not make it to the U.S. until late 2010. And even then there are no guarantees American drivers will want the tiny cars Fiat specializes in. During Fiat's last run at the U.S. market, in the 1970s and '80s, reliability problems led people to suggest the name stood for "fix it again, Tony."

With companies in no mood to hire, the unemployment rate jumped to 9.4 percent in May 2009 and to 9.5 percent in June, again the highest in more than a quarter century. If laid-off workers who have given up looking for new jobs or have settled for part-time work are included, the unemployment rate would have been 16.4 percent in May, the highest on records dating to 1994. As the recession, which is now the longest since World War II, bites into sales and profits, companies have turned to layoffs and other cost-cutting measures to survive the fallout. Those include holding down workers' hours and freezing or cutting pay. Factories and construction accounted for most of the losses in jobs. The employed worked fewer hours in May than at any time since the Bureau of Labor Statistics began counting in 1964. Part-time work is at a record high. Businesses cut total wages at a 6.2 percent annual rate in the first quarter. Off-setting some of the decline, federal, state and local governments increased spending on wages by 6.1 percent. Education, health care, leisure and hospitality were among the industries adding jobs in May. It is very difficult to be bullish on consumer spending when unemployment rates are so high.

## THE HOUSING AND BANKING CRISES: THE AFTERMATH

Having ignited the housing bubble in the first place, the Federal Reserve was not conventionally equipped to clean up in the aftermath. In mid-2008, the Fed tried to encourage lending by once again pushing interest rates down and the money supply up. But the banks — their capital depleted by the fall in value of their mortgage-related assets — had hoarded most of the cash they had received as a result of being able to borrow cheaply, rather than risk lending into a deep recession. Their hoarding, like that of consumers, is entirely rational, but it inhibits investment as well as consumption. Had Americans' savings not become concentrated in houses and common stocks, the banking meltdown would have had less effect on the general economy. When these assets — their prices having been artificially inflated by low interest rares — fell in value, credit tightened and people felt (and were) poorer. So people reduced their spending and allocated more of their income to precautionary savings, including cash, government securities and money-market accounts. No matter how much the money supply increased, the demand for it was insatiable. The money market was, as noted in Chapter 10, in a Keynesian liquidity trap! While conventional monetary policy, as noted, was initially ineffective, an easy money policy was essential in setting the stage for a rebound. Besides, more measures directed at housing were to be taken.

On June 5 regulators shut down Bank of Lincolnwood, a small bank in Illinois, marking the 37th failure in 2008 of a federally insured bank. More were expected to succumb amid the pressures of the weak economy and mounting loan defaults. Thus the banking crisis continued. Also in June homeowners who had applied for mortgage modifications found that banks typically were taking 45 to 60 days to respond to inquiries. Banks were dealing with even more demand for mortgages, including refinanced mortgages, than during the peak of the housing bubble in 2006, and the backlog was getting worse as more homeowners lost their jobs. Mortgage delinquencies had been growing in areas where unemployment had been rising fast, and even homeowners who successfully got modified mortgages could face trouble later if their income or home values fall. After all, the owner must have sufficient income to support the new mortgage debt.

Refinancing on terms favoring the homeowner does not favor the banker. And this problem is amplified by refinancing at historically low interest rates. Moreover, the bankers are being asked to do this during economic conditions not seen since the Great Depression. Bankers are not inclined to take such grave risks. The Obama administration is relying on the banking system that got us into the housing mess to get us out, and on terms not favorable to the banks. The administration was looking to foreign buyers of homes and condos — especially Canadians and Europeans — as a way out of the malaise.

Even fiscal policy was faced with rigid resistance. The biggest chunk of the income gain in May, 2009 came from one-time social security benefit payments of $13 billion. Millions of other workers benefited from the tax-credit part of the $787 billion stimulus plan. As noted, that program put $400 in the pockets of individuals and up to $800 for married couples. Workers began receiving that benefit in April in the form of less money withheld from pay, averaging about $10 per weekly paycheck. These benefits pushed incomes up 1.4 percent in May, but consumer spending rose only 0.3 percent. What happened? Households raised their savings rate to the highest level in more than 15 years in May. They chose to bolster nest eggs rather than to spend more. Like the bankers, households were avoiding risk. In June the Consumer Confidence Index dropped to 49.3, down from its revised May level of 54.8.

The global nature of the crisis was highlighted in early July at the meeting of the G-8 countries (USA, Japan, Germany, France, Britain, Italy, Canada and Russia). These countries pledged to coordinate efforts aimed at repairing the financial system, helping banks to rid their balance sheets of bad assets, while making sure that global competition remains fair. Underscoring these concerns, the IMF forecast a contraction of 1.4 percent in the world economy in 2009.

By July the U.S. housing market was facing new downward pressure as holders of subprime-mortgage bonds flooded the market with foreclosed homes at prices that were much lower than where many banks were willing to sell. A review of thousands of foreclosures in the Atlanta area show that trusts managing pools of securitized mortgages sold six times as many homes as banks during the six months ended March 31. And homes dumped by subprime bondholders sold for thousands of dollars less on average than bank-owned properties.

This was a bad omen for residential real-estate prices and homeowners trying to sell or refinance, because the fire sales, many to cover soured subprime loans, was putting downward pressure on the value of nearby homes. All of this undermined federal efforts to stabilize the housing market and revive the broader economy. In Atlanta, hit hard by foreclosures and declining home values during 2007–2008, mortgage-backed securitization entities completed 6,260 foreclosures in the fourth quarter of 2008 and the first quarter of 2009. That was more than double the 2,737 foreclosures by banks in the same period. Those tiered mortgages were creating the main problem.

Atlanta was typical of a pattern that was emerging across the U.S. In the first quarter of 2009, Atlanta had the 35th highest foreclosure rate out of 203 metropolitan areas with a population of at least 200,000. Related to the foreclosure crisis, nine Georgia banks had failed by the first quarter of 2009. (As noted earlier, these failures continued through at least October 2010.) On a nationwide basis, foreclosures were started on a record high of nearly 1.4 percent of all first-lien mortgages in the first quarter. U.S. home prices in 20 major cities fell an average of 0.6 percent in April, despite Alan Greenspan's admonition that this cannot happen.

Residential mortgage-backed securities helped feed the subprime boom, winding up in the hands of investment funds or more complicated pools [collateralized debt obligations (CDOs)], where underlying mortgage pools were ultimately sliced into different risk tranches. Insurance contracts or credit-default swaps often were sold on top of the CDOs. Securities sold by Bear Stearns, Lehman Brothers, and Merrill Lynch included residential loans from Atlanta.

The Obama administration decided to target directly those facing foreclosure on their homes. The administration created the Making Home Affordable program to help up to nine million homeowners in danger of losing their homes get lower monthly mortgage payments. That includes refinancing programs for more than four million homeowners with loans guaranteed by Freddie Mac and Fannie Mae, and $75 billion in incentives to provide mortgage modifications for up to four million "at-risk" homeowners who are in danger of falling behind on payments. Borrowers who are already delinquent on their mortgage will not qualify. Details of the plan were unveiled on March 4th, 2009. This action had very little imme-diate effect and did not aid the most distressed homeowners.

The difficulties with the Making Home Affordable program lay with its general conditions. (1) The home owner had to be current on home payments. (2) The amount owed on the first mortgage had to be about the same or slightly less than the current value of the home. (3) The homeowner had to have a stable income sufficient to support the new mortgage payments. Obviously, those facing foreclo-sure would not qualify for assistance. Still, it was better than no help at all.

Meanwhile, in the fourth quarter of 2008 and first quarter of 2009, Bear Stearns-issued trusts sold 29 properties in Fulton County, which includes Atlanta, for a total of $3.5 million. That was 60 per-cent of the combined original loan amounts of $5.8 million. The loans were pooled in the trust during a period of Bear securitizations that were sold to investors prior to the firm's sale to JPMorgan Chase in 2008. The depressed prices were representative of a housing mar-ket correcting itself in a period that was vastly different from a few years earlier. Many of the regions facing the largest decline in value were the same ones that soared and saw a frenzy of construction dur-ing the housing boom.

When the U.S. unemployment rate reached 9.5 percent in June 2009, 15 states had unemployment rates of ten percent. The jobless rate in the auto-producing state of Michigan surpassed 15 percent. A record 34.4 million people — or one in nine Americans — were participating in the food stamp program. This made consumers very cautious. With so much uncertainty, companies will stay in a cost-cutting mode and will be slow to make new investments in plant and equipment.

On July 24 regulators shut six more banks in Georgia and a small bank in New York State, raising to 64 the number of federally insured banks to fail in 2009. With these closings, 16 Georgia banks had failed in 2009, more than in any other state. Most of the failures con-tinued to involve banks in the Atlanta area, where the collapse of the real estate market brought economic dislocations. The once boom-town had gone bust.

The aforementioned "cash for clunkers" program took effect in late July. Car and truck owners looking to junk their gas guzzlers were flocking to dealerships to take advantage of the new program, boosting sales in showrooms across the country. With new vehicle sales down 35 percent for the first half of the year, this was a much needed stimulus for an industry devastated in the downturn. The program was so successful that dealers quickly ran through the initial $1 billion program. In August another $2 billion was approved by Congress. Smart-targeted, this was one fiscal program that was working. In the midst of this revival, General Motors announced that its forthcoming Chevrolet Volt electric car would get 230 mpg in city driving, making it the first American vehicle to achieve triple-digit fuel economy.

Still, by late August more than 13 percent of American homeowners with a mortgage had fallen behind on their payments or were in foreclosure. The record-high numbers were being driven by borrowers with traditional fixed-rate mortgages, rather than the shady subprime loans with adjustable rates. This was the effect of a recession throwing thousands of people out of work daily. Confidence had been shattered. The conditions in the job market were raising doubts about whether consumer spending would become vigorous enough to sustain an economic recovery anytime soon. The U.S. unemployment rate leaped to 9.7 in August, the highest since 1983.

Americans increasingly were putting their main hope for economic recovery on exports to Europe and Asia. Thanks in part to government stimulus efforts and consumer spending, Germany, Europe's biggest economy, grew at an annualized pace of 1.3 percent in the second quarter, while France, the region's second-biggest economy, expanded at an annualized rate of 1.4 percent. Both countries had recorded contractions for the previous four quarters. While this suggests that the region was joining the recovery under way in China and increasingly elsewhere in Asia, led by India's announcement that industrial production in June rose nearly eight percent from a year earlier, the growth rates in Germany and France were anemic. Previous global rebounds have relied heavily on U.S. shoppers. However, retail sales fell 0.1 percent in July, as American households continued to be hurt from job losses, a weak housing market and tight credit. At this juncture, no engine for sustained economic growth was on the horizon.

The banking system had not quite stabilized. In early September regulators shut down banks in Missouri, Illinois and Iowa, pushing to 88 the number of banks that had failed in 2009 under the weight of the soured economy and rising loan defaults. The giant banks such as Citigroup were still relying on loans from TARP funds.

The most encouraging news was the shrinkage in GNP of only one percent in the second quarter of 2009 (later revised to −0.7 percent). Some economists were talking of the possibility of a very slow recovery during the second half of the year. Still, we saw an unemployment of 9.5–10.2 percent during the second half with an *under*employment rate of about 16 percent. The recession measured in unemployment is not going to end in 2010, the National Bureau of Economic Research notwithstanding. What happens thereafter depends upon a number of things. The continuation of an easy monetary policy and low interest rates will be essential. The national savings rate will have to come down as people gain sufficient confidence to spend again. Business confidence and reduced uncertainty must be sufficient to renew investment projects. A sufficient number of educated and trained workers must match in skills the needs of an economy once again growing.

This is an opportune time to summarize some of these effects. The housing bubble propelled the economy in two ways. First, growth in the housing sector itself became an important source of aggregate demand. Housing construction averaged close to four percent of gross domestic product (GDP) throughout the post-war period, expanding to a peak of more than five percent in 2005. Since the collapse of the housing bubble, the sector has shrunk to less than three percent of GDP. Second, the housing bubble also drove the economy by stimulating consumption. The housing wealth effect says that each additional dollar of housing wealth is associated with an increase in annual consumption of five to seven cents. Some studies suggest that the effects may have been even stronger during the bubble because of the home ATM machine. In any case, even the modest five-to-seven-cents-on-the-dollar increase in consumption implies that the $8 trillion housing bubble led to additional consumption of $400 billion to $650 billion a year. Such an increase is consistent with the consumption boom witnessed at the peak of the bubble, when the savings rate fell to less than zero. The overall growth helped to spur a recovery in stock prices; additional stock wealth was in the range of $6 trillion to $8 trillion. Here the stock wealth effect on consumption is an estimated three to four cents on the dollar. All in all, the housing bubble indirectly caused an additional $180 billion to $320 billion in consumption.[2]

Come the burst in the housing bubble, the induced consumption fell. Moreover, there was a loss of more than $6 trillion in stock wealth. The saving rate soared to eight percent. Looking at the direct effects, the decline in housing construction reduced annual demand by more than $450 billion. The loss in consumption led to a further decline in demand of $580 billion to $980 billion. The total loss in annual aggregate demand was between $1,030 billion and $1,430 billion, which does not count the impact of the collapse of a secondary bubble in nonresidential real estate. The result: output would fall about 12 percent. The unemployment rate peaked above ten percent.

## UNEMPLOYMENT AND OUTPUT IN THE USA: A SUMMARY

It is useful to summarize in one picture of employment and output with currently available data. Table 11.1 shows the unemployment rate in the U.S. for March 2008 through December 2010. Although the unemployment rate peaked in October 2009, it remained stuck in the 9.5 to 9.8 range thereafter. By November 2010 the number officially unemployed had grown to about 15 million, enough to fill a state halfway between the populations of Pennsylvania and New York state. The "official" recession began with an unemployment rate of only 4.9 percent

---

[2] These estimates of multiplier effects rely on Dean Baker, *False Profits* (Sausalito, CA: PoliPoint Press, 2010), p. 35.

Table 11.1: Unemployment Rates in the USA

| | | | |
|---|---|---|---|
| December 2007 | 4.9 Percent | June | 9.5 Percent |
| January 2008 | 4.9 | July | 9.4 |
| February | 4.8 | August | 9.7 |
| March | 5.1 | September | 9.8 |
| April | 5 | October | 10.2 |
| May | 5.5 | November | 10 |
| June | 5.6 | December | 10 |
| July | 5.8 | January 2010 | 9.7 |
| August | 6.2 | February | 9.7 |
| September | 6.2 | March | 9.7 |
| October | 6.6 | April | 9.9 |
| November | 6.8 | May | 9.7 |
| December | 7.2 | June | 9.5 |
| January 2009 | 7.6 | July | 9.5 |
| February | 8.1 | August | 9.6 |
| March | 8.5 | September | 9.6 |
| April | 8.9 | October | 9.6 |
| May | 9.4 | November | 9.8 |
| | | December | 9.4 |

and ended with an unemployment rate of 9.5 percent. The unemployment rate did not peak until October of 2009, four months after the "official" recession was over. Moreover, the rate was 9.9 percent in April 2010 and got stuck at 9.6 percent by August 2010. What do we call the dreadful 18 months since the official recession ended?

Now we go behind the unemployment figures to industrial production in the basics industry and to the broader measure of Gross Domestic Product (GDP), which includes financial services. Let us look first at industrial production because this must be the measure used by the NBER to set the start of the recession in December 2007. The NBER still considered manufacturing to be the core of the economy. Figure 11.1 shows the pattern of percentage changes in industrial production for the U.S. from the first quarter of 2006 through the second quarter of 2010. Manufacturing declined in the fourth quarter of 2006, as a forewarning of unfolding events. There was a rebound during the next two quarters, to be followed by a weak 1.1 percent gain in the third quarter of 2007, only to be upended by

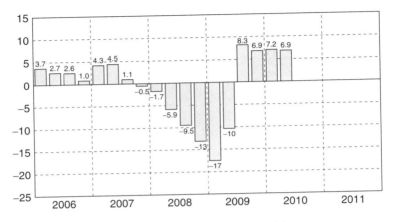

*Source*: Haver Analytics, Federal Reserve Board of Governors website.

**Figure 11.1:**   U.S. Industrial Production: Annualized Percentage Change.

the decisive blow of −0.5 percent in the fourth quarter. Thereafter we see the configuration of a deep recession in industrial output for seven quarters, with the jolting fall of 17 percent in the first quarter of 2009. This was an early warning of what was to come.

Alarms were set off at the Federal Reserve by the sharp deterioration in what I have called the basics industry. A −10 percent reading in the second quarter of 2009 was followed by rebounds during the last two quarters and the first two quarters of 2010. Most of this rebound — with a healthy 8.3 percent gain in the third quarter, followed by 6.9 percent in the fourth quarter — came from personal consumption expenditures unrelated to the automotive industry. Automotive sales, including that for parts and engines, nosedived after the cash for clunkers program ended. The rebound in consumption for other durables such as appliances stemmed from improvements in employment and personal incomes, much of which were companions of the stimulus package. The extraordinary near-deflation may have abetted this improvement even as it wreaked havoc on monetary policy. Still industrial production slowed to a 5.4 percent gain in September 2010 (monthly figures are not shown) compared with a 6.9 percent gain the previous quarter.

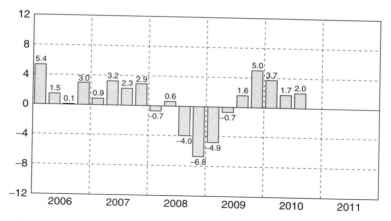

*Source*: Haver Analytics, Federal Reserve Board of Governors website.

**Figure 11.2:** GDP Growth: Annualized Percentage Change.

The broader measure of GDP growth rates are shown in Figure 11.2. As noted, this is the measure commonly used for economic growth. The first decline of the Great Recession came in the first quarter of 2008, a quarter after the NBER designated date for the start of the official recession. After a modest uptick for one-quarter, the GNP growth rate falls off a cliff with the low point being a growth rate of –6.8 percent in the fourth quarter of 2008. While the worst was behind us, modest growth resumed in the third quarter of 2009. Thereafter, the recovery was tepid despite a 5.0 percent gain in the fourth quarter of 2009. The gain then and the gains in 2010 were part of a "jobless recovery."

## UNEMPLOYMENT IN OTHER COUNTRIES

In February 2009, just prior to the "official" ending to the Great Recession, economists Mike Elsby, Bart Hobijn, and Aysegul Sahin made some interesting projections, which proved to be more accurate than those of the European Commission. Their rule of thumb is that the percentage increase in unemployment is well-approximated by the percentage increase in inflows plus the percentage increase in duration of unemployment.[3] In this view rises in unemployment are preceded by an increase in unemployment inflows as jobs are destroyed, followed by a rise in the duration of unemployment as workers fail to quickly find new job. Elsby, Hobijn, and Sahin find that the rapid inflow of workers into unemployment during what I have called the Great Recession confirms that this is one of the most severe recessions in U.S. history. They forecast a further weakening of the labor market, an outcome that proved to be true.

Their forecasts for the unemployment rates in Great Britain, Spain, France and Germany appear in Figure 11.3. They include the most recent unemployment rate available at the time. Germany and France both continue to enjoy declining unemployment rates, whereas Spain experiences a substantial rise in unemployment and Britain experiences a moderate rise. Upon closer inspection, since 2007 inflows rose by 50 percent in Britain and 23 percent in Spain, while outflow rates fell (and hence unemployment duration increased) by 23 percent in Britain and 14 percent in Spain. The role of job losses was more important in Europe. Inflow rates reached levels last seen in the mid-1990s, when Spanish unemployment soared above 20 percent and Britain was still recovering from the early 1990s recession.

Like in the U.S., both inflows and duration began to rise in Great Britain and Spain in 2007, suggesting that the origins of the 2009 slowdown also was apparent some time before the financial crisis of 2008–2009. This naturally raises the question of why the increase in British unemployment was more modest, at least through 2010. According to Elsby, Hobijn, and Sahin, the European labor markets are much less dynamic than their American counterparts. European workers take far longer to leave unemployment, whereas American

---

[3] Michael W. Elsby, Ryan Michaels, and Gary Solon, "The Ins and Outs of Cyclical Unemployment," *Macroeconomics*, 1(1), 84–110 (2009). For the annual estimates made on the VOX website as well, see Michael W. L. Elsby, Ryan Michaels, and Gary Solon, "Unemployment Dynamics in the OECD," *NBER Working Paper 14617* (2008). See also the contribution co-authored by the 2010 Nobel Prize winner in economics: Olivier J. Blanchard and Peter Diamond, "The Cyclical Behavior of the Gross Flows of U.S. Workers," *Brookings Papers on Economic Activity*, 1990–2, 85–155.

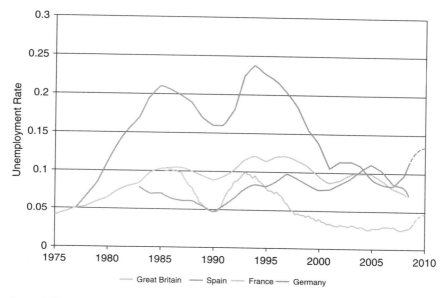

*Source*: Mike Elsby, Bart Hobijn, and Aysegul Sahin, "Unemployment in the Current Crisis," VOX website, February 14, 2009, p. 3.
*Note*: Dashed lines are future unemployment rates under the assumption that inflow rates and duration increase so further.

**Figure 11.3:** Unemployment Rates in Britain, Spain, France and Germany.

workers exit unemployment on average six times faster than European workers. In Europe, it takes time for unemployment to respond to changes in the rate at which workers flow in and out of the unemployment pool. My answer is somewhat different, at least for Britain. The quick implementation of Keynesianism is a part of the answer; Keynes has never been far from the minds of the British, the exception being during the Thatcher government. Moreover, much of Europe, Spain excepted, have very strong unemployment compensation programs which ease the income effects of unemployment. In Britain, at least, the social programs were being dismantled in October 2010, which is likely to change the unemployment rate increase from "modest." At about the same time France was raising its social security age retirement age from 60 to 62 in the face of violent protests.

Although Elsby, Hobijn, and Sahin show that changes in unemployment flows provide advance warning of unemployment increases, their admittedly "conservative" estimates of five percent unemployment in Britain, and 13.5 percent in Spain proved to be just that, conservative. According to Eurostat, the unemployment rate in Britain was 5.4 percent in 2006 and 5.3 percent in 2007. Elsby, Hobijn, and Sahin were assuming that labor market conditions would get no worse in either country. Notably, the actual unemployment rate in Britain stayed well below that of the United States in the 2008–2010 period.

According to the International Monetary Fund (IMF), the Spanish unemployment rate was 11.3 percent in 2008 and 18.2 percent in 2009. The official rate for February 2010 was 22 percent. In France, the IMF has an unemployment rate of 7.9 percent in 2008 and 9.5 percent for 2009. The International Labor Organization has an unemployment rate of 9.0 percent in 2008, 7.8 percent in 2009, and 8.2 percent in 2010. However, Germany's Federal Employment Office estimated a seasonally adjusted rate of 10.8 percent for 2008. The unemployment rates in Europe depend very much on who is doing the estimating. The sharp downward trend depicted by Elsby, Hobijn, and Sahin did not prevail through 2008–2010 for France and Germany. However, the earlier unemployment rates (official or IMF rates) were right on track. In contrast, China's unemployment rate in the four percent range remained lower than U.S. and European rates during 2007–2010, but the sheer number of unemployed Chinese was huge. Still, China remained isolated from the effects of the U.S. Great Recession, but much of the rest of the world did not.

We should not neglect Russia. The CIA has estimated Russian unemployment rates as 6.6 percent for 2007, 6.2 percent for 2008, 6.4 percent for 2009, and 8.9 percent for 2010. These too are conservative estimates. Until the fall of 2008, that pivotal year of the Great Panic, Russia appeared to be a safe haven with its steady, high growth rate of seven percent a year. It also had massive international currency reserves, which peaked at US$598 billion in August 2008. By October 2008, this all changed. The Russian stock market tanked, falling 80 percent from May to October 2008. In 2009 Russia's GDP fell by eight percent, more than any other country of the G-20 largest economies in the world. Among its high technology industries only computer software has emerged as a growth industry. It also has problems with its exports such as liquefied natural gas. Russia has chosen to remain mostly isolated from the United States and still remains aloof, despite overtures by the Obama administration. Thus far Russia has refused to join the World Trade Organization (WTO), which could improve its trade position.

## ROUBINI: A CASSANDRA WHO BECAME A PROPHET

Could much of the disaster been avoided? Alan Greenspan, by his own admission, did not see speculative bubbles emerging much less bursting. Ben Bernanke did not recognize the housing bubble until after the collapse. Both were busy creating the bubble environment. This raises the question of whether anyone correctly foresaw what was to come.

Among several who did see the future, Nouriel Roubini (1959–) stands out. Roubini is a professor of economics at the Stern School of Business, New York University and chairman of RGE Monitor, an economic consultancy firm. In September 2006, he warned to a skeptical IMF that: "The United States was likely to face a once-in-a-lifetime housing bust, an oil shock, sharply declining consumer confidence, and, ultimately, a deep recession." He also foresaw "homeowners defaulting on mortgages, a trillion dollars of mortgage-backed securities unraveling worldwide and the global financial system shuddering to a halt."[4]

In September 2006, Roubini outlined the end of the real estate bubble. He suggested that the trend for 110 years was for supply increases to lead to a fall in prices. But since 1997, real home prices have increased by about 90 percent. There was no economic fundamental — real income, migration, interest rates, demographics — that could explain this. It means there was a speculative bubble. He

---

[4] "Eight Who Saw it Coming," *Fortune*, August 2008.

went on to suggest that the bubble was now bursting. Furthermore, he argued, contrary to the conventional wisdom, that central banks should take action against asset bubbles.[5]

In Roubini's view, the U.S. has been growing through a period of repeated big bubbles. He suggests that too much human capital has gone into financing the most unproductive form of capital, namely housing, and would like to see the U.S. invest in more productive activities. Moreover, he saw housing bubbles in the United Kingdom, Spain, Ireland, Iceland, and in a large part of emerging Europe, like the Baltics all the way to Hungary and the Balkans. As of February 2009 he remained pessimistic about the U.S. and global economy. In *Foreign Policy* he writes: "Last year's worst-case scenarios came true. The global financial pandemic that I and others had warned about is now upon us. But we are still only in the early stages of this crisis. My predictions for the coming year, unfortunately, are even more dire: The bubbles, and there were many, have only begun to burst."[6] He does not see the end of what I have called "the Global Great Recession" until sometime late in 2010.

What has happened was predictable. To understand why Nouriel Roubini got it right when others failed, we only need to revisit our earlier chapters and the original John Maynard Keynes and his stress on uncertainty as well as the Post Keynesians such as Hyman Minsky. We next consider fiscal policy, which was always a part of the Roubini story. But it also is what I had recommended earlier. We will find fiscal policy in both its conventional and unconventional forms.

---

[5] Nouriel Roubini, "Why Central Banks Should Burst Bubbles," *International Finance*, Spring 2006.

[6] Nouriel Roubini, "Warning: More Doom Ahead," *Foreign Policy*, January/February 2009. See also Nouriel Roubini and Stephen Mihm, *Crisis Economics* (New York: The Penguin Press, 2010). For current assessments, go to Roubini Global Economics (RGE) Monitor blog on the Internet.

# 12

# THE UNCONVENTIONAL
# USE OF FISCAL POLICY

Despite a surplus of desperate workers and idle factories, a vicious circle of ever-falling demand, employment, production, and prices gripped the economy in a deflationary spiral. Along with deflation came the liquidity trap. It was a situation crying out for a dose of conventional Keynesian fiscal policy.

A little repetition can be a mighty useful thing. As noted, John Maynard Keynes saw the need for government intervention. In fact, the dramatic use of the government's fiscal powers was the only way out of a depression. The government would increase spending and reduce taxes, intentionally creating a federal budget deficit. It was the budget deficit which flew in the face of the then conventional wisdom. Keynes first published his ideas in 1936, but, as noted earlier, the New Deal policies of President Franklin Roosevelt anticipated his recommendations. As a result, from 1933 to 1937, unemployment fell from about 25 percent to a little under 15 percent. Unfortunately, a renewed commitment to a balanced budget along with a tightening monetary policy in 1937 caused a year long relapse into a severe recession. Thereafter, the Roosevelt administration resumed its earlier strategy of financing the New Deal with deficit spending. Finally, World War II, requiring massive government expenditures and unheard of budget deficits lifted the United States out of the lingering effects of the Great Depression. As a consequence, the actual unemployment rate began to fall faster than the official rate.

A variant of fiscal policy is the use of the transfer payment, whereby the government sends money to particular groups such as the poor, the unemployed or struggling states. Many New Deal programs threw lifelines to these groups. Like tax cuts, transfer payments are part of the standard arsenal for dealing with depression and include such things as unemployment benefits, food stamps, and funds for job retraining.

## THE STIMULUS PACKAGE

At first, all three conventional fiscal policies were deployed during the Great Recession. In January 2008 lawmakers fired the first of several shots by approving a $152 billion package of tax breaks aimed at individuals and businesses. This Economic Stimulus Act of 2008 was overshadowed fiscally by the American Recovery and Reinvestment Act of 2009, passed during the Obama administration. It passed the House with no Republican votes. Its total cost of $787 billion was directed at the three conventional policies of spending increases, tax cuts and transfer payments. Spending on infrastructure and energy projects topped $140 billion, while a miscellany of other spending projects, from fisheries to flood control systems, got billions more. But income tax credits took the lion's share of the package, as individuals received breaks worth some $237 billion. Some were applied across a broad spectrum of the public while others, like the tax credit for first-time homeowners and the one for the purchase of new fuel-efficient cars (cash for clunkers), targeted specific segments of the population. Finally, the bill directed billions to the unemployed, the elderly, and other vulnerable people through transfer payments. It also aimed to provide billions more to state and local governments.

These Keynesian policies went global. Nations around the world adopted comparable though mostly less ambitious fiscal stimulus policies. The European Economic Recovery Plan, adopted in the fall of 2008, provided some €200 billion to a variety of projects; nations such as Germany and France followed with their own smaller stimulus plans. Japan initially planned a massive stimulus package, but the government ultimately instituted a much more modest mix of tax cuts and new spending measures. China's more ambitious plan totaled US$586 billion, the bulk of which went to public works, rail lines, roads, irrigation, and airports. Smaller economies such as South Korea and Australia also initiated Keynesian policies.

These Keynesian policies did much to slow the global decline. The deficits led to growing debt relative to GDPs; this problem was postponed until recovery set in, also a Keynesian strategy. The United States issued more Treasury bills and bonds, most of which were bought by the Federal Reserve and added massively to the Fed's assets. The policies did not work perfectly. As noted earlier, the tax rebates and tax cuts led to increased savings in 2008 and 2009. Consumers spent only 25 or 30 cents on every dollar they received from the government; the balance was used to repair balance sheets.

Other policies were ground in the mill of unconventionality. Among unconventional Keynesian-style policies is the use of guarantees of other people's money. This is a kind of fiscal policy because the guarantees often end up costing taxpayers money. A typical guarantee is that the government will protect money that people have deposited in a bank from a run. As also noted earlier, during the Great Depression the United States adopted deposit insurance through the Federal Deposit Insurance Corporation (FDIC). The FDIC normally does not depend on taxpayer dollars; it assesses fees on the commercial banks. Also, the Federal Savings and Loan Insurance Corporation (FSLIC), was founded in 1934 to protect deposits in savings and loans institutions.

These bank deposit guarantees became an issue in 2008. The FDIC had been insuring deposits up to $100,000. (Similar insurance existed in other countries, though the ceiling varied by country.) In the United States alone, some 40 percent of the deposits remained uninsured, a problem underscored by the bank runs on Countrywide, IndyMac, and Washington Mutual. The threat of still more runs triggered a round of new government guarantees. In September 2008, Ireland had to increase its deposit insurance to €100,000, then fully guarantee all the deposits of its six largest banks. In the U.S., the FDIC raised the ceiling for insured bank deposits to $250,000. A few days later Germany guaranteed all of its private bank accounts; the next day Sweden extended insurance to all deposits to the sum of 500,000 kronas (about US$75,000). Then, a week later Italy announced that none of its banks would be allowed to fail and that no depositor would suffer any loss. The next month Switzerland increased its ceiling on deposit insurance. The European Union guaranteed its banks' bonded debt in October 2008. The same month the FDIC guaranteed the principal and the interest payments on debt issued by banks and bank holding companies up to a total of $1.5 trillion. Other countries followed with similar deposit and debt guarantees.

Ultimately it is the taxpayer that makes these guarantees good. This is highlighted by the FDIC funds dipping into negative territory in the third quarter of 2009. The taxpayer would need to shoulder part of the burden in the form of an FDIC bailout, much as it did in the wake of the savings and loan crisis.

Another kind of unconventional fiscal policy is the bailout. As noted, the big bailouts of the Great Recession in the United States began with Fannie Mae and Freddie Mac in September 2008. When the two mortgage giants came under government conservatorship, the Bush Treasury pledged $400 billion to underwrite the takeover. This made explicit the federal government's guarantee of their debt. The Treasury is on the line to cover some $5 trillion worth of obligations insured by the two institutions, along with another $1.5 trillion worth of debt that they issued. If housing prices continue to fall and many more mortgages go into foreclosure, the Treasury could end up sustaining considerable losses. Prior to the Fannie and Freddie bailout, the Housing and Economic Recovery Act of July 2008 pledged some $320 billion to help struggling homeowners refinance into mortgages that were insured by the Federal Housing Administration.

This was part of a cluster of bailouts and guarantees funded by the Troubled Assets Relief Program (TARP). As noted earlier, the legislation initially allocated $700 billion to purchase toxic assets. The money has been used to prop up banks and the automakers General Motors and Chrysler and their financial arms, GMAC and Chrysler Financial. This auto bailout amounted to $80 billion. This was just the beginning, as a sizable share of the TARP funds — some $340 billion — was given to nearly 700 different financial institutions, including giants like Citigroup, Bank of America, JPMorgan Chase, Goldman Sachs, and AIG, as well as a host of smaller banks. Most of the funds comprised capital injections, in which the government purchased preferred shares in the institutions. Besides a steady dividend payment, these shares provided a potential ownership stake in the companies. This marked a radical departure for fiscal policy; American taxpayers became owners of large swaths of the financial system.

The government formed a kind of insurance partnership with two giant ailing banks. The Treasury guaranteed several hundred billion dollars worth of impaired assets held by Bank of America and Citigroup. The pool of troubled assets totaled $118 billion in Bank of America's case, with a "deductible" of $10 billion. This kind of partnership was adopted widely in the United Kingdom.

All these measures combined managed to stabilize the global financial system. In turn, they prevented the Great Recession from becoming another Great Depression at a time when aggregate demand was in free fall.

## THE SHORTFALL

Obama's team went to Congress with a package that was clearly inadequate to meet the total loss of aggregate demand resulting from the housing crash. The proposed spending increases and tax cuts, most of which would be paid out in 2009 and 2010, was just over $800 billion. Why inadequate? The shortfall in yearly demand for 2009 and 2010 was around $1.3 trillion: roughly the $450 billion from lost housing construction, the $600 billion to $800 billion in reduced consumption, and the $200 billion from the collapse of the bubble in non-residential real estate. The proposed package would try to fill this gap with $350 billion a year in spending. Worse, close to half of the federal stimulus would be offset by spending cuts and tax increases at the state and local level. The Obama package was too small in part because the administration continued to underestimate the severity of the decline.[1]

Still, the package included several policies that addresses long-term problems. It increased unemployment benefits and changed the benefit formula so that many more part-time workers would be eligible. The plan also covered 65 percent of the cost of health-care insurance for unemployed workers. Moreover the overall stimulus package provided funding for investment in several areas, including the modernizing of the country's electric grid, computerizing medical records, and retrofitting public and private buildings to make them more energy efficient. There was also more than $80 billion for "shovel-ready" infrastructure projects, most of which were repairs to existing structures that could be undertaken quickly. Finally, the original package included more than $200 billion in assistance to state and local governments, but $100 billion was excluded in the final bill. This transfer of funds would made it only slightly easier for state and local governments to cope with their huge budget shortfalls. These effects would be immediate.

As it turns out, therefore, President Obama was forced to cut back the final package to $780 billion, which included a one-year adjustment to the Alternative Minimum Tax (AMT) for the effects of inflation. This AMT adjustment, which cost about $80 billion, was not stimulus, because Congress makes this adjustment for inflation every year, and probably not a single person in the nation ever expected to pay taxes at the unadjusted rate. This new package included only $700 billion in real stimulus money, less than $600 billion ($300 billion a year) of it to paid out out in the first two years. Taking into account the state and local government offset of about half of this stimulus with budget cuts and tax increases needed to balance their budgets, the net stimulus came to only about $150 billion a year, slightly more than one-tenth of what was needed to offset the demand lost from the collapse of the housing

---

[1] These estimates were made by Dean Baker in *False Profits* (Sausalito CA: PoliPoint Press, 2010), p. 101.

bubble.[2] This, according to economist Dean Baker, who assumes a conservative multiplier of only 1.5. If the multiplier were 2.0, which Lawrence Summers *later* surmised was the appropriate multiplier, then the net stimulus would have been larger, though nowhere nearly enough to close the unemployment gap.

Baker's reasoning goes like this. The standard rule of thumb is that it takes two percentage points of GDP growth to reduce the unemployment rate by one percentage point. The Obama administration had a baseline projection wherein the unemployment rate would peak at about nine percent in 2010 (in the absence of any stimulation). We can expect unemployment to fall at a rate of 4.5 to 5 percent; at the peak of unemployment the economy would have an additional 4 to 4.5 percentage points of unemployment. Take the 4.5 percent as the norm. Then we need nine percentage points of annual GDP, which is equal to $1.35 trillion to bring the economy back to absolute full employment, but this would be a projected unemployment rate of zero! With an Obama multiplier of 1.5, we need (1.35/1/5) $900 billion of annual stimulus over 2009 and 2010. If we desire a zero percent unemployment rate, Figure 12.1 illustrates what was needed. What we got was $150 billion a year in stimulus or only (1.5 × 150) $235 billion in GDP.

There are a couple problems with the Obama-Baker analysis, not the least of which is the zero unemployment rate as an ideal. In the end, nonetheless, I shall rescue the analysis. Frictional unemployment, persons between jobs and on the move, may be as high as 4.5 percent, though admittedly we may want to "downsize" this figure in a depression-like economy. If we make the objective of "full employment" as 4.5 percent, then the Obama stimulus package may have been sufficient during normal times with state and local budgets in balance, the banking system stabilized, and the federal funds rate at or near zero. The times were not normal. Let's look at actual outcomes. The realized GDP growth rate averaged one percent during

---

[2] We cannot ignore the ultimate effects of unconventional monetary policy, which were felt, however weakly, by 2010.

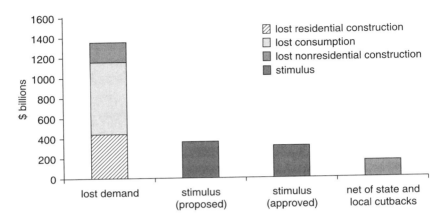

*Source*: Dean Baker, *False Profits, ibid*, p. 108.

**Figure 12.1:**   Loss in Annual Demand and Net Stimulus (from the government sector federal stimulus minus state and local cutbacks).

2009 and an estimated 2.4 percent in 2010. The rule of thumb, calculated in reverse, would yield only a 0.5 percent and 1.2 percent gain, respectively, in the unemployment rate. In reality, as we have noted, the unemployment rate peaked at 10.2 percent in October 2009 and has been higher than 9.4 percent for 13 months thereafter. This would seem to confirm Baker's 10:1 shortfall ratio.

Herein the economic problem becomes a political one. The 10:1 ratio gives the required annual net fiscal stimulus of $1.5 trillion a year (10 × 150) for the two years. The $700 billion stimulus was difficult to put together so that it would quickly pass the U.S. Senate.

Moreover, those budget outlays were on top of the $700 billion TARP expenditure to save the financial system from collapse. TARP was used to acquire toxic assets which did not provide Keynesian fiscal stimulus, but mimicked some of Bernanke's unconventional monetary policies. A near-depression is a very serious economic event, and a quick recovery would have required much more stimulus. Moreover, given the great uncertainty among both consumers and producers, the GDP growth needed to lower the unemployment rate did not materialize. Even Alan Greenspan, as late as November 8,

2010 said on "Meet the Press," "I have never seen so much profound uncertainty in the business community." (He went on to oppose more government spending.) This was a jobless situation bred in the direst of circumstances. People were made homeless by the foreclosures, and personal incomes had no stimulus from hourly wages. The meager growth in output in 2010 was the by-product of fewer workers working more hours at flat real wages. The situation called for increased employment by all governments, something that did not fit the times, only the circumstances.

The reasons for the Keynesian shortfalls were both ideological and political. Americans in both parties and the media have been conditioned to think that budget deficits are always bad, that government should behave like households and always balance its budget. This is pre-Keynesian thought. Besides this, economists and reporters began to raise the alarm about "looming inflation" even though wages were flat, many prices were falling and the unemployment rate had reached 10.2 percent. These were the same arguments used during 1937 that led to a continuation of the Great Depression. At its roots the confusion is about the difference between short-term stimulus and long-term balancing of federal budgets during good times.

## GLOBAL FISCAL LEGACIES

The housing and banking crisis had lingering fiscal effects; this is true for other countries and other crises. Declining revenues and higher expenditures, owing to a combination of bailout costs and higher transfer payments and debt servicing costs, lead to a marked worsening in the central budget. Figure 12.2 shows the increase in real government debt in the three years following a banking crisis in a large sample of countries. The buildup in government debt has been a defining characteristic of the aftermath of a banking crisis for over a century. The decline in government finances is striking, with an average debt increase of more than 86 percent. The increases in debt is driven primarily by a sharp falloff in tax revenue due to the deep recessions that accompany most severe financial crises. It should

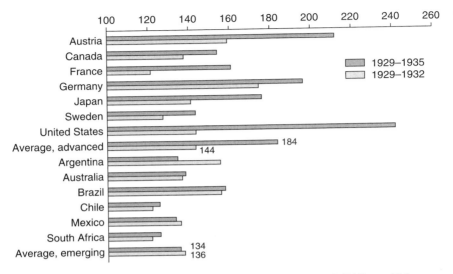

*Source*: Carmen M. Reinhart and Kenneth S. Rogoff, *This Time is Different* (Princeton, N.J.: Princeton University Press, 2009), p. 237.

*Notes*: The beginning years of the banking crises range from 1929 to 1931. Australia and Canada did not have a systemic banking crisis but are included for comparison purposes, because both also suffered severe and protracted economic contractions. The year 1929 marks the peak in world output and hence is used as the marker for the beginning of the Depression episode.

**Figure 12.2:**   The Cumulative Increase in Real Public Debt Three and Six Years Following the Onset of the Great Depression in 1929: Selected Countries.

be noted, however, that the global crisis that began in 2007 was accompanied by huge bailout costs for industry and banking (what is noted as "the 2007 crisis" is not in the figure.)

Increases in the U.S. federal budget deficits in the post-2007 crisis period were dramatic. The federal deficit topped $1 trillion on July 1, 2010 with three months still to go in the budget year. Still, that's down 7.6 percent from the $1.09 trillion deficit run up during the same period in 2009. Many economists are forecasting that the deficit for the entire budget year will come in about $1.3 trillion. This would be the second highest deficit on record (though not as a share of GDP), but it would be down slightly from 2009's all-time high of $1.4 trillion. The Obama administration predicts the imbalances over the next *decade* will total $8.5 trillion.

Worries about the size of the budget deficit have created political problems for the Obama administration. Congressional Republicans and moderate Democrats have blocked more spending on job creation and other efforts. Republicans also have held up legislation to extend unemployment benefits for the long-term jobless because of its effect on the deficit.

Excepting the 2007–2010 experience, the other post-World War II crises were contained. The most severe of these were either country-specific or at worst regional, none were global. Hence, it might be more instructive to compare the 2007–2010 experience with that of the Great Depression which is more comparable and global. The recessions accompanying the Great Depression were of much longer duration than the postwar crises. Many countries, including the United States and Canada, experienced a downturn of four years or longer, with Mexico and Romania experiencing a decline in output for six years. The average length of time over which output fell was 4.1 years in the Great Depression.

Consider the number of years it took for a country's output to reach its pre-crisis level. In the postwar crises, it took an average of 4.4 years for output to come back to pre-crisis levels. Japan and Korea were able to snap back more quickly, at only two years, whereas Colombia and Argentina took eight years. Things were much worse in the Great Depression. Countries took an average of ten years to increase their output back to pre-crisis levels, in part because no country was in a position to export its way to recovery as world aggregate demand contracted. The United States, France, and Austria took ten years to rebuild their output to its initial pre-Depression level, whereas Canada, Mexico, Chile, and Argentina took 12. Unemployment increases in the Great Depression were also far greater than those in the severe post-World War II financial crises. The average rate of unemployment increase was about 16.8 percent; in the United States, unemployment rose from 3.2 percent 24.9 percent. So the Great Depression sets more daunting benchmarks for the potential trajectory of the financial crisis of 2007–2009.

The growth in public debt follows a similar comparative pattern. The cumulative public debt increase was much greater during 1929–1936 than for 1929–1932. The growth was greatest in the United States, Austria and Germany; it was least in Australia, Chile and South Africa. In the Depression, it took six years for real public debt to grow by 84 percent compared with half that time in the postwar crises. Part of this difference reflects the very slow fiscal policy response that happened in the Great Depression. Nonetheless, asset prices and other standard crisis indicator variables tumbled in the United States and elsewhere along the same tracks laid down by historical indicators. The global nature of the 2007–2010 crisis has made it far more difficult, and contentious, for individual nations to grow their way out through higher exports or to smooth the consumption effects through foreign borrowing.[3]

All things considered, the aftermath of 2007–2010 will look more like that of the Great Depression than like the aftermath of the post-World War II crises. Moreover, the real estate bubble in the United States that began to deflate at the end of 2005 occupies center stage as a culprit in the recent global financial crisis, much as similar bubbles did in the post-World War II banking crises in advanced economies [especially Spain (1977), Norway (1987), Finland (1991), Sweden (1991), and Japan (1992)].

Not only were unconventional monetary policies used during the Great Recession, fiscal policies also followed innovative ways. The extreme use of policies illustrates not only the inadequacies of available policies but the severity of the decline. Fiscal policy continues to play at least a passive role as deficits continue because of shortfalls in tax revenue. As the historical data suggest, public debt is a natural consequence of severe downturns. This is fortunate because the Congress has little appetite for more deficit spending and monetary policy is as easy as it can ever be.

---

[3] This discussion relies on the tables presented by Reinhart and Rogoff, *This Time is Different, op. cit.,* pp. 233–237.

Increased inequality in incomes and wealth would be expected from any great contraction, the recent event being unexceptional is this regard. Worsening income and wealth distributions exacerbate the economy and a sliding housing sector hurts both the economy and the wealth distribution. Cause and effect does run both ways, as we next observe.

# 13

# THE GREAT INEQUALITIES

The Post Keynesians point to income and wealth inequalities as being critical to the analysis of economic conditions. In the spirit of Post Keynesianism, we address two kinds of inequalities. (1) The unequal income distribution of the United States. (2) The growing inequality in the U.S. wealth distribution. In turn, we consider whether these inequalities contributed to the global Great Recession and vice-versa. We will continue to draw comparisons with other countries.

## THE UNEQUAL INCOME DISTRIBUTION OF THE UNITED STATES

Wages comprise the greatest part of incomes in the United States. These have been growing unequally. In 1975, the 90th percentile earned, on average, about three times more than the tenth percentile, by 2005 they earned five times more. This growth was concentrated at the top. Wages of those in the middle relative to those at the tenth percentile have not gone up anywhere nearly as much as the wages of the 90th percentile.

Technological advancement is one element behind the growing wage gap. A second element is lagging education. There is a widening gap between the growing technological demand for skilled workers and the lagging supply because of deficiencies in the quantity and quality of education. A theory is required to explicate this gap. Some years ago I developed a vita theory of the personal income distribution to explain these inequalities.[1] I ask for the readers patience for just a few pages.

---

[1] E. Ray Canterbery, "A Vita Theory of the Personal Income Distribution," *Southern Economic Journal*, **46**(1), 12–48 (July 1979).

The main thrust of a vita theory can be simply stated. Assume that one labor market exists for each general human capital classification. Human capital is the accumulated skill set from birth, which includes education and experience, as well as age. It can be classified, for example, on a scale of one to ten. The individual's quantity of human capital determines *which* labor market the person enters. A person "qualifies" for a particular labor market by the state of his or her vita at that point in time. Determination of vita begins at birth when one's race, sex, religion, national origin, inherent mental and physical capacity, inheritances, and family background are duly noted.

The vita is "added to" over one's lifespan by education, other training, and experience. The individual has some control over the "length" and "depth" of his or her vita. Since labor demand is related to product prices and a changing technology, however, only the rare individual can predict with any accuracy the derived demand for workers with vitae of his or her type. Moreover, specific labor supply conditions are a collective consequence outside personal control. Then, *given* one's vita and the characteristics of the applicable labor market, as a first approximation, the individual's basic wage rate depends upon the wage of central tendency for such labor services. Upon further approximation, however, the individual's personal income exhibits differentials from potential labor market earnings. The differentials — occupational, geographic, inter-industry, union-nonunion, discriminatory, and so on — often can be traced all the way back to the first vita stage, which I called the *birth vita*. The configuration of the relevant labor market is determined more by technology than anything else; technology defines the requisite labor skills.

Empirical studies that find geographical, industrial, occupational, racial, and sexual wage and earnings differentials abound. Such studies, by their very design, do not explain all such differentials simultaneously. The eclectic nature of the vita theory offers a more complete explanation, and its complexity does not preclude empirical verification. Path analysis, a statistical model unfamiliar to most economists, is suggested. Parameter estimates from a prior study lend empirical support to the vita theory. Path analysis

I recommend because of the importance of identifying both direct and indirect impacts of numerous variables deciding personal incomes. We should add that the distribution of personal incomes goes a long way toward deciding the wealth distribution. Inheritances play a role in this configuration at the birth vita level.

It is instructive to summarize the path analysis of personal income determination. These findings are subject to updates. An occupational index has a special meaning within the context of the vita theory. The index — a two-digit score ranging from 00 to 96 — is highly correlated with the "performance demands" of an occupation. "Handlers," one category of occupation would have scores ranging between 00 and 20, while surgeons would score somewhere between 92 and 96.[2]

The effect of intelligence (IQ) on earnings, net of the effects of education and occupation, is appreciable. The direct effect of IQ on earnings is .10 while the sum of indirect effects via education and occupation is .12. The combined effect (net of the three social background factors) is .22. Therefore, white males aged 25–34 with the same schooling and in the same line of work received differential rewards for IQ because of social contingencies.

The direct effect of the family head's education upon income is .03 while the indirect effect through education and occupational choice is .04, for a total impact of .07. This excludes correlation due to common causes such as a person's number of children and the family head's occupation.

Path analysis can be used to calculate the total correlation between any two variables, including compound path coefficients. This explained variance includes that from the direct effect, indirect effects, and joint causes. In the path diagram genetic influence, capital costs, and family environment have greater total measured impacts upon education than upon (in turn) occupational choice and income. Each of the explanatory variables can be viewed as a

---

[2] Path analysis is further explicated in Canterbery, *ibid.*

stage in one's life plan in which new possibilities or life paths are diminished after each vita stage — genetic and family endowments, education, occupation — in turn is reached.

IQ alone accounts for 21 percent of the variance in education, number of children, four percent, the family head's education, five percent, and the family head's occupation, 13 percent. The shares of explained variances in occupational choice are 12 percent, two percent, five percent, and 15 percent, respectively. The family head's occupation is somewhat more important in determining occupation than in deciding years of education.

Consider the effects of IQ, capital-cost, family head's education, and family head's occupation. The total variance in education explained by these four initial state variables is 44 percent, occupation, 33 percent, and income, 13 percent. In the vita theory educational achievement does not translate proportionately into income even though the other genetic factors (sex and race) as well as (roughly) years of experience are held constant. Moreover, between occupation and income the effects of these four conditions are greatly muted by occupational types and labor market conditions that include differential geographic effects. However, this does not alter the reality of favorable initial endowments enhancing occupational (including locational) choice, nor does it alter vita theory conclusions about many labor market conditions being nonindividual choice variables.

White-black differentials or race effects are found. There is a total education gap of 2.3 years between white and black men, 1.2 accounted for by family background and number of children combined; an additional 0.9 years by culturally specific mental development, and only 0.2 years by unexplained causes. Net of family environment and number of children, culturally specific mental development accounts for 5.5 of the 22.9 points gap between black and white occupational status. However, 8.7 points of the remaining gap might be a result of racial discrimination. These differentials carry over into a income gap between white and black workers.

In passing we can note some policy implications. The weakness of individual control over certain human capital variables lead to policies often urged collectively by society to satisfy social goals. These policies often are urged on the basis of "equal opportunity." The advantageous birth vita starts the individual on the optimum vita path, aiding the selection of the "optimum" years of schooling and other training. Genetic and family endowments directly and indirectly affect occupational choice and thus earnings. In the mature vita, the genetic code can impinge again in the way of job and wage discrimination.

There are global implications. Peter Gray saw the vita theory as the "Rosetta Stone which enabled him to formulate all his misgivings about the interaction of rapid changes in trade patterns and the rate of employment in industrialized nations."[3] This comment motivated me to consider the implications of the vita theory in international trade and domestic employment adjustments.[4] My purposes were (1) to show how most trade theories can be summarized with a simplified production system that includes markup pricing, (2) to integrate my version of Vernon's (1966) product cycle theory with the vita theory, and (3) to suggest some broader policy implications. The production system, or the technical methods of production define labor requirements. Labor's vita decides which occupation in which industry is chosen. The product cycle is related to both product demand and supply conditions. The integration of the product cycle with the vita theory show the difficulties in long-term adjustments. In one view human capital deepening policies would be added to short-term protection. Then, irrespective of the source of trade competition, multinational firms could seek U.S. labor. In another view the U.S. could devise policies aimed at speeding the conversion of innovations into new commercial products, processes and industries.

---

[3] H. Peter Gray, *Free Trade or Protection: A Pragmatic Analysis* (London: Macmillan; New York: St. Martin's Press, 1985), p. x.
[4] E. Ray Canterbery, "A General Theory of International Trade and Domestic Employment Adjustments" in M. Landeck, editor, *International Trade: Regional and Global Issues* (London: Macmillan Press and New York: St. Martin's Press, 1994), pp. 147–185.

Because of the importance of technology and markup pricing, I also developed a theory of technical change at the firm level.[5] The price markup is determined by a firm's industry cost position, its ability to accomplish product differentiation, and the relative power that the firm enjoys within its industry. Although internal financing requirements are part of the markup strategy, the amount of fundable gross investment depends upon whether economic profits exist. With economic profits, the firm (or industry) maintains itself or expands, and without economic profits, it contracts. Part of the investment strategy of the firm is to innovate. Hence, the markup is used, in part, to generate the internal funds that affect a firm's ability to reduce costs. In this way investment depends on changes in net economic profits as well as a planned level of internal funding. In turn, the growth in these net economic profits is positively related to price.

According to the vita theory, part of what economists call the "college premium" in wages can be accounted for by additional years of college education. Indeed, the ratio of the wages of those who have only a bachelor's degree to those who only have a high school degree has risen steadily since 1980. This has probably been spurred on by technological change and the redefinition of skill requirements by occupation. According to the 2008 Current Population Survey (U.S. Census Bureau), the median wage of a high school graduate was $27,963, while the median wage of someone with an undergraduate degree was $48,097 — about 72 percent more. Those with professional degrees (like an MD or MBA) earn even more, with a median wage of $87,775. The college premium goes a long way toward explaining the 90/10 differential. The increase in the college premium may be due to technological change that gives rise to even more demand for skills (skill-biased technical change).

American years of education have not kept pace with technological change. Between 1930 and 1980, the average years of schooling

---

[5] E. Ray Canterbery, "An Evolutionary Model of Technical Change with Markup Pricing" in William Milberg, editor, *The Megacorp and Macrodynamics* (Armonk, NY and London, England: M.E. Sharpe, Inc., 1991), pp. 87–100.

among Americans aged 30 or older increased by about one year every decade. But between 1980 and 2005, the pace of increase in educational attainments was glacial — only 0.8 years over the entire quarter century. There are several possible reasons for the slowing pace. The fraction of the population with high school degrees has not increased since 1980, and other countries have caught up and surpassed the U.S. Students have been dropping out of college. College graduation rates for young men born in the 1970s are no higher than for men born in the 1940s. At the same time the demand for workers with college degrees has been increasing rapidly. Finally, there may be a natural limit to how much education a population can absorb. Whether or not that is the case in the U.S., much of the rest of the world does not seem to have such a limit. The U.S. has fallen behind 12 other rich countries in four-year-college graduation rates.

Inequalities in income and wealth create inequality in the distribution of education. Rich families can afford to live in better neighborhoods, can give the children the health care and nutrition that allow them to grow up healthy, and can hire tutors and learning aides if their children fall behind. Family instability, too, is harder on the poorer children. Divorce affects the childrens' health and schooling far more in a poor family than in a rich family.

The vita theory suggests that in the short run inequalities can only be addressed by a central government through fiscal policy, changes in the tax code and spending distributions. In the long run, the funding of education at the federal level plus that at the state and local levels can make the playing field fairer. Next, we turn to one of the longer-playing roles of the U.S. Government that helped to create the housing bubble.

## THE FORCED DOMINANCE OF FREDDIE MAC AND FANNIE MAE

How is inequality related to the 2007–2009 financial crisis? Economist Raghuram G. Rajan has gone a long way toward connecting the dots.[6] The political opposition to transfer payments and tax rate changes that redistribute income is strong. Since the early 1980s, the trend has been toward easier credit, especially for housing. The decline in the use of fiscal policy and the rise of monetary policy has aided and abetted this trend. Easier housing credit pushes up house prices, making households feel wealthier, allowing them to finance more consumption. Furthermore, easier credit creates more profits and jobs in the financial sector as well as in real estate and housing construction. The effects of easy credit is large, positive, immediate, and widely distributed, whereas the costs lie in the future.

Fannie Mae and Freddie, those government-sponsored enterprises, were created to facilitate the move toward affordable housing. They are exempt from state and local income taxes, and have a line of credit from the U.S. Treasury. The full faith and credit of the U.S. stands behind these agencies, especially since their bankruptcy. Fannie and Freddie can thus raise money at a cost that is barely above the rate paid by the Treasury. The purpose is to support housing finance. As more and more Americans faced stagnant or declining incomes in the early 1990s, politicians began to look for ways to help them with quick fixes. Affordable housing for low-income groups was the answer, and Fannie and Freddie provided the channels. There was more to come. In 1992, the U.S. Congress passed the Federal Housing Enterprise Safety and Soundness Act to promote home-ownership for low-income and minority groups. The Department of Housing and Urban Development (HUD) was instructed to develop affordable housing goals for the government agencies and to monitor progress toward these goals. The Clinton administration argued that the financial sector should find creative ways of getting people who could not afford homes into them, and the government would help wherever it could.

All this activity combined with low interest rates at the Fed led to a housing boom in the administration of George W. Bush. The Bush administration pushed up the low-income lending mandate on

---

[6] Raghuram G. Rajan, *Fault Lines* (Princeton, NJ: Princeton University Press, 2010), pp. 31–45.

Fannie and Freddie to 56 percent of their assets in 2004, even as the Fed now began increasing interest rates in fear of the housing boom. Relaxed lending standards in the housing industry soon followed. Subprime lending alone (including financing through the purchase of mortgage-backed securities) by Fannie and Freddie and the FHA started at about $85 billion in 1997 and went up to $446 billion in 2003, after which it stabilized at between $300 and $400 billion a year until 2007. These entities accounted for 54 percent of the market across the years, with a high of 70 percent in 2007. By June 2008, Fannie and Freddie, the FHA, and various other government programs were exposed to about $2.7 trillion in subprime and Alt-A loans. About 59 percent of total loans were in these categories.

Housing was a market driven by government mandates and money. Although housing booms took place around the world, driven by low interest rates, the boom in the U.S. was especially pronounced among borrowers who had not had prior easy access to credit, the subprime and Alt-A players in the market. Rajan concludes that growing income inequality in the USA stemming from unequal access to quality education led to political pressure for more housing credit.

The connection of the ensuing subprime mortgage mess to the financial crisis of 2007–2009 was established earlier in this book.

# A GLIMPSE AT GLOBAL INCOME INEQUALITIES

It is difficult to pin down information on income inequalities in the broader world. An important attempt to remedy this is taking place. James K. Galbraith heads the University of Texas Inequality Project (UTIP). He and fellow researchers have replaced the Gini coefficient, which is used to measure income inequality between individuals, with the Theil index, which measures inequality between groups and regions. Among the Organization for Economic Co-operation and Development (OECD) countries, Galbraith finds that all but Denmark had an increase in inequality from the beginning of the 1960s. The trend was similar among non-OECD countries. Most of the OECD countries have high incomes and a high development of human capital.[7] Inequality of pay has fallen in the USA, whereas inequality of income has risen. Stock earnings and bonuses account for the "unearned income" contributing to the inequality.[8]

Using the UTIP results, Robert Skidelsky draws comparisons between two broad eras. The Bretton Woods period is defined as from 1951 to 1973, a period dominated by the Keynesians. The Bretton Woods era ended when the fixed-exchange-rate system collapsed between 1971 and 1973. The first OPEC oil shock marks the end date. The Keynesian commitment to full employment was abandoned from the late 1970s onward. The second period, the Washington Consensus era, was dominated by the theory of the self-regulating market. The Washington Consensus era begins with Ronald Reagan in the early 1980s and continues; it, of course, could end in exchange-rate wars. As we have noted (in narrower historical segments), neither system was purely Keynesian or purely neoliberal. Exchange rates did not have to remain fixed during Bretton Woods and some countries retain fixed exchange rate regimes during the Washington Consensus era. Still, argues Skidelsky, the first age embodied a Keynesian philosophy, the second, a neoliberal one.[9]

UTIP has inequality stable during the Bretton Woods era, but rising sharply in the Washington Consensus era, beginning in 1982 (Reagan tax policies) and continuing into the new millennium. An exception is South America, where inequality diminished since the financial crises in the late 1990s and the early 2000s. This, Galbraith concludes, is the result of "that region's retreat from neoliberal

---

[7] The OECD, founded in 1961, is comprised of 34 member countries as diverse as the United States, Japan, Spain, Portugal, Estonia, and Denmark. Chile is the only member classified as less developed, but the GDP of the member countries vary widely. OECD's parent organization is the Organization for European Economic Co-operation (OEEC), which originated in 1948 to help administer the Marshall Plan.

[8] James K. Galbraith, "Inequality, Unemployment and Growth: New Measures of Old Controversies," *Journal of Economic Inequality*, 7(2), 189–206 (June 2009).

[9] Robert Skidelsky, *Keynes: The Return of the Master* (New York: Public Affairs, 2010), pp. 114–115.

orthodoxy."[10] In Argentina, the financial collapse led to a downsizing of the previously disproportionately dominant financial sector and a Keynesian-like increase in public sector employment. Whether something similar will happen in the USA during the post-2008 era remains to be seen.

Skidelsky draws even broader global conclusions for the two eras. The Bretton Woods age had less unemployment, higher growth, lower exchange rate volatility and lower inequality. The Washington Consensus era suffered through five global recessions, the last being the largest and deepest since the Great Depression.[11] Though there is debate about whether it is getting worse, global inequality is probably greater than it has ever been in human history. In part this is due to rising industrialization in developing countries and in part the consequence of a move toward market economies in East Asia, China, and eastern Europe. The richest one percent of persons in the world receive as much as the bottom 57 percent. The ratio between the average income of the top five percent in the world to the bottom five percent increased from 78 to 1 in 1988 to 114 to 1 in 1993.[12]

Geographically, what is the source of world income inequality? The greatest contributors are the large countries at either end of the spectrum, the "Twin Peaks," as defined by Quah.[13] One peak represents the 2.4 billion people whose average income is less than US$1,000 per year and includes persons living in India, Indonesia and rural China. With 42 percent of the world's population, these areas received only nine percent of the world's income. The other peak is the group of 500 million people whose average income exceeds US$11,500. The nations include the United States, Japan,

---

[10] James K. Galbraith, *op. cit.*
[11] Skidelsky, *op. cit.*, p. 123.
[12] See B. Malanovic, "True World Income Distribution, 1988 and 1993: First Calculation Based on Household Surveys Alone," World Bank, 1999.
[13] See Danny Quah, "Empirics for Growth and Distribution: Stratification, Polarization and Convergence Clubs," London School of Economics and Political Science, Center for Economic Performance, Discussion Paper No. 324, 1997, pp. 1–29. Income is adjusted by purchasing power parity.

Germany, France and the United Kingdom. Combined, they account for just 13 percent of the world's population but garner 45 percent of the world's income. The gap between these two peaks is so large it comprises the main component of the world's income inequality. Populous countries with average income between the two peaks, such as Brazil, Mexico and Russia, contribute to world inequality, but to a much lessor degree.

China embodies both causes of rising inequality. In the great transition to a market-based industrialized economy, there has been migration from rural areas of poverty to urban environments with rising standards of living. Still, the inequality has increased in urban areas, while leaving country-wide inequalities intact.[14] In November 2010, three bottles of 1869 vintage Bordeaux at Sotheby's auction in Hong Kong sold for US$232,692 each, about the price of a new Ferrari in the United States. Thirst is not the issue. There are wealthy people in China who can afford to forgo a luxury car for three bottles of wine (so, it's Bordeaux!). In short, today it is easier to stimulate economic growth than it is to maintain a reasonable income distribution. Where income distributions are unequal, wealth distributions are even more unequal.

## WEALTH INEQUALITIES IN THE USA

Household net worth or wealth is comprised mostly of the values of financial holdings and the value of homes. Low income earners generally have zero or negative wealth. Middle income earners rely on the prices of houses for their wealth. The upper income earners hold most the wealth represented by financial holdings. Thus, changes in home prices differentially affect the low and middle income earners, those whose "savings" are tied up in the value of their homes.

House price inflation at the peak of the housing bubble created more than $8 trillion in housing wealth. With this heightened perception of wealth, the low-income and middle-income homeowners

---

[14] For details on fairly recent changes in the income distribution in China, go to www.msu.edu/~gileri/BBGW.

changed their saving and consumption patterns. In many cases they borrowed directly against the equity in their homes, either taking out home-equity loans or refinancing for amounts that were larger than the original size of the mortgage. In most cases, they opted not to save, believing their homes were saving for them; they saw the rise in house prices adding perhaps $20,000 a year to the equity in their homes. Saving rates fell to zero and people stopped accumulating any wealth aside from home equity.

The subsequent collapse in housing prices as the bubble burst greatly altered reality. Tens of millions of middle-class households have seen much or all of what they thought of as their savings disappear. The loss of $8 trillion in wealth is equal to $110,000 per homeowner. At the same time, the stock market lost more than one-third of its value compared with the pre-recession peak, adversely affecting the richer part of the population. As noted earlier, the stock market has since rallied.

The aforementioned economist Dean Baker has calibrated the effects of the housing collapse and the stock market decline on wealth-holders by age group.[15] Figure 13.1 shows the net wealth for late baby boomers (those between the ages of 45 and 54 in 2009) in 2007 along with a projection for 2009 that takes into account the fall in house prices and the drop in the stock market.[16] In 2007, when the price of a typical home in the U.S. cost $219,000, typical people in this age group had $215,000 in net wealth. This effectively means that if they cashed out all retirement benefits, savings, and checking accounts; sold all stocks and home(s); and paid off their mortgage, credit cards, and other debts, they would have $215,000. This is the typical or median homeowner in 2007. Half of this age group had even less wealth. Roughly a fifth of this group had zero net wealth, including equity in their homes, which means that their mortgage, credit card debt, and other liabilities equaled or exceeded the value of their homes and other assets.

---

[15] Dean Baker, *False Profits* (Sausalito, CA: PoliPoint Press, 2010), pp. 48–55.
[16] As luck has it, data on wealth are not as current as data on personal incomes.

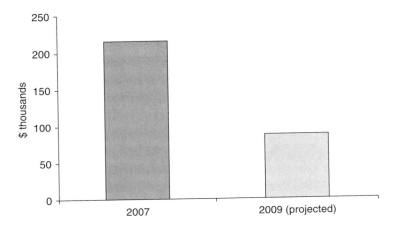

*Source*: Dean Baker, *False Profits*, p. 49.
*Note*: FRB 2007 SCF and author's calculations.

**Figure 13.1:**   Net Wealth of Late Baby Boomers (Ages 45–54).

In the wake of the housing collapse, matters were much worse. According to Baker, the typical or median late baby-boomer household is projected to have only $88,000 in wealth after the collapse of the housing bubble and the stock market's plunge. This is somewhat more than enough to pay off half the mortgage on the median home, which now sells for about $170,000. Once again, half of the later baby boomers have even less wealth than this. Close to a third now have zero net wealth. Some $70,000 will not go very far toward supporting a couple through a 20-year retirement; it would provide only about $4,000 a year in annual retirement income to supplement Social Security payments. Even the wealthiest families in this age group are likely to be almost totally dependent on Social Security to support their retirement.

The retirement situation is not very different for the early baby-boomer households (those between the ages of 55 and 64). Figure 13.2 shows the net wealth for early baby boomers in 2007 along with a projection for 2009 that comes after the fall. In 2007, typical people in this age group had $268,000 in net worth. Since wealth rises somewhat through the 50s, peaking around age 60, this

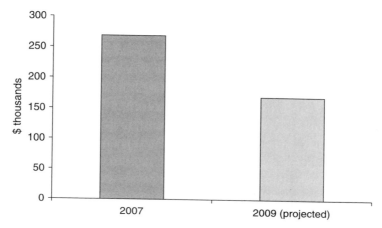

*Source*: Baker, *False Profits*, p. 51.
*Note*: FRB 2007 SCF and author's calculations.

**Figure 13.2:** Net Wealth of Early Baby Boomers (ages 55–64).

amount is somewhat more than what the typical late baby boomer had in the same year. Still, the wealth for a typical family in this age group is projected to fall to $168,700 in 2009; the net wealth of the typical early baby boomers would be reduced to about $50,000 after paying off their mortgages. This amount would provide the very modest supplement of around $3,000 a year to the family's Social Security benefits. Almost a fifth of the families in this age group will have zero wealth in 2009. Even the better-off families will have relatively few assets to support them in retirement. Those in the upper-middle class (the fourth wealth quintile) do somewhat better. They are projected to have wealth equal to $397,000 in 2009, leaving them with about $230,000 after paying off the mortgage on a typical home. Their wealth would provide only about $12,000 a year in retirement benefits.

All in all, the collapse of the housing bubble means that the vast majority of baby boomers will be almost completely dependent on Social Security in their retirement. This is so for even the upper-middle-class. Many baby boomers will attempt to work more years to offset this loss of wealth. Their ability to accumulate savings in these additional years of work will depend on their vitae and conditions in the labor market. Since it appears that high unemployment from the housing and financial crisis will persist into 2011, and even 2012, the opportunities to make up for the lost wealth will be severely limited. (Again, an optimist would say it is possible to marshal public policy to reduce unemployment in such a rich country.) Baby boomers will be struggling to find work along with everyone else. Employment is likely to be part-time, and the wages might be considerably lower than what they once had expected. Homeownership, instead of being a source of additional wealth, will be a drag on the baby boomers.

What to do with the home will be on the minds of the baby boomers. Figure 13.3 shows the percentage of homeowners in each age group who will have to bring cash to complete the sale of their homes, because the sale price will not be sufficient to pay off the mortgage and cover the closing costs. These calculations assume six percent closing costs, but often additional expenses will accrue when selling a home. Some 32.4 percent — almost one-third — of younger baby boomers would need to bring cash to complete the sale of their homes. But the situation is much worse for low- and moderate-income homeowners in this age group. Almost three-quarters of these families would have to bring money to a closing. Even many

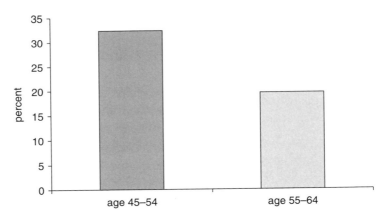

*Source*: Baker, *False Profits*, p. 54.
*Note*: FRB 2007 SCF and author's calculations.

**Figure 13.3:** Percent of Homeowners Needing Cash to Sell Their Houses (2009).

upper-middle-income families would have to pay out cash to sell their homes; more than 20 percent of families in the fourth wealth quintile would be in this situation.

Things are slightly better for the older baby boomers but still rather bleak. About a fifth, or 19.5 percent, would have to pay money to sell their homes. Among moderate income homeowners (the bottom wealth quintile of homeowners), 64 percent will need to put up cash to sell their homes. All things considered, homeownership has not been a path to wealth accumulation for this group. Even among upper-middle class homeowners, 14 percent would have to bring money to the table at closing.

This lack of sufficient equity in the home also affects workers' efforts to seek employment. With jobs shifting between industries and geographical regions, many workers may have to leave their locale and seek work elsewhere. Being tied to homes they cannot sell is a serious impediment; mobility is limited, a condition found in the vita theory. This is on top of having been misled with trillions of dollars of imaginary housing-bubble wealth.

## THE WEAK USA WELFARE NET

With several years of near double-digit unemployment rates, the attention naturally shifts to the welfare system and its viability. This is important because in the United States workers are not automatically supported if a recession is deep and prolonged. This is unlike the experience of workers in other rich industrial economies. The U.S. welfare system is adequate only if the recessions are short. As luck has it, most of the post-World War II recessions had rapid employment recoveries prior to 1990. The 1990–1991 recession was different; output growth came back quickly, but jobs did not. Production recovered within three quarters in 1991, but it took 23 months from the trough of the recession to recover the jobs lost in the recession. That experience is eclipsed by the Great Recession, in which the presence of near double-digit unemployment rates is already measured in years. Once again, there is extraordinary political pressure on Congress and the Federal Reserve to somehow produce jobs.

Why the urgency? There is a great difference between the United States and most continental European countries in the level and duration of unemployment benefits. In the 1989–1994 period the United States, on average, replaced 50 percent of lost wages, while France replaced 57 percent and Germany 63 percent. Moreover, in the United States these benefits ran out fast, in about six months. In France benefits last for up to three years, and in Germany they last indefinitely. Worse, there are holes even in the scant unemployment benefits in the U.S. While 90 percent of workers are covered by unemployment insurance, only about 40 percent of them receive benefits upon unemployment. Some do not qualify for benefits because they have not worked long enough, others because they left voluntarily, yet others because they are involved in labor disputes, and still others because they do not make themselves available for work while unemployed. The weaknesses in unemployment benefits is compounded by the absence of universal health care or affordable private medical insurance.

The judgment regarding unemployment benefits apply more or less equally to social welfare generally. The United States, alone among the rich countries, is parsimonious. For example, the U.S. spent seven percent of its GDP on old-age pensions and disability payments in 1998, whereas France spent 13.17 percent and Germany 12.8 percent. Looking at retirement benefits, they were only 19.3 percent of the average worker's pre-tax income in the U.S. for people over age 65. This compares with 58.6 percent in France and 37.2 percent in Germany. Worse, Americans do not have personal savings to compensate for the shortfall.

Rajan has provided some reasons for this disparity.[17] There are aspects of the U.S. historical experience that drives its antipathy toward welfare benefits. Among these are the libertarian tradition in politics, the absence of strong nationwide workers' organizations, the concentration of poverty in segments of the population that are racially different, the large size and easy mobility within the economy,

---

[17] Rajan, *op. cit.*, pp. 93–97.

and the existence of competing economic jurisdictions that make centralized legislation difficult.

The liberalism is fundamentally classical or Lockean, which embraces the freedom of the individual and resists significant government intervention in ordinary life. This is seemingly embedded in the cultural and political ethos of the United States. The beliefs still expressed by many Americans in surveys is that the United States has virtually unlimited opportunities, where everyone has the capacity to become rich if they only work hard enough, and that anyone who remains poor probably has not tried hard enough. All of this corresponds with the desire for limited government and welfare. This despite American opportunity and mobility being a myth for the immobile and poor underclass and increasingly the middle class.

There also is the absence of strong workers' organizations in the U.S. In contrast to the United Kingdom, a national workers' movement never really took hold in the U.S. This has left labor unions fragmented in a society that highly values the individual work ethic. This fragmentation was further augmented by the size of the country wherein workers could simply pull up stakes and move if they found local conditions oppressive. By contrast to Europe, socialist parties commanded little voting power in the United States.

Eighteenth-century liberalism has supported business interests and money power as an important force in the U.S. Firm owners were individually much more powerful than any of their workers, even when owners as a group were not well organized. Moreover, if business conditions become oppressive in one state, owners can move investment to another state. Factories are more mobile than labor. This threat of loss of business investment and associated taxes gives states a strong incentive to support business profitability.

This is not to say that the American government fails to respond to business downturns. However, policy made during the midst of a downturn is often hurried, opportunistic, and poorly thought out. This was the case during the recent crises. About one-third of the stimulus package passed by the Obama administration in its early months consisted of one-time tax rebates, which had little effect on spending. Housing, as ever, was not overlooked. A "temporary" tax break to first-time home buyers was passed to try to prevent further declines in house prices. It was quickly renewed and may become permanent. This is a subsidy to first-time buyers, brokers, and construction firms and may simply substitute current sales for future sales. As noted in Chapter 12, the overall pure fiscal stimulus was inadequate to restore full employment. The reasons for meager welfare benefits are similar to those for the shortfall. The difficulties with fiscal policy leave a heavy burden for monetary policy during a period when zero interest rates are failing to provide enough stimulus as well. Deficit spending was the proper Keynesian tool, even if underutilized.

We next consider recent policies and suggest some from my earlier writings which remain fresh.

# 14

# POLICIES: OLD AND NEW

*You see things; and you say, "Why?" But
I dream things that never were; and I say, "Why not?"*

George Bernard Shaw, *Back to Methuselah* (1921), pt. I, act I

Only the federal government can spend more than its revenues and
run budget deficits: Most states and cities must balance their budgets
annually or face default. There is the recourse of states and some large
cities to issue bonds but at increasingly high rates of interest as they
become junk. The magic at the federal level is found in the way
budget deficits are financed. Because of the willingness of financial
institutions and households to hold government bonds, the Treasury
can issue U.S. Treasuries equal in value to budget deficits. In turn,
the Federal Reserve can keep interest rates stable or at zero, if need
be, by buying a large share of these T-bills or bonds. As luck would
have it, many foreign central banks and treasuries have been buying
the bonds as well. They will continue to do so as long as the international value of the dollar is fairly stable. At the margin, China and
India can only sell their U.S. dollar holdings at some loss. Even
Japan, however, is considered a safe haven for non-yen currencies.

## THE FINANCIAL CRISIS IN THE STATES
## OF AMERICA

States and cities had no choice except to cut back on the provision
of services to balance their budgets during the Great Recession.
Their balancing act in mid-2010 cut state and municipal

285

employment at a time when the national unemployment rate remained very high (9.5 percent in July 2010). In fact, state spending had fallen for two years in a row for the first time in four decades. These cutbacks contributed to the national unemployment rate (9.6 percent in August, September and October).

This fiscal fiasco was playing out on a grand scale in California and New York. Both states boast economies larger than Greece, which so disturbed the world economy in spring 2010 with its threatened default. In 2009 the Golden State was reduced to issuing IOUs: the 2010 year's budget was in no better shape, being in the hole some $19 billion. In New York there was the difficulty of finding cost cuts acceptable to the public-employee unions that helped elect Democrats there. The mid-2010 deficit in Albany was $9.2 billion.

There are the tried and true responses to declines within the business cycle, but as the woes drag on from year to year, the task of closing budget gaps grows more difficult. Larger issues and harder choices are being laid bare, beginning with the problems with Medicaid. Medicaid was created by Congress, but administered by the states and paid for by a patchwork of federal, state and local governments. It is the health care system for America's poor. With enrollments growing rapidly, Medicaid has become a train wreck. The number of people covered by Medicaid will grow an estimated 5.4 percent in 2011. Meanwhile, anticipated funding is expected to grow hardly at all. It is worse in states that are foreclosure-racked. In Arizona officials were planning for a jump of more than 17 percent, and the budgetary pressure there is enormous. By mid-2010 government revenues had sagged to 2004 levels, while Arizona's Medicaid rolls had grown by 475,000 patients since 2004.

A quick run-down of the state-by-state situation in mid-2010 highlights the breadth of the financial crisis.[1] In Missouri Governor Jay Nixon still needed to ax $350 million for a $23.3 billion

---

[1] David von Drehle, "The Other Financial Crisis," *Time*, June 28, 2010, pp. 26–27.

budget. Some cuts have gone to the bone: only five liquor-control agents now monitored 12,000 licenses statewide. Despite having $200 million from Washington next year, the state will likely cut health services for the poor. The state's lack of cash had already curtailed home-care services for the elderly. In Kentucky the legislature made cuts to almost all agencies. In Georgia tax cuts for property owners and the elderly softened the sting of tax hikes on hospital revenue as legislators closed a $785 million deficit. The state's 2011 budget will be $3 billion less than it was in 2008. In Florida then Governor Charlie Crist closed a $3.2 billion hole by slashing university funds and cutting a gambling deal with the Seminole tribe. He killed a plan to borrow cash from a highway trust fund to pay for schools. In Ohio Governor Ted Strickland decreased the state's workforce by one in 12, cut $2.5 billion in across-the-board spending and sought to add gambling. Ohio's rainy-day fund had been drained to 89 cents. New Jersey was deferring $3.1 billion in pension payments because raising property taxes was not enough to close a $10.7 billion shortfall. Funds for schools would have plunged without $1.2 billion stimulus help from Washington D.C. In Connecticut rainy-day funds and stimulus money filled a $4 billion deficit in 2009, but the red ink may top $3 billion by 2012. For now, residents, promised no tax hikes, will pay utility surcharges. In Michigan lawmakers in Lansing were arguing over how to cut a final $300 million and was planning to extend their session through the summer to hash it out. This cut was from an original $1.7 billion deficit. The Minnesota legislature cut aid to local governments and health services to cover a $3 billion deficit. Many of these cuts provided only temporary relief; the state budget office estimated that the shortfall would almost double by 2013. And so it goes. In many states the cuts in aid to local governments guarantee deficits there.

Going *within* the states, the Great Recession has affected some *cities* in surprising ways. In Georgia, at least a dozen Atlanta-areas municipalities and agencies embraced the high-risk derivative securities called swaps in hopes of lowering the cost of bond issues. They paid nearly $300 million in fees for the privilege to such investment banks as Goldman Sachs, JPMorgan and UBS. When the deals went sour, the same governments paid another $100 billion to cancel the contracts. It was worse in Birmingham, Alabama. Former mayor Larry Langford was sentenced to 15 years in federal prison for bribery in a pay-for-play scheme involving sewer-bond swaps in 2002 and 2003. That particular debt was only a part of a municipal spending spree for a domed stadium, transit improvements and a scholarship program — worthy causes but unaffordable in a city even with a sales tax of ten percent. To clean up the mess required budget cuts. The new mayor was proposing a 12 percent wage cut for city workers, closing libraries and recreation centers and canceling a city program to provide laptops for grade school students. Meanwhile, sewer rates have quadrupled, and speculation on the rates has Birmingham headed for bankruptcy. In San Diego, a grand jury was probing that city's troubled financiers fund of a recurring practice of skipping required payments to the city's pension fund while simultaneously awarding ever more generous pensions to public employees. A once solvent system is now billions of dollars in the red. There is the question of whether San Diego is still a "viable" financial entity.

This is an appropriate moment to summarize. The total estimated gap between states' income and obligations in 2011 is $62.3 billion. The expected growth in the number of Medicaid recipients on average in 2011 is 5.4 percent. Some 31 states were projecting a 2011 shortfall of ten percent or more as a percentage of their 2010 budgets. An additional $53.4 billion shortfall was expected in the 2012 fiscal year. Moreover, the bankruptcy word has crept into many conversations in communities around the country: The bonds of these cities may end up being of little value, spelling bankruptcy.

In short, the states of the United States could be the trigger for the next financial crisis. What is a potential crisis is really a tragedy. The estimated $115.7 billion shortfall for 2011–2012 is a gigantic sum for the states but a meager amount for the federal government. The same conclusion applies to future years of state deficits. If the crisis comes because the Treasury was unwilling to make a $115.7 billion transfer, that will be a tragedy. In late July 2010 the Senate approved a meager $26 billion package of aid to states in the hope of saving the jobs of teachers and other public workers. Approval by the House was expected in fall 2010. The proposed state and local aid, however, is less than a quarter of what was needed.

In terms of employment, the state-local tragedy was already in play. State and local budget gaps were so vast that up to 30,000 public jobs would be cut each month at least through the end of 2010. Since their peak in 2008, state and local payrolls have shrunk by 316,000, a figure that does not include private sector jobs tied to government spending. And private companies that contract with states and localities were likely to cut even more deeply. All told, 600,000 to 700,000 jobs likely will vanish during the 12 months ending July 2011.

## POLICIES AT MID-YEAR 2010

Congress passed and President Obama signed into law on July 21, 2010 the stiffest restrictions on banks and Wall Street since the Great Depression, clamping down on lending practices and expanding consumer protections to prevent a repeat of the 2007–2009 meltdown. This came 22 months after the collapse of Lehman Brothers which triggered a worldwide panic in credit and other markets. The law will give the government new powers to break up companies that threaten the economy, create a new agency to guard consumers in their financial transactions and shine light into shadow financial markets that escaped the oversight of regulators.

Large, failing financial institutions would be liquidated and the costs assessed on their surviving peers. The Federal Reserve's powers were being expanded while falling under greater congressional scrutiny. From storefront payday lenders to the biggest banking and investment houses on Wall Street, few players in the financial world are immune to the bill's reach. Consumer and investor transactions, whether simple debit card swipes or the most complex securities trades, face new safeguards or restrictions.

The legislation does not offer a quick remedy, however. Rather, it lays down prescriptions for regulators to act. In many cases, the real impact will not be felt for years. Still, one of the top regulators who will be charged with implementing the law, Federal Reserve Chairman Ben Bernanke, said the bill represents a "far-reaching step toward preventing a replay of the recent financial crisis." The law injects transparency into transactions involving financial instruments such as derivatives and will restrict banks from making risky bets with their own capital. It directs agencies to write hundreds of new rules.

One provision that barely survived will have the most direct bearing on millions of ordinary people's lives: the new agency meant to protect consumers from abusive financial products, called the Bureau of Consumer Financial Protection. The proposal was the source of some of the most intense debates in the long struggle over the financial-regulatory overhaul, and the battles are far from over. The biggest looming one was over who would head the agency, a fight that heated up as union leaders met with Treasury Secretary Timothy Geithner[2] to lobby for giving the job to Elizabeth Warren of Harvard Law School — whose idea the agency was. Banking groups were urging key senators to oppose Ms. Warren, calling her an activist who would impose policies they argue would hurt the availability of credit, especially for those with low incomes.

With Democratic leaders in Congress joining liberal consumer groups and unions in pushing for Ms. Warren — and with many Republicans opposed — the contest was shaping up to have the interest and drama of a Supreme Court nomination. Senate confirmation was needed. It is an important appointment; the agency will have a roughly $500 million annual budget that doesn't require approval from Congress.

There are advantages of the new agency being housed in the Federal Reserve. Placing the agency within the Federal Reserve presumably insulates it from politicians. The new consumer regulator will have independent powers to write and enforce rules governing how loans and other financial products are offered, bearing on everything from the type of mortgages people can get to the fees on their credit cards. The agency will be able to enforce its rules against any

---

[2] Geithner plans to leave his post at Treasury at the end of 2010.

bank with more than $10 billion of assets, as well as all large mort-gage lenders, student-loan companies and payday-loan firms. It will have an army of examiners to probe these companies' practices. Small banks will have to follow the new rules written by the agency but they will be examined by other federal regulators. The bureau's policies and rules could be overturned by *other* regulators only if they would put the safety and soundness of the U.S. banking system or the stability of the financial system of the United States at risk.

Ms. Warren's connection to the bill predated its inception. In April 2009, White House chief economic adviser Lawrence Summers[3] and Ms. Warren, long-time acquaintances from Harvard, met for three hours at an Indian restaurant in Washington, hashing out ideas about the possible design of such an agency. Playing a devil's-advocate role he often employs in policy debates, Dr. Summers questioned how such a bureau could be insulated from political influence. Ms. Warren left with a sense she had Mr. Summer's support of the agency. In early September 2010 the naysayers won as Ms. Warren was denied the position, though she was allowed to build the agency.

Consolidating powers of multiple regulators, the new agency would write and enforce rules affecting a range of companies, from Wall Street banks to payday-loan stores. Almost any company that offered a financial product to consumers would have to answer to it. Administration officials thought the concept would resonate so strongly with the public that it would smooth the passage for the entire financial overhaul. But bankers and Republicans went on the attack, saying it would create an ungovernable bureaucracy and restrict credit. This opposition continued and was joined by the U.S. Chamber of Commerce.

The bill nonetheless moved forward and the financial-protection bureau, as noted, was approved. Now that the bureau has been approved — and is expected to be fully operational within a year — it remains to be seen what effect it will have on credit. Some consumer

---

[3] Dr. Summers plans to leave his post as chief economic adviser to President Obama at the end of 2010.

advocates acknowledge that certain borrowers, particularly low-income people, are likely to find less credit available, as products such as payday lenders are more tightly regulated. They say, nonetheless, that tighter controls will prevent borrowers from being hit with abusive loans.

This Dodd-Frank financial regulation bill, as it was called, was already forcing the restructuring of some investment giants on Wall Street. Goldman Sachs, under orders from Washington, must break up its principal strategies group, the wildly successful trading unit that has helped power the bank's profits. Goldman was considering several options, including moving the traders to another division or shutting the unit altogether.

Across Wall Street, other financial giants are embarking on the task of complying with the new rules governing their trading and investments. Morgan Stanley is considering ceding control of its $7 billion hedge fund firm, FrontPoint Partners. At Citigroup, executives have sold hedge fund and private equity businesses and are now discussing paring back proprietary trading, which relies on a bank's own capital to make bets in financial markets. JPMorgan Chase has already begun dismantling its standalone proprietary trading desk and is now preparing to wind down One Equity Partners, its internal private equity business. Some of these changes will take years to fully implement.

## PROSPECTS FOR MONETARY POLICY

We must not forget that the Federal Reserve is also the driver of conventional and unconventional monetary policies. Federal Reserve Chairman Ben Bernanke told Congress at mid-year he is prepared to take further action to support the economy if the outlook deteriorates, but indicated the Fed's reluctance to do so, given limited options and questions about the effectiveness of any new measures.

Presenting the Fed's semiannual report to the Senate Banking Committee on July 21, 2010 Mr. Bernanke said the Fed still expects the economy to show moderate growth this year despite a "somewhat weaker outlook" that he blamed on financial market turmoil, largely stemming from Europe. But pronouncing the outlook "unusually uncertain," he said, "We remain prepared to take further policy actions as needed to foster a return to full utilization of our nation's productive potential in a context of price stability."

Wall Street did not welcome the remarks as stocks declined sharply. In answering questions, Mr. Bernanke outlined three options for supporting the economy, if necessary. The Fed could verbally emphasize its commitment to keep short-term interest rates low for a long time. It could lower the interest rate it pays on reserves that banks store at the central bank, to encourage more lending. (The fed funds rate remains near zero.) And it could reinvest proceeds from maturing or prepaid mortgage securities, instead of letting them come off the Fed's balance sheet, or make additional purchases. The latter is among the unconventional policies. As we shall see in the final chapter, Bernanke was to return to the policy of quantitative easing.

Mr. Bernanke emphasized that the labor market remains a key worry. The U.S. has lost 8.5 million jobs since the downturn started, and he said the pace of private payroll growth in the first half of 2010 — 100,000 a month, on average — is "insufficient to reduce the unemployment rate materially." The Fed sees the unemployment rate falling even more slowly than it previously expected, leaving it at a still high 7 percent to 7.5 percent at the end of 2012.

As to pure fiscal policy, Mr. Bernanke said the recent large federal budget deficits are appropriate, considering the weak economy. He said additional fiscal support from Washington could help, given weak private spending, but acknowledged concern that markets might react adversely if the deficit is not brought under control. "The best approach, in my view, is to maintain some fiscal support for the economy in the near term, but to combine that with serious attention to addressing what are very significant fiscal issues for the United States in the medium term," Mr. Bernanke said. "I don't think its either/or, I think you need to really do both. If the debt continues to accumulate and becomes unsustainable...then the only way that can end is through a crisis or some other very bad outcome."

Meanwhile, the White House was championing the stimulus already in place. President Barack Obama and top officials were stepping up the pace of their travel to promote the economic stimulus package to skeptical voters — particularly in states with close mid-term election contests in the fall. The increased activity came as Republicans are making an issue of the administration's spending and selling the stimulus. Under the banner of "Recovery Summer," the president had recently made visits to Holland, Mich., Kansas City, MO., Las Vegas and Columbus, Ohio. In all, administration officials made 70 stimulus-themed trips to six states which had competitive elections in November, and will be pivotal in the 2012 Presidential campaign: Ohio, Pennsylvania, Florida, Michigan, California and Missouri. Except for extending unemployment benefits, the White House has had trouble in advancing any new fiscal stimulus policies. This places still more of the burden on the Federal Reserve and Bernanke.

## EUROPEAN STIMULUS?

Any new source of stimulus is unlikely to come from Europe. Growth in the eurozone is expected to slog along at less than a two percent pace through 2012, the International Monetary Fund forecast in July, as many of the region's countries focused on getting their debt problems under control. The IMF said three major areas need to be addressed to establish a durable recovery: tackling weaknesses in the banking sector, implementing ambitious fiscal-consolidation plans, and moving ahead with fundamental structural reforms such as entitlement programs and labor markets.

After the 17-nation eurozone sharply expanded its overall fiscal deficit in 2009 to fight the global recession, the IMF forecast that the eurozone would take a "neutral aggregate fiscal stance" in 2010, and would reduce its deficit somewhat over the following two years. While the tighter fiscal stance would limit growth, it was necessary to stabilize the eurozones' debt. In particular, the Greek financial crisis in 2010, with its threat of sovereign-debt default, has accelerated the effort by other heavily indebted eurozone nations to limit spending.

There are consequences for employment. The IMF forecast for unemployment in the eurozone, which was 7.6 percent before the global recession in 2009, is expected to average 10.2 percent in 2010 and fall only to 10.1 percent in 2012. There is one bright spot. The decline in the value of the euro over 2010 should give European exports a boost. The deeper risk for Europe is a renewal of a credit crisis. A credit crunch on the scale of 2009, the IMF estimated, could reduce eurozone gross domestic product by two percentage points from 2010 to 2011, resulting in a zero growth rate.

## ADDRESSING INCOME INEQUALITIES IN THE USA

As noted above, a highly unequal income distribution in the U.S. led to the use of easy housing credit and easy money policy generally. Subprime mortgage lending was a byproduct of easy housing credit. In turn, inequalities in income stem from the relative scarcity of workers with abundant human capital. The opportunity to acquire greater human capital is the way out of this dilemma.

Earlier the vita theory of the personal income distribution was used to explain the sources of human capital and wage inequalities.[4] Human capital refers to the broad set of capabilities, including health, knowledge and intelligence, attitude, social aptitude that persons bring to the workplace. These characteristics begin with the birth vita. While we cannot do anything about the genes a child is endowed with, we can influence nutrition during pregnancy and in early childhood. Poor nutrition in a child's early years seems to be associated with the early onset of degenerative diseases of old age. Moreover, nutrition makes an enormous difference to a child's intelligence and pre-career health. In other words, disadvantageous human capital

---

[4] E. Ray Canterbery, "The Vita Theory of the Personal Income Distribution," *op. cit.* The lay reader can read between the differential equations to get the jest of it. Later, the vita theory was expressed in matrix algebra and input-output analysis in E. Ray Canterbery, "A General Theory of International Trade and Domestic Employment Adjustments" in Michael Landeck, editor, *International Trade: Regional and Global Issues* (New York: St. Martin's Press and London: Macmillan, 1994), especially pp. 152–153.

begins early in life. Children of the poor and the poorly educated perpetuate the cycle of poverty.

The vita is first added to by early education. Early education is crucial. By the age of eight, intelligence, as ordinarily measured, seems pretty well set. Therefore it is important that young children have access to quality pedagogic resources. Moreover, early childhood learning programs tend to reduce the likelihood that a child will drop out of high school, and increase the likelihood that the child will enroll in college, the next step in building a vita.

The family is part of the birth vita that continues to contribute to development over the life cycle. The 1966 Coleman report concluded that family background was a greater influence on school achievement than any measure of the school environment, including per student expenditures. The income of the parents is important because it provides access to resources and the kind of environment that enhances learning. Children of high-income parents grow up with educational games, books, and summer programs, all of which contribute to their learning outside of school. Income tax credits and a progressive income tax system can contribute to more equal chances at the family level and can enhance the birth vita.

Success in school and in the workplace depends significantly on noncognitive abilities, such as perseverance, determination, and self-discipline. These are abilities that can be enhanced as the vita develops. Good schools inculcate values that serve students well throughout life. It is likely that both the learning environment and the learning of noncognitive skills could be improved through attempts to teach behavior as well as impart knowledge. Some of the noncognitive skills can be learned in extracurricular activities such as sports and being on the debate team.

The quality of teaching and class size affects a child's educational experience. Along with good teaching comes accountability, the key to which is a national standard of student achievement, coupled with testing at regular intervals. The Obama administration has proposed nationwide testing standards, evaluation of teachers based on student test performance, and the entry of more charter schools, using the lever of additional cash for states and districts that adopt reforms.

The aforementioned college premium accounts for wide wage differentials. Its achievement depends very much on income of the household. Only 34 percent of youths from households in the bottom quintile of income distribution enroll in college, whereas 79 percent of those from households in the top quintile of family income do so. What's more, only 11 percent of youngsters from the bottom quintile graduate, whereas 53 percent from the top do so. The college dropout rate is also disproportionately high among the poor. Once again, the income distribution is critical.

In the vita theory human capital can be augmented by on-the-job training. Apprenticeships can be important in inculcating work habits and behavior that can help disadvantaged youths hold a steady job. Because of the rapid turnover rate of workers in the U.S., firms will need tax incentives to offer these apprenticeships to compensate for the fact that they are unlikely to keep an apprentice in the long run.

According to the vita theory, as the quality of the human capital of the disadvantaged improves, wage inequality will diminish. The redistribution of opportunities can lead to a more equal income distribution and, ultimately, to a more equal wealth distribution.

## GLOBAL CONSUMPTION PATTERNS

Current global consumption patterns are unsustainable. The United States and a few other industrial countries like Spain and the United Kingdom have been spending more than they produce or earn and thus borrowing to finance the difference. Countries like China and Vietnam have been doing the opposite. Energy use is one indicator of consumption of goods. In 2003 each person in the United States used 7.8 tons of oil, which was about twice the amount used per person in France, Germany, and Japan; about seven times the amount used in China; and 15 times the amount used in India. Despite per capita income in the U.S. being among the highest in the world, the U.S. financed its spending in 2006 by borrowing 70 percent of the world's excess savings.

The U.S. spending was facilitated by a massive financial system and by the role of the dollar as a reserve currency. Moreover, U.S.

policies encouraged debt-fueled spending in normal times and as a way out of recessions. Countries like Chile, China, Germany, Japan, Malaysia, Saudi Arabia, and South Korea supplied the United States by following a pattern of growth led by exports and financed by being willing to hold U.S. debt. This mutually beneficial but unsustainable equilibrium has been disrupted by the financial crisis and the subsequent downturn.

Sustained high U.S. unemployment is compounding uncertainty for the middle class already hit by stagnant wages. Households in the United Kingdom and Spain are in a similar situation, while smaller countries like Greece and Portugal are on the verge of crisis.

Ideally, consumption growth will shift from rich deficit countries to developing ones. The developing countries would have to give up on their export-led growth policies. There is room for multilateral organizations to improve the availability of loans to some countries, if nothing else so that nations do not run trade surpluses only to build up foreign exchange reserves. For this to happen, the IMF and the World Bank will have to operate differently than in the past. The IMF operates through a process of exhortation that fails to move anyone except those who need the Fund's money. There is a real problem of gaining agreement on policy reforms across a set of countries on a case-by-case basis, as the Fund has to do if it is to bring down trade imbalances. To give discretion to one agency, such as the IMF, would require countries to give a tremendous amount of sovereignty to an international bureaucracy. Moreover, the IMF's recommendations are not backed by any power of enforcement: most industrial countries and large emerging-market countries do not need IMF funding, which constitutes its main means of persuasion. Still, IMF prescriptions often hit the mark simply because the Fund is apolitical.

## EMPOWERING THE IMF

One way of increasing the power of the IMF is to make Special Drawing Rights (SDRs) more important as global reserves and by giving the IMF more power over exchange rates. Many years ago I recommended a wide gold band that moves as a delayed peg.[5] The widening of the gold band would have required a minor modification in the IMF Articles of Agreement. At the time exchange rates were calibrated in terms of the price of gold. This has changed with nations divided between those with completely flexible exchange rates such as the United States and those with managed exchange rates such as China. Many exchange rates are tied to the U.S. dollar or the British pound. Today I recommend that exchange rates be calibrated in terms of the SDR. The combination of a wide SDR band and delayed peg would be good compromise between flexible and fixed exchange rates. The band would be six percent, a fluctuation of three percent either side of the SDR par value.

The wide SDR band and the allowance of rates to move freely within it would have several distinct advantages: (1) There would be considerable uncertainty for potential currency speculators and thus tend to lessen speculation based on too narrow a fluctuation. (2) Purchasers of foreign securities who do not always "cover" exchange risks under a narrower band would now be virtually compelled to enter forward exchange markets and "cover" their exchange position. This would broaden the forward exchange market in several maturities, providing a wider market for export-importer covering against the risk of exchange rate fluctuations. (3) With smaller "hot money" flows from anticipated devaluation, short-term capital flows would probably be more stable. (4) Moderated short-term capital flows would eliminate one excuse for a monetary policy geared to "international considerations." (5) World liquidity needs would be lessened because balance-of-payments adjustments within a wide band would reduce the frequency of intervention and hence the level of required international monetary reserves.

The second step would be to move to even more exchange rate flexibility under the International Monetary Fund. Because exchange prices would still have upper and lower limits, there would be an

---

[5] See E. Ray Canterbery, *Economics on a New Frontier* (Belmont, CA: Wadsworth, 1968), pp. 212–216.

"early warning system" for identifying a par value level that differed greatly from the natural market exchange rate. If the U.S. exchange rate, for example, had to be supported near the lower end of its six percent range (losing foreign exchange reserves) for several months, that necessity would be a signal for reducing — not devaluing — the par value of the dollar in terms of SDRs. The SDR band would be lowered with the old lower limit as the new par value. The announcement of the new band would come several weeks after its adoption in order to deter speculators. Because the exchange rate can be pegged until the economy catches its breath, this delayed peg would allow for some domestic adjustments. This par rate would be precisely supported to give those traders not covered against exchange risks an opportunity to scurry for cover in the forward exchange markets. Moreover, the maintenance of this level for an indefinite period plus a slow rate of depreciation would further deter heavy speculation in the appreciating currency. In order to prevent the lower limit from becoming a "fixed-for-all-times" rate, the IMF would be empowered to alter currency par values under a semi-automatic market rule. This new role for the IMF would insulate exchange rate adjustments from political stress. Nations would have already agreed to the IMF rules.

The objections voiced by opponents to more flexible exchange rates are clearly modified under the delayed peg. But would great uncertainty about rates still disrupt trade and capital flows? Quite the opposite would be true. The forward markets which cover against exchange risks would be even more viable than they are today. The necessity of trade covering would generate heavier markets in very long maturities, so that every reasonable exchange risk could be offset.[6]

---

[6] Short-term capital flows are self-limiting when exchange rates are sufficiently flexible. With forward covering, interest-rate parity occurs: the cost of covering rises to equal the interest-rate differential. For a theory that explains the consequences for speculation, see E. Ray Canterbery, "A Theory of Foreign-Exchange Speculation Under Alternative Systems," *Journal of Political Economy*, May–June 1971. Among the systems explained is the wide band with a delayed peg. Lay readers can read between the mathematical equations.

The adoption of a wide SDR band with a delayed peg can be briefly summarized.

1.  The implementation of a six percent SDR band would cause short-term capital flows to stabilize. This width would be sufficient for substantial adjustments in trade accounts.
2.  When, and if, the exchange rate of any nation rises or falls toward the new exchange rate limits for a prolonged period of reserve losses, the band could be moved with the new par value centered on the violated limit.
3.  The new par value would be sustained for an indefinite period. Speculators could not be certain whether the rate would then appreciate or depreciate.
4.  Under the delayed peg and wide SDR band, monetary policy would be free to perform its domestic duties.
5.  The timing and moving the peg would be determined by the IMF. Rules for such changes should, however, be made explicit, but sufficiently vague in actual implementation to fool most speculators.

The advantages to the adoption of this reform plan are several and can be briefly summarized.

1.  The powers of the IMF would be enhanced as well as the role of the SDR in international finance.
2.  Fixed exchange regimes would be relics of the past.
3.  The role of the International Monetary Fund (IMF) would be strengthened in the global community.
4.  The dilemma of the reserve-currency nation whereby deficits are required to supply foreign exchange but the accumulation of reserves abroad threatens devaluation would be ended.
5.  Currency wars could be avoided.

China's currency was overvalued by about 40 percent against the dollar in the fall of 2010. The yuan, the Chinese currency, is presently tied to the dollar. Under a wide SDR band with a delayed peg, the yuan could be brought down gently, thereby stimulating U.S. exports and dampening U.S. imports from China. China is a problem because it holds a substantial volume of U.S. dollars as official foreign currency reserves. At the margin a fall in the value of the dollar might lead to a greater shift by the Chinese into Japanese yen or even South Korean won.

## FUTURE INCOME TAX POLICIES

The Bush tax cuts of 2001 and 2003 were set to expire at the end of 2010. An epic fight brewed over what Congress and President Obama should do about the expiring tax cuts, with such substantial economic and political consequences that it could shape the 2012 elections and fiscal policy for years to come.

Democratic leaders, including Mr. Obama, were intent on letting the tax cuts for the wealthy expire as scheduled at the end of the year. But they had pledged to continue the lower tax rates for individuals earning less than $200,000 and families earning less than $250,000 — what they are calling the middle class. Letting the tax rates expire for the rich would provide an estimated $850 billion to the Treasury through 2012. At the same time, this expiration of the tax would make the income tax more progressive and go along way toward making incomes less unequal. An added bonus: such a tax would place a limit on available funds for pure speculation. Most Republicans wanted to extend the tax cuts for everyone, and some Democrats agreed, saying it would be unwise to raise taxes on *anyone* while the economy remains weak. If no action were taken, taxes on income, dividends, capital gains and estates would all rise.

Beyond the implications for family checkbooks, the tax fight will serve as a proxy for the bigger political clashes of several years, including the size of government and the best way of handling the tepid economy. On December 7, Pearl Harbor Day, Obama was forced to surrender to the GOP. The Democrats in the House of Representatives wanted extension of low tax rates for those below $250,000 only. The GOP wanted an extension of low tax rates for the top two percent or those above $250,000. Obama agreed to a compromise that included an extension of the 2001 Bush tax rates across the board for two years. This plan was being considered by the U.S. Senate; the Democrats in the House were up in arms. We will return to the final outcome and the prospects for these tax programs in the final chapter.

The uncertainty over the outcome has many businesspeople sitting on their hands, because they don't know what tax rates will be during the near term. That is suppressing investment and hiring, surveys suggest, contributing to economy's current sluggishness. As John Maynard Keynes had it, any uncertainty is bound to adversely affect business investment.

Table 14.1 shows the current tax rate schedule alongside the scheduled rates in 2011 if the tax cuts were allowed to expire. The rate for the lowest income bracket would go from 10 percent to 15 percent and the rate for the highest bracket would go from 35 percent to 39.6 percent. Taxes on capital gains and dividends would soar. The estate tax, which is currently zero, would go up to 55 percent in 2011. These latter tax increases could hurt stock prices.

Given the state of the current economy and forecasts for the next two years, allowing tax rates of the lower income and middle class to rise would be a disaster. These income classes comprise the wellspring of consumer expenditures. The tax rates on the rich, which include those on capital gains, dividends and estates can be allowed to rise. The rich consume a lower share of their incomes and such taxes have very little disincentive for real investment. After all, the economy prospered under these tax burdens in the past, while the Great Recession happened with the 2001 lower tax rates on the better-off.

The overall tax system has become more regressive over time with lower income families paying larger shares of taxes than the rich. The federal government has transferred ever greater fiscal burdens to state and local governments that have always relied on regressive taxes. The tax burden of the working class has steadily increased with each increase in social security tax payments. Federal income taxes remain modestly progressive.

**Table 14.1:**   Tax Rates

| Current | Income Level | Scheduled Rate in 2011 |
|---|---|---|
| **Income taxes** | | |
| 10% | $0–$16,750 | 15% |
| 15 | 16,751–68,000 | 15 |
| 25 | 68,001–137,300 | 28 |
| 28 | 137,301–209,250 | 31 |
| 33 | 209,251–373,650 | 36 |
| 35 | $373,651 and above | 39.6 |
| **Capital-gains taxes** | | |
| 15% | couples up to $250,000 | 20% |
| 15 | couples over $250,000 | 20 |
| **Taxes on dividends** | | |
| 15% | couples up to $250,000 | up to 36% |
| 15 | couples over $250,000 | up to 39.6% |
| **Estate tax** | | |
| Rate | 0% | 55% |
| Exemption | N.A. | $1 million |

*Sources*: 1. *Wall Street Journal*, July 15, 2010, p. A5.
       2. Tax Foundation; WSJ research; amended by the author.

*Note*: Income-tax ranges based on 2010 taxable income. Income levels for capital gains and dividends based on adjusted gross income.

The present income tax structure could be greatly simplified and made more progressive at the same time. Table 14.2 shows only three tax rates (if the zero tax rate is ignored). Most tax exemptions could be eliminated in order to bring in more revenue. Those with incomes of $16,750 or less would continue to receive transfer payments. Elsewhere, I, and others, have presented detailed plans for tax reform.[7] Such low rates of taxation would

---

[7] See E. Ray Canterbery, Eric W. Cook, and Bernard A. Schmitt, "The Flat Tax, Negative Tax, and VAT: Gaining Progressivity and Revenue," *Cato Journal*, 5(2), 521–536 (Fall 1985). See also E. Ray Canterbery, *Wall Street Capitalism* (Singapore/New Jersey/London/HongKong: World Scientific, 2000), pp. 280–294.

**Table 14.2:** A Simplified Federal Income Tax Schedule.

| Income Level | Tax Rate (%) |
|---|---|
| $0–$16,750 | 0 |
| $16,751–$68,000 | 15 |
| $68,001–$137,300 | 25 |
| $137,301 and above | 35 |

require the elimination of most exemptions, including that for mortgage interest. Presently low-income wage earners receive an Earned Income Tax Credit (EITC), which during 2007–2010 was the country's largest anti-poverty program. Income from capital gains, dividends and interest would be taxed as ordinary income. Robert Reich, Labor Secretary under President Clinton, has suggested that the EITC be extended as a "reverse income tax." Full-time workers earning $20,000 or less (in 2009 dollars) would receive a wage supplement of $15,000. These wage supplements would cost the federal government $633 billion yearly and would presumably allow the elimination of most other welfare programs. The reverse tax would be funded by a carbon tax and much higher progressive tax rates on the wealthy (the top three percent). Reich's plan would be highly progressive.[8]

A progressive tax system has several advantages beyond fairness. Historically lopsided income and wealth distributions have always led to speculative excesses, and, more often than not, economic depressions. Also a truly progressive tax provides a built-in fiscal stabilizer for the economy. When the economy is growing rapidly, rising tax revenues can prevent the growth from being overly exuberant. When the economy is tilting toward recession, households fall into lower tax brackets reducing the government's revenue but providing a natural

---

[8] Robert Reich, *After Shock* (New York: Alfred A. Knopf, 2010), pp. 129–132. Reich also recommends a reemployment system to replace the unemployment benefits system (pp. 133–137) at the modest cost of $3 billion yearly. The vita theory would support the latter proposal. The present House and Senate are unlikely to buy such a package, but it provides excellent left-Democrat talking points.

stimulus for the economy. The simplified tax plan would be implemented alongside an initially modest value-added tax and the aforementioned VATIP proposal.

## A TRANSACTIONS TAX ON WEALTH

Still, there is a need for an additional tax revenue source besides the otherwise potentially regressive VAT. The fattest target is the oversized financial sector which has grown disproportionately to the industrial sector. A small financial tax on financial assets could be levied. A minor tax would raise considerable revenue because of the presently vast size of financial assets outstanding. Beyond this, there is a need for a financial transactions tax on speculators.

Long-term capital gains — taking place over several years — within an industrial firm have long been considered the flywheel of capitalism. Rare is the economist who suggests that long-term capital gains are undesirable. I am with the majority on the blessings of strong *long-term* capital gains. Quick capital gains on secondary financial instruments are of a different character; generally, the purpose of such sudden sales is to make money out of money, something accomplished in a time too brief and too indirect to produce goods and services. If we prefer lasting to fleeting capitalism, we would discourage speculative gains. Such speculation led to the recent banking and money panic.

A long time ago Nobelist James Tobin recommended a small transactions tax on foreign exchange and stocks to dampen speculation in such markets. I endorse the Tobin tax but suggest it be substantially greater than half a percent. A transactions tax also recommends itself for other kinds of domestic financial transfers. The purpose would not be to punish manufacturers for earning profits or stockholders for unearned dividends. The 30-year bond, for example, was not designed to change hands daily. It and ten-year bonds were intended to provide funds for long-term, real investment. Mortgages for financing housing is another example that comes easily to mind. Even equities were originally considered "long-term capital investments" both because perpetual corporations used them to provide finance for new factories and because households held them such a long time.

A properly designed financial transactions tax would discourage speculation in securities. I recommend a transactions tax, not as a levy on productivity, which it isn't, but as a penalty for pure speculation. It is intended to punish people for the misuse of money and wealth. Such a tax, sufficient to sting but not so great as to eliminate all gains, would be directed at the new leisure class of wealthholders, who have increased financial market volatility and made speculation more lucrative, moving from bonds into stocks and back again, and sometimes into derivatives.

Any person or institution buying and selling General Motors or any other stock in less than a year has either been imprudent in its purchasing decision or is speculating. A transactions tax, graduated from a high percentage near term and vaporizing at the end of a two-year holding period, would discourage short-term speculation in the stock markets. The design of the tax itself should be subject to long-term study.

Still, as a starting point for discussion, I would recommend a transactions tax of 12 percent on the value of the spot purchase (or sale, in the case of a short position) for all stocks held for less than thirty days. Thereafter, the transactions tax would be reduced by a half percentage point for each month that the shares are continually held. The tax would be introduced gradually but would eventually be applied to all stock holdings. The same tax would be applied to financial derivatives based upon stocks.

The purpose of a transactions tax penalty is not to discourage the buying and selling of securities. If speculators can gain more than 12 percent (after other fees) during the first holding month, they will still make a profit, though a smaller one. Moreover, the government will have additional revenue going toward deficit reduction (and reduced interest) or toward particular programs.

Because most mature in less than a year, U.S. Treasury bills are not a speculative threat. However, U.S. Treasury bonds and corporate bonds are intended to be long-term investments. Federal, state, and municipal bonds have a variety of maturities. The same 12 percent transactions tax could be levied on bonds maturing in one year and held for less than 30 days with a downward-sliding penalty equaling a full percentage point less every 30 days thereafter. If the bonds are held to maturity, no transactions tax would apply. For bonds maturing in two years, the 12 percent transactions tax would be phased out by a half percentage point every 30 days. The same kind of structure would apply to the transactions tax on bonds maturing in three or four years. Further, a tax good enough for standard financial instruments should be applied, perhaps with even greater enthusiasm, to financial derivatives based upon bonds.

After four years, we are looking at truly significant holding periods, and we do not wish to discourage individuals and institutions from buying such long-term bonds. The 12 percent transactions tax would be phased out at zero after holding a bond for five years, whatever its final maturity date. Thus, a bond maturing in ten years or 30 years would be subject to no transactions tax if sold at the end of five years. A transactions tax structured to encourage the buying of long-term bonds would have a surprising benefit. By encouraging the purchase of long-term bonds, that part of the bond market would be deepened and would enjoy greater liquidity, making it less subject to sudden collapse.

Still, some will say that a transactions tax on financial debt instruments and equities will take some excitement out of the markets. They justifiably indict such a tax. However, the gaming tables and slot machines will still be open for business in Las Vegas, Reno, New Orleans, Atlantic City, and even Biloxi. Leisure-class speculators lusting after fast gains or losses can enjoy them in the same manner as the working class. Of course, to the extent that a transactions tax subdued financial speculation, real returns in industry would begin to supersede the paper profits from paper.

## INTEREST-FREE LOANS FOR INFRASTRUCTURE

What I next propose — to counter partly the adverse effects of high long-term interest rates — is not an original idea. Tax supported bodies — state and local governments — should be able to borrow money, interest-free, directly from the U.S. Treasury for capital projects and for paying off existing debt. Such a loan — not a grant — would be for capital projects only, not day-to-day expenses. For example, public schools could borrow to build new classrooms but not to pay teachers. Moreover, such investments are in need of stimulation. Though public investment had averaged 30.0 percent of GDP from 1955 through 1980, it averaged only 2.3 percent from 1981 through 1997, even less in recent years. State and local governments typically account for 85 percent of such investment.

Other benefits would soon flow from interest-free loans for infrastructures. Research has shown that public capital investment stimulates *private investment*, suggesting that President Clinton's initial focus on public infrastructures was sound. A study shows that private business fixed investment from the late 1960s through the late 1980s would have been 0.6 of a percentage point higher as a share of GDP had the nation devoted an additional ten percentage points of GDP to public investment.[9] Lower interest rates alone would make private investment projects more attractive and they would stimulate real investment. Of course, to the extent that a transactions tax subdued financial speculation, real returns in industry would begin to supersede the paper profits from paper. State borrowing also currently tends to be a substitute for federal infrastructure spending.

Furthermore, public investment has a very high rate of return because it stimulates economic growth and employment as better highways, schools, airports, and cleaner water boost the output and sales of private industry. According to a study using state-level data, an increase in the ratio of public to private capital stock from a current 0.45 to 0.50 would increase output growth by 0.8 percent

---

[9] See David A. Aschauer, "Is Public Expenditure Productive?" *Journal of Monetary Economics*, **23**(2), 177–200 (March 1989) and David A. Aschauer, "Dynamic Output and Employment Effects of Public Capital," Working Paper No. 191, The Jerome Levy Economics Institute, Annandale-on-Hudson, N.Y. (April 1997). For a summary of some of the early research on this topic, see Sharon J. Erenburg, "The Real Effects of Public Investment on Private Investment: A Rational Expectations Model," *Applied Economics*, **25**, 831–837 (June 1993).

per year and employment by 0.3 percent per year (peaking at 0.5 percent after 15 years). Moreover, the positive effects are sustained for centuries. At the end of two centuries output climbs by some 27 percent and employment by nearly 21 percent.[10] Even if the effect on economic growth were only half as large as the research suggests, the nation's wealth and income would now be about a fifth higher if the 1955–1980 pace of public investment had been maintained. Virtually every nook and cranny of the private economy benefit from improved roads, airports, and schools.

The advantages of using interest-free loans for funding public infrastructures are many. The U.S. Treasury would get the money not from the federal budget but from Congress which would create the money [as authorized in the U.S. Constitution: Article 1, Section 8, Clause 5]. The action by the Congress and the Treasury would increase the money supply — which is otherwise an exclusive privilege reserved today for private commercial banks and the Federal Reserve. Not only would such loans reduce interest costs, they could be used to reduce taxes on both income and property, even while serving, to an enhanced degree, the necessary and legitimate needs of communities and the nation. Money supply additions from such loans (if not neutralized by securities sales by the Federal Reserve) would be subtracted by an equal amount when the loans are repaid to the Treasury.

Vital infrastructures — bridges, roads, airports, schools, court houses, and so on — could be built without adding to deficits. (Alternatively, existing loans could be exchanged for interest-free debt and taxes could be reduced.) Since the interest cost on state, county, city and schools *doubles* the cost of a project funded by interest-bearing bonds of more than 20 years maturity and *triples* the cost of one of more than 30 years, the public presently pays taxes for two or three schools while getting *only one*. Not only would the payrolls of private contractors be enhanced, employment would rise even as construction costs and inflation cooled. The presence of zero-interest

---

[10] See David A. Aschauer, "Dynamic Output and Employment Effects of Public Capital," *op. cit.*

loans would exert downward pressures on average private loans rates for automobiles, appliances, and houses. If this is such a win-win idea, we might ask, why hasn't it been done?

The answer will surprise many. Such interest-free loans for public infrastructure have been deployed several times, even in this country! It was done by the colonies and by the founding fathers. Later, during the prolonged depression of 1837–1843, Congress enacted a special national bankruptcy law in 1841 to provide relief to debtors; the Treasury Department, faced with rising budgetary deficits, also issued non-interest-bearing government notes. Abraham Lincoln issued similar interest-free notes (mixed with periodic rallies for interest-bearing bonds during the Civil War). More recently, the Federal Reserve cooperated with the Treasury during World War II to yield virtually the same effect, when the federal government borrowed money at less than one percent interest.

When proposed by President Lincoln, a Republican, he said, "the privilege of creating and issuing money is not only the supreme prerogative of Government, but is the Government's greatest creative opportunity. By the adoption of these principles, the taxpayers will be saved immense sums of interest." After all, the money supply *is* a public good. As one of humans' greatest inventions, it was not supposed to serve primarily the purposes of the wealthholding class. Though the bondholders would have us believe that the money supply was invented to threaten the value of its bonds (and hence, indirectly, of its shares of stock), money was originally invented as a means to improve the production and sale of real commodities — grains, timber, textiles, and so on.

New Zealand introduced a modified version of interest-free loans. During the Depression of the 1930s, the central bank of New Zealand issued money to plant trees and build roads and housing, enabling the country to be the first to recover economically (and go on for 30 years of prosperity). Until 1981 its central bank gave loans at one percent interest to the Dairy Board, helping to establish the dairy industry. The Federal Reserve did the opposite during the Great Depression, calling in discount loans from a failing private banking system.

The longest and most resolute use of interest-free public funding of infrastructures has been in the island state of Guernsey, in the English Channel. In 1816 Guernsey's sea walls were crumbling, its muddy roads only four-and-a-half feet wide, and its debt, £18,000. Out of an annual income of £3,000, £2,400 was used to pay interest on the debt. Unemployment was very high.

The government created and lent £6,000 of interest-free state notes. It continued to issue more notes over time until, by 1837, £50,000 had been issued interest-free for sea walls, roads, a marketplace, a church, and a college. By 1958, more than £500,000 had been issued. Contrary to what monetarists would tell us, no inflation followed these issues.

By 1990, the island had 60,000 permanent residents with the equivalent of US$13 million in interest-free notes in circulation. Guernsey has no public debt, its unemployment rate is zero, the average family owns 3.3 cars, and the price of gasoline is US$2 a gallon compared with US$5 in England. Its income tax is a flat 20 percent, and a surplus of government funds earn interest. Even with such interest-free public infrastructure funding, Guernsey has a small but humble bondholding class. The state of Guernsey has become a "cash cow."

A not-for-profit organization of taxpayers, Sovereignty, in Freeport, Illinois has recently renewed the proposed the idea of interest-free public debt. Not only has the group drafted a bill for Congress, its proposal has been endorsed by at least 64 cities, including St. Louis, Missouri, Cleveland, Ohio, Independence, Missouri, and Lansing, Michigan, pus the Southwest (Chicago) Conference of Local Governments, the St. Louis County Municipal League, many school districts, townships and counties. The idea has widespread, even popular grass roots support.[11]

The idea of interest-free loans seems to be catching on. S. Jay Levy and Walter M. Cadette of the Jerome Levy Economics Institute propose the establishment of a Federal Bank for Infrastructure

---

[11] More information can be obtained directly by writing to Ken Bohnsack, Chairman, Sovereignty, 1154 West Logan Street, Freeport, Illinois 61032.

Modernization (FBIM), which would buy and hold approximately $50 billion annually of zero-interest mortgage loans to state and local governments for capital investment in projects recommended by Congress and the President.[12] The $50 billion annual investment would return public capital spending only to the standards of the 1955–1980 period. They suggest a maximum mortgage of 30 years, the period of repayment depending on the type of project, with the principal repaid in annual installments.

As stated earlier, the authority to provide interest-free loans for infrastructures is available to Congress. It is the same authority that allows the Federal Reserve and the commercial banking system to create bank credit in the same manner.

If Congress created the money for interest-free loans to tax-supported bodies, the Federal Reserve would have several options. First, if the Fed did not want the money supply to increase by the amount of the new loans, it could sell government securities of an equal amount from its huge portfolio, reducing the reserves of the banking system, thereby negating potential expansion of the money supply. Second, the Fed could raise banks' reserve requirements by the amount of the interest-free loans and then allow banks to create the same amount of money they otherwise would. The new, higher reserve requirements would make the banking system safer. Third, the Fed could deploy both policies in mixed amounts.

## INTEREST-FREE BONDS AND THE BUSINESS CYCLE

Just as with golf swings, timing is vital with most reforms. The Treasury could introduce interest-free loans during economic recessions or periods of slow economic growth, such as the period we are in. In fact, interest-free bonds could become a flexible, new fiscal policy. The size of deficits and the national debt since the early 1980s has

---

[12] S. Jay Levy and Walter M. Cadette, *Overcoming America's Infrastructure Deficit*, Public Policy Brief No. 40 (Annandale-on-Hudson, N.Y.: The Jerome Levy Economics Institute, 1998).

decimated the traditional use of fiscal policy as a means of countering the business cycle. In turn, the absence of fiscal policy has placed too great a burden on monetary policy as the sole available policy for combating recessions and inflation. Though counter-cyclical timing of new issues of interest-free bonds could resurrect fiscal policy, its effectiveness, like the success of low interest rates during the financing of World War II, would require the cooperation of the Federal Reserve. With the central bank's cooperation, the timing of new issues of such bonds during recessions could increase employment without adding to the federal budget deficit or to the national debt.

The lending of funds to state and local governments has enormous public appeal. It would be especially timely now with the state budgets in crisis. The amounts lent could be based on the populations of the tax-based creatures. It would be a short, though perhaps more controversial, step for Congress to issue interest-free bonds for financing national infrastructures, much as earlier Congresses have done. If such loans are good enough for wartime killing, why not use them to sustain the domestic peace, if not democracy?

Conservatives ceaselessly demand that the federal government behave more like a business firm. If the government kept its books in the manner of business firms — one budget for current revenues and expenses, another for investment — interest-free bonds could partly fund the investment side of the budget. Becoming more businesslike at the Office of Management and Budget also would add still more flexibility to the use of the new fiscal policy by the White House and Congress.

All this raises the question of where we are headed. At mid-2010 and beyond the economic indicators were very mixed. Consumer sentiment was down one month and up the next. The unemployment rate first was stuck at 9.6 percent, rising to 9.8 percent in November and to 9.4 percent in December. The ten months ending in November were the worst for unemployment since the Great Depression. As ever, the stock market was highly volatile. While September began with a rapidly rising stock market, October and November brought some bad news, and December began with a lot of uncertainty.

# 15

# PROSPECTS

*The United States will do its part to restore strong growth, reduce economic imbalances and calm markets. A strong recovery that creates jobs, income and spending is the most important contribution the United States can make to the global recovery.*

President Barack Obama in a letter sent November 9, 2010 to leaders of the Group of 20.

A strong recovery in the United States is necessary to revive the global economy. Yet, in December 2010 the most depressing news was about employment. Job growth was anemic; the unemployment rate was 9.4 percent, which meant that almost 15 million people were unemployed. Some 4.6 unemployed Americans were competing for each job opening, whereas only 1.8 people were vying for each job before the Great Recession. Only 49 percent of people laid off from 2007 through 2009 were reemployed by January 2010. The economy lost 95,000 non-farm jobs in September 2010, the result of a 159,000 decline in government jobs *at all levels*. Some 155,000 non-farm jobs were added the next month, but 300,000 were needed just to match population growth. One out of seven Americans were on food stamps. The USA needs full employment as well.

Bank failures and foreclosures were exceeding 2009's levels. As noted, the pace of bank failures in 2010 exceeds that of 2009, already a brisk year for shutdowns. The $787 billion stimulus finally passed by Congress to restart a halting economy is running out, shutting off the cash flow just as the states compound the dampening economic effect with severe budget cuts and layoffs of their own. Capping this off, the Great Recession wiped out huge amounts of middle-class wealth. With wealth eroding and paychecks flat, consumers generally were keeping their hands firmly in their pockets, except for Christmas.

All this raises the question of where we are headed. We may be trapped in the economic doldrums, on the way to a lost decade like the one Japan had in the 1990s and 2000s under similar circumstances. Worse, we could be headed for a terrifying reprise of 1937, when the U.S. economy, fighting its way out of the Great Depression, crashed a second time. Perhaps we can count on Ben Bernanke to continue to avoid the policy mistakes the Fed made back then. As noted, the world seems dependent on monetary policy, especially that of the Federal Reserve.

The record speaks for itself. In a gesture to business in early September, 2010, President Barack Obama proposed that companies be allowed to write off 100 percent of their new investment in plant and equipment through 2011. According to estimates by White House economists, this would cut business taxes by nearly $200 billion over two years. About the same time he proposed an expansion of the research and experimentation tax credit, which would provide $50 billion more in spending on roads, railways and airport runways. But the expansion of private credit for investment was still a matter of pushing on a string. The one exception was the corporate bond market.

As we look around the globe, we see China and India as the only other growth engines of significant size, but China is fixated on an export-led model of modernization. The Chinese trade surplus grew to US$27.1 billion in October 2010. Other sources of export demand include Europe, especially Germany and Great Britain. They still feel a need to *export more to the U.S.* The USA importing more than it exports weighs heavily on the growth rate of its GDP.

The trade deficit is important too because it is a measure of the demand pull or lack thereof from the rest of the world. The U.S. trade deficit of almost US$50 billion for June 2010 is the biggest in almost two years; in August it was US$46.3 billion. The U.S. deficit with the European Union alone increased 26 percent in June. The contribution of net exports to real GDP was −3.5 percent in the second quarter and −2.0 percent in the third quarter. As a result, the economic growth for the second quarter, which came in at a sluggish rate of 2.4 percent in early estimates, turned out to be only 1.7 percent.[1] The initial value of GDP growth was 2.0 percent in the third quarter, barely an improvement. We detail these various contributions to GDP growth below.

Exports to Europe are falling behind as that region of the world struggles with fallout from its own sovereign debt crisis. This happened during a period when import prices were flat or falling. In short, the United States cannot rely on demand overseas to make up for its own weak economy at home. Overshadowing all this is the reality of a U.S. economy nearly three times larger than second-ranked China.

The situation with China was especially worrisome. On September 29th the House of Representatives by a wide margin passed legislation to penalize China's foreign-exchange practices. The concern was with the aforementioned overvaluation of the yuan. The measure would allow, but not require, the U.S. to levy tariffs on countries that undervalue their currencies, with China uppermost in mind. The faltering U.S. economy was very much on the minds of

---

[1] The great global divide is between the current account deficit countries and those running surpluses. Besides the trade account, the current account includes income outflows and income inflows, mostly from financial ownership earnings. The U.S. current account deficit in 2010 is running about nine times the total of other deficit countries: these countries are, in the order of deficit sizes, Spain, Brazil, U.K., France, and India. The 2010 U.S. current account deficit is an estimated −US$466.5 billion. China currently has the largest surplus at US$269.9 billion, followed by Germany (US$200.2 billion) and Japan (US$166.5 billion), while in turn Russia, the Netherlands, and Saudi Arabia have smaller surpluses. No single surplus country has enough surplus credits to balance the shortfall of the U.S. The current account deficit is sustainable only as long as foreign institutions and individuals are willing to hold U.S. securities. The USA key/reserve currency position depends on the same willingness. The dilemma of the key/reserve-currency nation is highlighted by the Great Panic. The U.S. net foreign investment position deteriorated by more than US$2 trillion in 2008, which led to a fall in the international value of the dollar.

the lawmakers. Treasury Secretary Timothy Geithner had already tried to use the threat of congressional action to press China to let its currency appreciate. Nonetheless, the Obama administration did not positively endorse this House bill, perhaps hoping to avoid the infamous Smoot-Hawley tariff practices of the 1930s. On October 6th the IMF forecast China's growth to be 10.5 percent in 2010, while pointing to lingering weakness in the United States and Europe.

China is not alone in trying to gain a competitive advantage. The Japanese government intervened in currency markets for the first time in years on September 15th. Then, fears of a full-blown currency war flared up on October 7th. The U.S. dollar fell to an eight-month low against the euro and the U.S. stepped up pressure on China to let its currency rise. Soon, however, the dollar would rise again. By December 2010, the euro was in free-fall against the U.S. dollar, endangering the eurozone area. Germany warned speculators that it was intervening to save the euro. Meanwhile, the Federal Reserve's low fed funds rate and newly inspired quantitative easing are driving down interest rates, keeping the dollar lower than it otherwise would be. The Fed bought a batch of Treasury bonds on November 12, the first step in its latest stimulus attempt. In theory, pushing $600 billion into the banking system should ripple across the economy, encouraging banks to lend, companies to invest in equipment and employees and Americans to open up their wallets. The chain reaction, it is hoped, will knock the unemployment rate below 9.0 percent, and ignite a stock market rally. As we will see, the timing of this action had adverse repercussions in the world community. But first, we will provide a summary.

The Great Recession in the USA can be summarized by looking at changes in consumption (C), investment (I), government spending (G), and net exports (X − M). These GDP components are derived from Keynesian economics. In the domestic part of GDP, Keynes considered I to be the most volatile component. In a world of mostly flexible exchange rates, however, (X − M) becomes almost as volatile and has recently been suppressing GDP.

In Keynesian theory, $C + I + G + (X - M) = GDP$. What we see in Table 15.1 are annualized percentage changes in these sources of

**Table 15.1:** Percentage Points Contribution to Changes in U.S. GDP

|      | 07Q4 | 08Q1 | 08Q2 | 08Q3 | 08Q4 | 09Q1 | 09Q2 | 09Q3 | 09Q4 | 10Q1 | 10Q2 | 10Q3 |
|------|------|------|------|------|------|------|------|------|------|------|------|------|
| C    | 1.0  | -0.5 | 0.1  | -2.5 | -0.5 | -0.3 | -1.1 | 1.4  | 0.7  | 1.3  | 1.5  | 1.8  |
| I    | -1.5 | -1.5 | -1.2 | -2.0 | -6.3 | -6.8 | -2.3 | 1.2  | 2.7  | 3.0  | 2.9  | 1.5  |
| G    | 0.2  | 0.4  | 0.7  | 1.0  | 0.3  | -0.6 | 1.2  | 0.3  | 0.3  | -0.3 | 0.5  | 0.7  |
| X – M| 3.2  | 0.8  | 1.0  | -0.6 | 1.6  | 2.9  | 1.5  | -1.4 | 1.9  | -0.3 | -3.5 | -2.0 |
| GDP  | 2.9  | -0.8 | 0.6  | -4.1 | -6.7 | -4.8 | -0.7 | 1.5  | 5.6  | 3.7  | 1.4  | 2.0  |

*Source:* Haver Analytics, Federal Reserve Board of Governors website.

*Note:* All values are seasonally adjusted at annual rates in real dollars. I includes inventory adjustments, G includes both consumption and investment, and X – M equals net exports of goods and services.

aggregate demand. These are final figures, since the multiplier effects have already taken place. Among these, G is partly discretionary. Thanks to the net export balance being strongly positive, the GDP growth in the first full quarter of the official recession was 2.9 percent. The official recession, as noted early on, did not begin until December of that quarter when the unemployment rate rose to 4.9 percent. The recession officially ended at the end of the second quarter of 2009 when GDP growth was −0.7 for the full quarter. The unemployment rate for June 2009, the official end date, was 9.5 percent. Although GDP growth was positive thereafter despite a deteriorating trade balance, the unemployment rate soared to 10.2 percent in October, leveled off at 10.0 percent thereafter, and was never below 9.5 percent through November 2010 (Q4). In terms of GDP growth, the worst period was from the third quarter of 2008 through the second quarter of 2009. Government spending's contribution to growth was very positive in the third quarter of 2008 and the second quarter of 2009; otherwise G was anemic. Luckily the trade balance was strong from the fourth quarter of 2008 through the second quarter of 2009. Thereafter, except for the fourth quarter of 2009, the contribution of the trade balance was decidedly negative. The trade balance remains a major point of contention in the struggle among the U.S., China, Japan and and the eurozone countries.

The USA gained little at the mid-November 2010 Group-20 summit in Seoul, South Korea. Among other things, President Obama was attempting to negotiate (though his Treasury) a free trade agreement with S. Korea. Smelling blood in the water, the S. Korean negotiators rebuked the USA despite Obama's argument that U.S. leadership was necessary to restore global economic growth. Obama's bargaining power was partly undercut by weak U.S. economic growth and a falling dollar. Worse, the Fed's quantitative easing was cited as "manipulating" the dollar downward and giving the U.S. an unfair advantage in global markets, this despite the whopping current account deficit of an estimated US$467 billion in 2010. By early December the U.S. and S. Korea had a trade agreement but it fell well short of "free trade." As a consequence, the world moved closer to a currency and trade war like that which worsened the Great Depression (see Chapter 2).

The foreign currency and trade crisis could have been avoided through the implementation of a universal wide SDR band cum delayed peg and an empowered IMF. Inflation anxiety in China threatened tighter monetary policy at its central bank and may yet slow China's growth. As the end of 2010 neared, the government's plan to limit inflation to near three percent and new bank lending to 7.5 trillion yuan (about US$1.1 trillion) were perilously close to being violated.[2] U.S. GDP growth would have been a respectable four percent in the third quarter of 2010 if it had not been for a net export change of –2.0 percent, driven by deflation in durable goods and flat capital goods prices abroad. A freely convertible international standard throws the main burden of balance of payments adjustment on the debtor nation, especially the U.S. It would be far better if the creditor nations (enjoying current account surpluses) bore more of the burden of adjustment.

Keynes did not recommend a delayed peg but in principle his idea of a fixed but adjustable exchange rate is consistent with the idea. (Moreover, he had recommended the establishment of a world central bank with one currency.) As noted, the problem under the Bretton Woods conference agreement was the undue fixity of rates; the problem now is the reverse. After World War II, the Marshall Plan combined with other aid from the United States to Western allies substituted for dollar exchange rate movements. However, it is unlikely that the rest of the world will try to balance the U.S. trade deficit with economic aid to the by-far largest economy in the world! Paul Davidson, probably the leading American Post Keynesian, has written a concise history of the post-WWII story.[3]

---

[2] As a share of GDP, China's stimulus program during the Great Recession was much larger than the USA's. China's Politburo, the body that oversees the Communist Party, does not always agree with the central bank head. This tension is being relieved with the central bank prevailing.

[3] Paul Davidson, *The Keynes Solution* (New York: Palgrave Macmillan, 2009), pp. 129–133. Davidson is now the sole editor of the *Journal of Post Keynesian Economics*.

Rather than a world central bank, Paul Davidson goes on to recommend an International Monetary Clearing Union (IMCU). International payments, for imports or financial funds crossing national borders, would go through this clearing union. Each nation's central bank would set up a deposit account with the IMCU and any payments made would have to clear through each nation's central bank deposit account. Accumulated credits by the creditor nation would be used to settle debtor nations' accounts. As the creditor nation spends its excess credits, this spending should increase profit opportunities in the debtor countries. To work, the onus would have to be placed on the creditor nations to make the appropriate adjustments, including the provision of economic aid.

While Davidson is right in arguing that simply tinkering with the IMF's role will not suffice, it is difficult to imagine the dismantling of the IMF. It is more likely that the IMF and World Bank would be merged into a more powerful instrument for currency adjustments. Keynes' original plan included a supranational bank and the use of "bankcors" or "bank money." Still, Davidson's plan should have its day in court.[4] Since central bankers presently conduct most of the stimulus policy in the industrialized world, perhaps central bankers will have to be relied on even more. However, I have provided some cautionary reasons why their powers may be too great.

The situation in Ireland in mid-November 2010 highlights the need for international financial reform. Ireland's central bank has borrowed the maximum from the European Central Bank (ECB) and from the Paris Club. Therefore, it is getting a loan from the European Union and the IMF to the tune of almost €90 billion

---

[4] Only a brief summary of Davidson's IMCU is presented herein. For the details and full defense, see Davidson, *Ibid.*, pp. 136–142. For other policy recommendations in line with the original Keynes, see the balance of his book. If you don't want to read Keynes's *The General Theory of Employment, Interest and Money* (1936), you will find many direct quotes from Keynes in Robert Skidelsky, *Keynes: The Return of the Master*, paperback edition (Public Affairs: New York, 2010). Moreover, the original plan of Keynes for an international Clearing Union, which dates from September 8, 1941, is found on pp. 180–181.

(US$122 billion). Ireland faces a trio of problems: its private banks are facing insolvency, it suffers from an extraordinary public debt, and it has become part of the global recession. Only a few years ago, it was called the "Celtic Tiger." Portugal, Spain, Italy, and Greece (once again) may be next. Since these nations comprise more than 30 percent of the membership of the eurozone, the fallout from its current loans to these countries could further endanger the euro.[5] This, in turn, could drive the U.S. dollar up, worsening the U.S. trade balance, and slowing GDP growth. In December Germany was leading the eurozone in aiding fellow nations, but was struggling to keep the euro out of the hands of speculators. Rather than having so many competing agencies offering assistance, it would be far better to have a supranational IMF-based bank issuing SDRs or one international currency.

Today the White House sees the need for more Keynesian stimulus. Whether we get enough stimulus is problematic. We have argued earlier that the original stimulus bill was too little too late. We must remember the dire conditions of the economy with a collapsing housing sector and a money and banking panic ongoing. On top of this was the prospect for deflation and liquidity traps. We had to go back to the Great Depression and its lessons in order to attempt to grapple with these difficulties. Without the stimulus, however, the job loss would have been another 2.5 to 3.6 million jobs. The recovery has been lackluster with a summer slowdown in 2010 in reaction to wealth losses, the unwinding of debt, housing foreclosures, and the reductions in economic stimulus. By December the jobless rate had been at or above 9.5 percent for 16 straight months, the longest such stretch since the Great Depression.

It will not be easy to muster public support for the kind of economic stimulus required for full employment. Mid-2010 polls by *Time* reveals just have hard the task is: Two-thirds of respondents say

---

[5] The eurozone comprises 17 European member nations that have adopted the euro currency as their sole legal tender. It currently consists of Austria, Belgium, Cyprus, Estonia, Finland, France, Germany, Greece, Ireland, Italy, Luxembourg, Malta, the Netherlands, Portugal, Slovakia, Slovenia, and Spain.

they oppose another government stimulus package. Worse, some 53 percent say the country would have been better off without the first stimulus package. Polls show that many voters either don't understand or don't buy the long-established economic theory of John Maynard Keynes, which calls for more government spending (even if it means running large deficits) to help the economy through hard times. Hopefully, this book will educate the public on the needs for Keynes and even Post Keynesianism as a way out of the malaise.

At first blush, the mid-term elections in the U.S. did not seem like an endorsement of Keynesianism, much less Post Keynesianism. The House went overwhelmingly to the Republicans while liberal Democrats were outnumbered in the Senate. Like Alan Greenspan, however, the Republicans (including Ronald Reagan, as we have noted) turn to fiscal stimulus during downturns. Granted, this is no ordinary situation because there is nothing remotely resembling full employment. President Richard Nixon in 1971 famously said, "We are all Keynesians now." Robert Lucas, who won a Nobel Prize for his application of rational expectations to macroeconomics is quoted during the Great Panic in 2008 as saying, "I guess everyone is a Keynesian in a foxhole."[6] When the ocean is turbulent, Greenspan, the rational expectationists, and the Republicans join hands in the same boat.

Between the beginning of the recession in December 2007 and September 30, 2010, nearly six million people have signed up for Medicaid, funded by the states and the federal government. That period includes the biggest 12-month increase since the program's early days: 3.7 million new participants from December 2008 to December 2009. Starting in the fall of 2008, the federal government provided more than $100 billion in additional Medicaid funding to the states. In early October, 2010 California still faced a $19 billion shortfall in its budget, and had cut the pay of its employees by about 14 percent. In mid-November it tried to float a new bond issue with little success (at the offered interest rate), a bad omen for states and

---

[6] "The Comeback Keynes," *Time* magazine, October 23, 2008.

local governments. Estimates for the total of states' deficits have gone up since *Time* magazine published its summary. Estimates run as high as $500 billion. A federal transfer of $300 to $400 billion more to the states to halt the massive layoffs there should be an easy sell. Such a transfer might be necessary to prevent a collapse in the bond market. As explained earlier, the issuance of zero-interest loans to states and cities for needed infrastructure would be very timely.

The original $700 billion TARP financial bailout officially ended on October 4, 2010. It largely achieved its goal of propping up the financial sector. But some banks have yet to be weaned from the program. More than 600 banks are sitting on about $65 billion in bailout funds. Federal officials believe some larger institutions can repay the government but have chosen not to because it would require them to raise additional capital and weaken existing shareholders. The government is mostly out of the biggest companies it helped save, including Citigroup and Bank of America. The U.S. Treasury garnered $35 billion in profits from the sale of Citicorp stock in early December. American International Group (AIG) is expected to announce a plan to repay the United States. The AIG plan could reduce the Obama administration's ownership stake in the company, though the final outcome is unclear. General Motors (GM) has started to return its bailout funds with a record IPO of $18.1 billion common shares and $5 billion in preferred stock. The government's stake in GM has dropped to about 25 percent. Continued positive profits for GM depend on low auto wage-benefits rates and rising consumer demand.

Ben Bernanke at the Federal Reserve, a keen student of the Great Depression, is aware of the precariousness of the economy. On August 10, 2010, he announced that the target for the federal funds rate would remain near zero. This was reaffirmed in September. He now sees deflation as a less probable risk, though the overall inflation rate for October was a record low. According to the September 21st minutes of the FOMC, the Fed nonetheless was concerned that the economy was growing slower than they had expected, and though they didn't see the economy slipping back into a recession, they worried it had become vulnerable to "potential negative shocks." The

December minutes of the FOMC simply reaffirmed the September concerns. The Fed was once again buying long-term government bonds in an effort to lower long-term interest rates still further. As noted, this unconventional quantitative easing or QE2 is borderline fiscal policy, as the buying of Treasury's long-term debt helps to finance deficit spending. Ben Bernanke also urged commercial banks to lend to small businesses, the source of job growth. However, this appears to be a part of the liquidity trap wherein low interest rates do not spur business investment. Uncertainty prevailed among both small and large businesses.

Bernanke remains profoundly pessimistic. His views were expressed in a remarkable "Sixty Minutes" interview on December 5th. When asked whether the weak recovery in GDP was sustainable, he replied, "It may not be; it's close to the border." He went on to say that a 2.5 percent growth rate is required to keep the unemployment rate from rising. He said it may take four to five years before the unemployment rate reaches "normal levels" of "five to six percent." (This is a new norm for defining full employment.) Moreover, he said that small business was not getting needed credit because of perceived risk at private banks. He defended the extreme monetary ease of the Fed and said that "the fear of inflation is overstated." Though the Federal Reserve "cannot influence the income and wealth distributions," Bernanke expressed a concern that two separate societies were being created in the U.S., mostly decided by differentials in education.

Bernanke, like all Fed chairmen before him, stressed the importance of independence of the central bank. This is easier said than done. The head of the Federal Reserve appears frequently before Congress and meets often with the president. Few understand the arcane making of monetary policy, policy that became more complex and enmeshed in Wall Street during the Great Recession. And there is the strong tendency to make fiscal policy recommendations. In the present crisis this is understandable since the GOP has created a stalemate on fiscal spending. On "Sixty Minutes" Bernanke said that tax rates should not be allowed to rise with unemployment so high. Congress recognizes the expanding powers of the "independent"

Federal Reserve. We can conclude that the central bank should have as much independence as possible, but no more.[7]

On September 12, 2010, the Basel III agreement was reached. Representatives of major central banks, including the European Central Bank and the U.S. Federal Reserve, agreed to the deal at a meeting in Basel, Switzerland. The deal was presented to leaders of the Group of 20 of rich and emerging countries at their meeting in November. It must be ratified, however, by national governments before it is enforced. In the agreement the central banks will be required to hold additional capital as reserves. Under current rules, banks have to hold back at least four percent of their balance sheet to cover their risks. Starting in 2013, this reserve, also known as tier 1 capital, would have to rise to 4.5 percent, reaching six percent in 2019.

The dispute between Democrats and Republicans over tax rate extensions at the end of 2010 was worthy of a Doonsbury cartoon strip. House Democrats wanted to retain the Bush era tax rates for the middle class, defined as less than $200,000 for a single household and $250,000 a year for a couple, but wanted to allow the expiration of those tax rates for those earning more. This had no chance in the Senate where the Democrats had a slim majority and divided opinions. Republicans were united on tax relief for the rich, or those earning $200,000 or $250,000 a year or more. The rich, in the GOP view, had suffered enough! This comes on the heels of a bailout of big banks and Wall Street. As noted, on December 7th a frustrated President Obama compromised with the Republicans by endorsing an extension of *all* Bush era tax cuts (except the zero estate tax). We cannot leap away from an overwhelming reality: the Great Recession happened with this nearly identical tax structure.

---

[7] We need the monetary equivalent of the non-partisan Congressional Budget Office to provide independent estimates of the overall effects of Federal Reserve policies. It would include academic economists as well alumni of the central bank. Such a committee or office could operate as a "shadow" FOMC.

As it stood, President Obama had surrendered to the GOP. With former president Bill Clinton, one of the most compromised presidents, at his side, Obama defended his own compliance. As he put it, the choice was between no tax rate extensions for the middle class and tax cut extensions for the richest Americans as well. Worse, the GOP was refusing to extend unemployment benefits for two million unemployed workers. The unemployed had been taken hostage at Christmastime. The Bush era tax rates would be extended "temporarily" for two years. At the same time the social security payroll tax would be reduced by two percentage points for one year on the first $105,800 of income. The estate tax, payed mostly by the upper one tenth of one percent of the wealth distribution, would be lowered to 35 percent with a $5 million exemption. Current rates will be extended for capital gains and dividends. Unemployment compensation was extended for 13 months. Businesses will be allowed to deprecate new equipment investments at 100 percent in 2011 and 50 percent in 2012. Liberal Democrats in the House were furious. With time running out (the tax rates would have expired on January 1, 2011), this tax deal prevailed in the Senate and House.

The tax package will add an estimated $858 billion to the budget deficit through 2012. While 2010 income tax rates are extended, the main new net stimulus comes from the reduction in Social Security deductions. The average taxpayer with an adjusted gross income of $50,000 will get a $1,000 break from the Social Security tax reduction; for the average $100,000 a year taxpayer, the break will be $2,000. This will add about $112 billion to the income stream during 2011 and is likely to have a high multiplier effect. Unemployment compensation was extended through 2011; this will add about $57 billion to incomes and will be mostly spent, also having a high multiplier effect. The rapid-fire depreciation on equipment should lead to a bunching of businesses' investment expenditures in 2011. The estate tax rises from zero, but its effect with the large deduction affects only a few thousand taxpayers.

The dispute was mostly ideological, as the Democrat Party has been, since the time of Franklin Roosevelt, the party favoring the middle class and the poor. The Republicans have been, especially since the time of Herbert Hoover, the party of the upper middle class and the rich. Since the income distribution favors the rich, there is less likelihood for stimulus there, mostly more savings. Welfare programs would cover the poor. As we also know, real saving comes from real investment. A tax cut for the middle class and aid to the poor would add more to consumption since the middle class and below spend reliably on necessities. The social security tax at payroll would lead to a full multiplier effect, so it would probably add about $168 billion to GDP. The new estate tax with its huge exemption will have little effect except to benefit the tip of the top. As we argued earlier, consumption is closely allied with necessities, which has a multiplier effect on national income and real investment. The total package would probably prevent the erasure of 0.5 to 1 percent from the GDP.

In a desperate attempt at stimulus, the Congress passed the Small Business Jobs Act. It promises that investors who put money into small companies will get full relief from capital-gains taxes on any returns, but there is a catch, perhaps a Catch 22. The tax break was only for six months ending January 1, 2011. Moreover, to get a 100 percent tax break, the tax filing must take place within three months. This may add only confusion at tax time. It is unlikely that such a tax break will spur real capital investment in plant and equipment. Worse, the Sraffa and Kalecki trade-off between wages and profits continues with profits winning. As explained, this worsening condition leads to declines in consumer sentiment.

The cost-of-living adjustments or COLAs in Social Security went the way of the deflationary trend. The COLAs are automatically set each year by an inflation measure that was adopted by Congress back in the 1970s. Based on near-zero inflation in 2010, the trustees who oversee Social Security say there will be no COLA for 2011. This would be the second year in a row of no increase for more than 58 million Social Security recipients, who comprise nearly a fifth of the U.S. population. Thus, social security *benefits* cannot be counted on for a positive stimulus.

On September 24, 2010, the Federal Reserve and the Treasury announced a rescue of the nation's wholesale credit unions, underpinned by a federal guarantee valued at $30 billion or more. Wholesale unions don't deal with the general public but provide essential back-office services to thousands of other credit unions across the U.S. The majority of retail credit unions are sound, but they nonetheless will have to shoulder the losses. This marks the latest intervention by the U.S. Government into a financial system weakened by the real-estate bust. Since the start of 2008, 66 retail unions have failed, compared with many more failed banks or savings institutions. Still, credit unions are an important source of credit, including mortgages.

As we have seen, derivatives and mortgages were near the heart of the problem afflicting the economy. As of September 27, banks were directed to share in the risk when they sell holdings of these kinds. The Federal Deposit Insurance Corp. (FDIC) is requiring banks to hold at least five percent of the securities on their books, as part of new rules the regulator adopted that were required under the new financial overhaul law enacted in July. The securities may contain bundles of mortgage, credit card or auto loans. Banks will be required to purchase their share of the securities beginning January 1, 2011. Although financial industry executives opposed the requirements, the so-called "skin-in-the-game" requirement was mandated. The banks failure to hold reserves in these risky securities contributed to the financial meltdown, but it is problematical whether five percent is sufficient for the banks to behave.

In a sign of the new regulatory times, the Federal Bureau of Investigation (FBI) began raiding hedge funds just after mid-November. The FBI and other law enforcement agencies are investigating insider trading by hedge funds, mutual-funds and investment bankers. Among the companies are Level Global Investors I.P. and the Stamford, Conn. Headquarters of Diamondback Capital Management LLLC. Diamondback manages about $4.71 billion, and Level Global manages $3.09 billion. The allegations involve tens of millions in illegal profits using secret information about mergers. Shortly thereafter, the Justice Department opened a criminal investigation into Swiss regional banks that it suspects may have helped scores of wealthy Americans evade taxes despite a crackdown on Swiss giant UBS, one of the world's largest private banks. UBS paid a US$780 million fine in 2009 and agreed to turn over 4,450 names of American clients — a rare rip in the traditional veil of Swiss secrecy. These investigations are likely to roil financial markets, including stock markets.

Stock market volatility continues. The Dow Jones industrials gained a whopping 7.7 percent in the month of September, the largest September gain since 1939. However, that run-up followed a dismal August, and the Dow was only up 3.5 percent for the year and was 3.7 percent below its closing high for 2010 reached on April 26. It was 20 percent below its peak in October 2007. Stocks were drifting in mid-October, 2010, as players waited to see how much Treasury debt the Fed would buy. That old relic gold continued to make new highs as it otherwise tampered the rise in stocks. On October 5th a surprise move by the Bank of Japan to cut its key interest rate to virtually zero also lifted stocks worldwide. The price of oil reached a new high for the year of about US$77 a barrel, a modest rise that nonetheless competed for stock investors' attention. Just when it appeared that a new speculative bubble in gold may continue, the Chinese made moves to slow its inflation, which dropped Asian stock markets sharply, and spilled over into the U.S. Dow industrials for a decline of 90.52 points (November 12). The price of gold plunged 2.7 percent to a still historic high of $1,365.50 an ounce. Oil and gold continue to be wild cards.

Just as the income and wealth distributions are connected, so too is the stock market and the wealth distribution. Since the housing bubble peaked in 2007, there has been a drop of 36 percent in the wealth of median income earners, the income that divides the income distribution in half. The drop in the wealth of the top one percent of households has been only 11 percent. The middle class depends on the value of housing as the basis of its wealth; the rich, especially the super-rich, depend not only on housing values but also on their holdings of stocks, bonds, and other financial assets. The top one percent now own 34.6 percent of all privately held wealth. The next 19 percent (managers, professionals and small business owners) own 50.5 percent. This leaves only 14.9 percent of the wealth for the bottom 80 percent of households. As we have noted more than once, the concentration of financial assets in the hands of the few can lead to speculative bubbles just as speculative bubbles can worsen the wealth distribution.

Investors who stuck with the U.S. stock market through the worst financial crisis in 70 years were still down about 20 percent from the boom days after accounting for dividends on October 10, 2010, wondering whether their accounts will ever recover. It took 15 years for investors to recover from the Crash of 1929 if they reinvested their dividends, and 25 years for the stock market to come back if they didn't. As noted, however, the top fifth of wealthholders continued to do extremely well. Whether another stock market bubble expands depends on the balance between low interest rates in the U.S. and tightening monetary and fiscal policies in China and Europe.

Some 18 months after the recession officially ended, the U.S. government's latest measures to bolster the economy have led some forecasters and policy makers to express cautious optimism that the recovery will gain substantial momentum in 2011. Despite persistently high unemployment, consumer confidence is improving. Giant corporations are reporting healthy profits, and the Dow Jones industrial average reached a two-year high at the end of 2010. Of course, all this could be simply irrational Christmastime exuberance, which so far isn't being shared by wage-earners.

The Federal Reserve, which has kept short-term interest rates near zero since the end of 2008, has made clear it is sticking by its controversial decision to try to hold down mortgage and other long-term interest rates by buying long-term government securities. Meanwhile, President Obama's tax-cut compromise with Congressional Republicans is putting more cash in the hands of consumers through a temporary payroll-tax cut and an extension of unemployment insurance for the long-term unemployed. Then, too, there are the tax incentives for private business investment. With low long-term interest rates and 100 percent tax write-offs, surely business will invest in new equipment during 2011.

However, this measured optimism is reminiscent of the mood in late 2009, when the economy seemed to be reviving, only to stall again in the spring amid widespread fears caused by the debt crisis in Greece and other European countries. Indeed, there are significant caveats to the more positive outlook, the housing market remains weak, and another sustained drop in prices could badly undercut the economy. At the end of 2010 Sarah Palin's daughter bought a house in a Phoenix, Arizona suburb at half price. Financial markets and the banking system remain vulnerable to a new round of jitters in Europe over the debt burdens of countries like Ireland and Spain. Worse, there is mounting concern about the tattered balance sheets of state and local governments. There are rising health and long-term fiscal concerns. A widespread fear that a debt crisis will soon infect U.S. cities and states would be an unwelcome shock. Overriding all the dark clouds on the horizon is the immediate unemployment crisis.

A cautionary tale comes from the also mature industrial Japan; it too has an aging population. At the end of 2010 Japan was struggling to keep its economic recovery alive while attempting to cut back on its massive public debt. Japan's central bank continued to hold interest rates at virtually zero and said the recovery "seems to be pausing," while noting that exports are flat. A central bank survey found that business sentiment fell for the first time in seven quarters. In November the government passed a US$61 billion stimulus package under a massive US$1.11 trillion budget plan, aimed at creating jobs and injecting life into the economy. The government also announced plans to cut the country's corporate tax rate by five percentage points in a bid to help Japanese businesses stay competitive. A falling international value of the yen would help Japanese exports at the possible expense of U.S. exports.

Japan's recovery was overshadowed by a 9.0 earthquake and a 30-ft tsunami. The devastation may leave as many as 17,000 dead. Compounding the tragedy was a nuclear meltdown at Fukushima Daiichi. Supply lines, including auto parts going to General Motors, were interrupted and stock markets around the world fell. These cataclysmic events cloud prospects for the global recovery. Meanwhile, unrest in the Middle East was driving oil prices upward.

Those who advocate doing nothing more to stimulate the USA economy are placing ideology above knowledge. The new financial regulations should take some of the risk out of financial markets. Everyone, however, is not in agreement. For example, the European Banking Federation warned that the new global rules forcing banks to put aside more capital could keep the eurozone economy in or close to recession through 2014. Then, the Great Recession would continue, at least in the United States and Europe. However, the central bankers at Basel concluded that the new capital rules will lead to long-term financial stability, and economic growth will be substantial. Then, the Global Great Recession would end. Though there remain financial institutions too large to be allowed to fail, recent experience should tell us what to do when that happens again. Meanwhile, the White House and Congress will have to be increasingly innovative in the conduct of fiscal and incomes policies. The Federal Reserve will need to continue its unconventional monetary policy despite the risks. The global economy awaits a rational redistribution of wealth and income that would foreclose the next debacle. This is something that the best of capitalism cannot deliver without the appropriate fiscal-incomes policy. Most of all, a civilized society depends on policies in pursuit of full employment.

# INDEX

Atlanta, GA, 238–239
Atlantic City, NJ, 308
Atlantic Ocean, 14
Australia, 157, 159, 253, 260, 262
Austria, 261, 262, 323n5
Authers, John, xv
AutoNation Inc., 165

**B**
*Back From the Brink: The Greenspan Years* (Steven K. Beckner), 111n26
*Back to Methuselah* (George Bernard Shaw), 285
Bagehot, Walter, 201
Baker, Dean, xv, 242n2, 256n1, 257–258, 277–278
Bakersfield, CA, 129
Balkans, 250
Baltics, 250
bank credit, 194–197
Bankers Trust, 181
bank failures
  in 1970s and 1980s, 76
  during 2007–2009, 173–174, 236, 239
  in 2010, 10, 315
  draining the FDIC, 105
  during Great Depression, 17
  of small banks, 192–193
Banking Act of 1933, 182, 203
Bank of America
  acquisition of Merrill Lynch, 155, 190, 191, 223–224, 229
  federal directive on capital levels and, 233
  financial deregulation and, 180

TARP and, 255, 325
too-big-to-fail status, 186, 192
write-downs, 188
Bank of Canada, 210, 225
Bank of England, 201, 210, 217, 218, 225
Bank of Israel, 210
Bank of Japan, 210, 225, 331, 333
Bank of Lincolnwood, 236
Bank of New York Mellon, 186
Bank of the United States (New York), 17
Bank One, 178
Barclays, 188, 223
Bartiromo, Maria, xv, 188n4
Bartlett, Bruce, 86, 87
Basel III agreement, 327, 334
basics industry, 243–244
Bear Stearns
  collapse, 4, 154–155, 191
  JPMorgan Chase and, 161–162, 178, 187
  subprime holdings, 145, 154, 215, 238, 239
Beckner, Steven K., 111
*Beckoning Frontiers* (Marriner S. Eccles), 37n4
Belgium, 323n5
Bell, Daniel, 193
Bentsen, Lloyd, 113
Bernanke, Ben. *See also* Federal Reserve
  Bear Stearns collapse and, 162, 187
  burden on, 294
  chairmanship of FOMC, 210
  on economic outlook, 325–326

European Union, 254, 316, 322
Eurostat, 248
eurozone, 294–295, 323, 334
"Evolutionary Model of Technical
    Change with Markup Pricing,
    An" (E. Ray Canterbery),
    270n5
Exxon, 99
Eynsford-Hill, Clara, 41, 43

**F**
Fabian socialism, 38, 43
"Falling Rate of Profits" (William
    D. Nordhaus), 65n14
*False Profits* (Dean Baker), xv,
    242n2, 256n1, 257–258,
    277–279
Fannie Mae
    Alan Greenspan and, 133–135
    Bush stimulus and, 6
    in foreclosure prevention plan,
        238
    government takeover, 222,
        224, 228–229, 231, 254
    nature of debt, 215
    post crisis, 191
    purpose behind creation,
        272–273
    role in housing crisis, 126,
        145, 168, 180, 188, 195
    too-big-to-fail status, 214
*Fault Lines* (Raghuram G. Rajan),
    xv, 272n6
FDIC. *See* Federal Deposit
    Insurance Corporation
    (FDIC)
*Fearful Rise of Markets, The* (John
    Authers), xv

Federal Bank for Infrastructure
    Modernization (FBIM),
    312–313
Federal Bureau of Investigation
    (FBI), 330
federal deficit spending, 11, 259,
    285
Federal Deposit Insurance
    Corporation (FDIC)
    Community Bank & Trust
        failure and, 193
    creation, 3, 26, 199–200, 203,
        253
    depletion by bank failures, 105,
        192
    deposit and debt guarantees,
        254
    directive on bank securities,
        330
    loan guarantees, 229
    nationalization of Illinois
        Continental Bank, 76
    role in 2007–2009 financial
        crisis, 5, 174, 196
    seizure of Washington Mutual,
        224
    South Carolina Bank & Trust
        failure and, 193–194
Federal Emergency Relief
    Administration (FERA), 25
federal funds rate
    Alan Greenspan and, 125, 127,
        136, 167
    current level, 293
    FOMC and, 210, 227
    liquidity trap and, 211, 213
    monetarist experiment and,
        84–85

on German reparations
payments, 17
on government intervention,
251
Great Depression and, 2,
11–12, 38, 44
on income distribution, 43–44,
78
on interest rates, 9
liquidity trap and, 211
on money, 36, 76
New Deal and, 37, 82
as Post Keynesian, 81
proposal for supranational
bank, 322
on savings, 93
on Victorian virtue of thrift, 23
voters and, 324
Keynesianism. *See also* fiscal
Keynesians; neo-Keynesians; Post
Keynesians
aggregate demand, 90, 95
Anglo-American
macroeconomic policy and,
11–12, 247, 259
Bretton Woods era and, 274
Bruce Bartlett and, 87n3
disequilibrium economics, 80
fiscal and monetary policy in,
68, 251–255
Great Recession and, 229
nadir, 95
offshoots, 3
"primal," 3, 25–40
stagflation and, 41, 86
uncertainty in, xvi, 6, 42, 75,
250, 303
*vs.* Reaganomics, 4, 120

*Keynes Solution, The* (Paul
Davidson), 321n3
*Keynes: The Return of the Master*
(Robert Skidelsky), 274–275
Kindleberger, Charles P., 19, 76–77
Klaner, Arjo, 82n22
Knickerbocker Trust Company,
199–200
Knowledge Universe (KU), 105
Kohlberg Kravis Roberts & Co.
(KKR), 100–101
Krugman, Paul, 36
Kuwait, 176
Kwak, James, xv, 117, 184, 192n5

L
labor force, 59
Laffer, Arthur, 89
Laffer curve, 89
Lampman, Robert J., 13n1
Landeck, Michael, 269n4, 295n4
Land Rover, 164
Langford, Larry, 288
Lansing, MI, 287, 312
Las Vegas, 96, 294, 308
Latvia, 157
Lehman Brothers
Atlanta mortgage securities
and, 238
bankruptcy filing, xvi, 155,
187, 191, 214, 224, 289
bid to survive, 223
CEO, 163
Federal Reserve bailout, 162
write-downs, 188, 189
lenders of last resort, 76, 77. *See
also under* Federal Reserve
Leno, Jay, 57